Attribution Theory

To the memory of Henri Tajfel (1919–1982)
teacher, friend and colleague

Attribution Theory

Social and Functional Extensions

Edited by Miles Hewstone

Basil Blackwell

© Basil Blackwell Publisher 1983

First published 1983
Basil Blackwell Publisher Limited
108 Cowley Road, Oxford OX4 1JF, England

British Library Cataloguing in Publication Data
Attribution theory
  1. Attribution (Social psychology)
  I. Hewstone, Miles
  155.2   HM132

  ISBN 0–631–13257–0
  ISBN 0–631–13322–4 Pbk

Typeset by Oxford Publishing Services, Oxford
Printed in Great Britain
by the Camelot Press Ltd, Southampton

Contents

ARIE W. KRUGLANSKI, MARK W. BALDWIN and SHELAGH M.J. TOWSON

PART II Social Foundations of Attribution

SERGE MOSCOVICI and MILES HEWSTONE

GURNEK BAINS

MICHAEL H. BOND

. . . common-sense psychology guides our behaviour forward other people. . . . We interpret other people's actions and we predict what they will do under certain circumstances. Though these ideas are usually not formulated, they often function adequately.

Fritz Heider

Preface

Attribution theory is concerned with how and why ordinary people explain events; its subject matter is everyday, common-sense explanations. Although such matters are not by any means the jealously guarded property of social psychologists, they have been extensively and enthusiastically explored in this discipline. Thus attribution theory has now become one of the most popular conceptual frameworks in social psychology.

This book provides an integrative introductory overview, to guide students and newcomers to the area, and ten specially commissioned chapters which deal with extensions of previous work. The term 'extension' is chosen deliberately, to convey 'enlargement' as well as 'addition'. For these chapters build on the sturdy foundations of previous work as well as pushing research in several new directions. The common aim is to light some candles, rather than curse the darkness. The two themes that permeate the volume emphasize the social foundations and consequences of explanations, and the functions that they fulfil. Both themes converge on a richer analysis of explanations in common sense and the wider aspects of attribution. For the final chapter I invited John Harvey, an eminent scholar in the field, to begin what I hope will be a constructive reaction to the volume. I am grateful to him and to Ben Harris for paying the contributors (including myself) the compliment of honest, careful and critical attention.

The view offered herein is neither a polemic, nor a blinkered defence of orthodoxy. The contributors share a belief in the strengths of attribution theory, but are also aware of its shortcomings. This spirit of consensus began to emerge at a conference on 'New Developments in Attribution Theory' which I organized at the University of Oxford in July 1980. Many of the contributors were present, and this meeting provided a springboard for the present volume. The development of my own ideas, interests and contacts suggested the additional chapters.

Many people and foundations have helped me towards the completed work. My debt begins with the financial support provided by the Social Science Research Council and the British Council for the Oxford conference. I also gratefully acknowledge the unstinting encouragement for publication provided by two of my most influential teachers, Howard Giles and Jos Jaspars. The book took shape during my sojourn at the Laboratoire Européen de Psychologie Sociale, a division of the Maison des Sciences de l'Homme, Paris. There, I was generously funded by the Leverhulme Trust and blessed with an obligation simply to think and write. My very happy time in that establishment was in no small way due to the administrative acumen of M. Clemens Heller and the unceasing kindness of Mme Adriana Touraine. Intellectual stimulation was supplied in full by Serge Moscovici, who shared with me his ideas – and lunches – during 15 months on the Left Bank.

Finally, my thanks to Rebecca Holmes, Katherine Gardner and Brigitte Churchill for their help in translating parts of chapter 6, and to my long-suffering family for their contribution towards final preparation of the manuscript.

Miles Hewstone

Contributors

Robert P. Abelson, Department of Psychology, Yale University, New Haven, Connecticut

Tony Anderson, Department of Psychology, University of Glasgow

Gurnek Bains, Department of Experimental Psychology, Oxford University

Mark W. Baldwin, Department of Psychology, University of Waterloo, Ontario

Michael H. Bond, Department of Psychology, the Chinese University of Hong Kong

J. Richard Eiser, Department of Psychology, University of Exeter

Robert M. Farr, Department of Psychology, University of Glasgow

Frank D. Fincham, Department of Psychology, University of Illinois at Champaign-Urbana, Illinois

Ben Harris, History and Sociology of Science Department, University of Pennsylvania, Philadelphia

John H. Harvey, Department of Psychology, Texas Tech. University, Lubbock, Texas

Miles Hewstone, Psychologisches Institut, Universität Tübingen, West Germany

Jos Jaspars, Department of Experimental Psychology, Oxford University

Jennifer King, Department of Experimental Psychology, Oxford University

Arie W. Kruglanski, Department of Psychology, Tel-Aviv University, Israel

Mansur Lalljee, Department for External Studies, Oxford University

Serge Moscovici, Laboratoire de Psychologie Sociale, Ecole des Hautes Etudes en Sciences Sociales, Paris

Shelagh M.J. Towson, Department of Psychology, University of Waterloo, Waterloo, Ontario

1 Attribution Theory and Common-sense Explanations: An Introductory Overview

Miles Hewstone

> Common sense is the most widely shared commodity in the world, for every man is convinced that he is well supplied with it.
>
> René Descartes

PREAMBLE

The study of how people understand the causes of behaviour has a long and distinguished philosophical tradition. Yet, as Simon (1968) has pointed out, questions raised by philosophers in relation to causation are purely logical; they do not necessarily parallel the beliefs of the lay person, nor do they deal with *why* such beliefs are important and *how* they are arrived at. It is with such questions that psychologists, and especially social psychologists, have been concerned. The causal explanations of lay people have been central to attribution theory; they are one of the cornerstones of contemporary social psychology, and the one on which all the chapters in this volume are built. This introductory chapter considers, first, the three central pillars of attribution theory, and then some of the current critiques. This assessment paves the way for the remaining chapters in the volume. Its major themes – social and functional extensions – are outlined and then highlighted in overviews of the following chapters. Finally, a look to the future considers what might be made of a common-sense psychology. Although we often decry common sense as folklore and fiction, it may provide an understanding of why people act as they do and why such beliefs are often firmly held.

Much ink has flowed in recent years over definitions of what 'attribution' is and is not (see Antaki, 1981; Buss, 1978; Fincham and Jaspars, 1980; V. L. Hamilton, 1980; Jaspars, Hewstone and Fincham, 1983; Shultz and Schleifer, 1983). Such discussions have argued about whether attributions are always explanations, and about whether explanations are always causal. Debate continues over whether people in effect answer the question 'Why?' or 'For what reason?' something happened; and, if the explanation is causal, over the notions of causality that may be involved. It is not necessary to tread this ground again, but rather to make clear the meaning adopted in this volume. A cursory glance at the voluminous attribution literature makes clear that researchers show a general interest in *common-sense explanation*, or in how and why ordinary people explain events. This is the most common thread that runs through the following chapters.

Another observation that has gained some currency in recent debate is that the major expositions of attribution theory (Heider, 1958; Jones and Davis, 1965; Kelley, 1967) constitute not a theory in the formal sense, but rather a set of loosely structured propositions or, at best, a conceptual framework. Resolving this question would raise issues in the philosophy of science that go well beyond the present undertaking and are *not* peculiar to attribution theory. Suffice to say that attribution theory is not a 'monolithic theory' and certainly not a 'hegemony' (see Semin, 1980, and a rejoinder by Harvey, 1981). However, the central theories do deal with essentially common questions, and, if not set out in terms of formal logic, they have at least been presented in the form of systematic hypotheses the exploration of which has proved remarkably fruitful for experimental social psychology.

In fact, the psychological study of causality did not begin in social psychology at all – the first major psychological investigations were those of Piaget and Michotte.[1] Piaget (1930) dealt with the origin of the idea of causality in children and with their use of causal language (see Fincham, 1983). Michotte (1946) studied the perception of causality through the apparent movement and collision of geometrical shapes. He revealed that it was possible to experience phenomenal causality directly, provided that the perceiver's total impression of causality was not dissected into pieces by the investigator (cf. Duncker, 1945; Maine de Biran, 1942 edn). This process was, furthermore, subconscious and perceptual, rather than conscious and inductive. Michotte's emphasis on the perceiver's subjective experience shows that he was clearly influenced by Gestalt psychology. The ideas of the Gestalt school (e.g. Köhler and Wertheimer) also played an important role in introducing the study of causality into social psychology, through the work of Heider (see Heider, 1973), which is considered below.

THEORIES OF ATTRIBUTION

The 1970s ushered in the halcyon days of attribution theory – it now accounts for 11 per cent of all social psychological research (Pleban and Richardson, 1979), and the progress of this blossoming area has been regularly charted (Harvey, Ickes and Kidd, 1976, 1978, 1981; Jaspars, Fincham and Hewstone, 1983). However, as several authors have noted (Eiser, 1980; Jones and McGillis, 1976; Kelley and Michela, 1980; Shaver, 1975), conceptual advances have been limited, and the historical background to the vast majority of those studies is supplied by Heider (1958), Jones and Davis (1965) and Kelley (1967). These three theories are outlined briefly below, in a form that should guide the attributional neophyte but may also be of some service to more advanced readers. The focus is on the 'body', rather than on the 'tentacles', of this literature, which seems a more useful and practical option than to attempt a review of this vast area in the space available (see Kelley and Michela, 1980).

Heider's theory of the 'naive analysis of action'

Heider's 'naive psychology' attempted to formulate the processes by which an untrained observer, or *naive psychologist*, makes sense of the actions of others. His early work (Heider, 1944), like that of Michotte, was simplified and abstract. It examined perceptions of the movement of geometric figures (Heider and Simmel, 1944). But he also introduced the important notions of 'unit formation' and persons as the 'prototype of origins' (Heider, 1944), to which we now turn.

Unit formation referred to the process whereby origin (cause) and effect, actor and act were seen as the parts of a causal unit. Heider was particularly interested in the varying degrees of similarity between the two parts of the unit, in which he was influenced by Wertheimer's (1923) principles of perceptual organization. Thus, factors such as similarity and proximity were seen as determining the locus of attribution. If two events were similar to each other, or proximate, then the one was likely to be seen as the cause of the other. This was shown by Zillig's (1928) experiments, in which a 'bad' act was more easily connected with a 'bad' person (cf. Allport and Postman, 1947). Heider frequently cites Fauconnet (1928) in noting some of the serious social implications of these tendencies – such as the varying standards of evidence used to evaluate people with good and bad reputations. As George Orwell remarked, 'When a man has a black face, suspicion *is* proof.'

The most important consequence of this ineluctable link between actor and act is that, in general, a 'person' attribution is more likely than a 'situation' one (cf. Ichheiser, 1949), as persons are seen as the 'prototype of origins'.[2] But Heider also recognizes the functions served by this tendency, namely, that people can be punished and hence some control over the cause can be effected. A further point that deserves mention is the 'ego-protective' tendency to attribute one's failures to others. Although subject to some current controversy (see Zuckerman, 1979), this idea has certainly had an impact on later research.

Heider's early paper, despite its striking insights with respect to social categorization and social functions of attribution, has received far less attention than it deserves. In contrast, Heider's (1958) monograph has become a 'bible' for attribution researchers and at least some of its contents merit discussion here. Questions of attribution were just one aspect of the naive, or common-sense, psychology in which Heider was so interested. This was held to be important for two main reasons. First, whether 'true' or not, it was these lay beliefs that were assumed to guide behaviour, describing and predicting events as a science should do. Heider thus states: 'If a person believes that the lines in his palm foretell his future, this belief must be taken into account in explaining certain of his expectations and actions' (Heider, 1958, p. 5).

The second reason for which this common-sense psychology was considered relevant was for the truths that it might contain. It might also entail a web of erroneous myths and proverbs, but Heider maintained that scientific psychology could learn from common-sense psychology.

Heider proposes that causal analysis is in some respects similar to the perceptual process, as conceived in Brunswik's (1952) 'lens model'. An object 'out there' and with objective properties is the distal stimulus, but what is psychologically important is the proximal stimulus, the way the object appears to the perceiver. For social perception, Heider suggests that the important distal stimuli, dispositional properties linked to the proximal act, often refer to psychological states. It is these invariant dispositional properties that are needed to explain the behaviour of others and render the perceiver's world stable, predictable and controllable.

The naive analysis of action (Heider, 1958, chapter 4) deals with how observable behaviour is linked to unobservable causes. It is a fundamental activity that enables individuals to create organization from chaos and relate continuously changing stimuli to stable properties of the environment. This activity leads, in turn, to the crucial distinction between internal and external causes. Internal causes are factors within the person (e.g. effort, ability and intention), while external factors lie outside the person (e.g. the difficulty of the task, and luck). Understanding which set of factors should be used to interpret the behaviour of another person will make the perceiver's world more predictable and give a sense of control.

Heider's contribution to attribution theory is not always presented in the form of directly testable propositions, but his insights provided the blue-print for succeeding theories. This overview has chosen to emphasize certain ideas. Heider also saw the analogy between causal analysis and experimental methods, which led to Kelley's work; he considered the importance of intentionality in assessing personal causality, which was taken up by Jones and Davis; and he elaborated a model of responsibility attribution based on levels of interaction between personal and environmental forces. He is therefore unquestionably the founding father of contemporary attribution theory, and his influence is reflected and respected throughout this volume.

Jones and Davis's theory of 'correspondent inferences'

As Heider acknowledged, the criterion of intentionality is critical to personal causality. Understandably, then, Jones and Davis's (1965) theory is an attempt to formalize how individuals make inferences about a person's intentions and, in turn, dispositions (see also Jones and McGillis, 1976).

The perceiver's problem is to decide which effects of an observed action, if any, were intended by the actor. Two essential criteria for making this judgement concern the knowledge and ability of the actor. To infer that any of the effects were intended, the perceiver must believe that the actor 'knew' the consequences of his or her action. In addition, the actor must be seen to be 'capable' of intentionally producing the observed effects. These then are the preconditions for the assignment of intentions, which themselves are prerequisites for inferences concerning underlying personal dispositions of the actor. The aim of correspondent inference theory is 'to construct a theory which systematically accounts for a perceiver's inferences about what an actor was trying to achieve by a particular action' (Jones and Davis, 1965, p. 222). The central concept of the theory, the correspondent inference, refers to the perceiver's judgement that the actor's behaviour is caused by, or corresponds to, a particular trait. Thus underlying dispositions are directly conveyed in behaviour, or, as Jones (1979) put it, 'the heart is on the sleeve'. A simple example of such an inference would be to ascribe someone's aggressive behaviour to the trait 'aggressive'.

Jones and Davis's paper is, in short, an exposition of the conditions that facilitate the making of correspondent inferences. First, the principle of 'non-common effects' suggests that any characteristics shared between two areas of choice (e.g. in the original paper, the choice between teaching psychology at Harvard or at Yale) do not help to explain why one alternative, rather than the other, was chosen. It is non-common effects, characteristics that differentiate between the two universities (e.g. perhaps one is biologically and the other sociologically inclined) that are important. These should guide the perceiver to the dispositions, or the intentions, of an actor. The fewer such differentiating characteristics, the less ambiguous is the attribution.

The second principle of the theory, 'social desirability', concerns the perceiver's beliefs about what other actors would do in the same situation. Although Jones and Davis acknowledge that effects that are normally desirable to actors are more diagnostic of their intentions, they also realize that universally desired effects tell the perceiver little about an individual's unique characteristics. Thus in a study by Jones, Davis and Gergen (1961), an interview candidate's behaviour that was *at variance with* the interviewer's ideal (i.e., 'out-of-role') was seen as more informative than socially desirable (i.e., 'in-role') behaviour. It is behaviour that conflicts with expectations that tells us most about an actor.

Two further factors which influence correspondent inferences concern the rewarding or punishing implications of an action for the perceiver. 'Hedonic relevance' refers to the positive and negative effects of an actor's choice for the perceiver. The authors predict that the more relevant an act is for the perceiver, the stronger will be the correspondence between act, intention and disposition (Jones and De Charms, 1957). 'Personalism' refers to the actor's intention to benefit or harm the perceiver specifically. This variable is introduced to distinguish between cases where an actor's behaviour has general (positive or negative) relevance, and those where the behaviour is directed towards the perceiver. Both these additional factors appear to be an extension of Heider's view that the perceiver's needs and values may distort attributions.

Thus, Jones and Davis provide a set of ideas concerning how a perceiver searches for the dispositional cause of an intention. As the title of their paper conveys, they are concerned with how perceivers make the inferential leap 'from acts to dispositions'. Although the proposed relation between behaviour, intentions and dispositions has been challenged (Eiser, 1980, 1983), this approach has stimulated, and been supported by, many empirical studies. These have provided a fertile basis for further theorizing (e.g. Jones, 1979; Jones and Nisbett, 1971; Ross, 1977), which has culminated in a more complete and systematic analysis of biases in attribution and other social judgements (Nisbett and Ross, 1980).

Kelley's theories of 'covariation and configuration'

Kelley's contributions to attribution theory build on Heider's proposal that understanding of the distal environment is gained by means of a causal analysis that is similar to the experimental method. He begins with the question of what information is used to arrive at a causal attribution and goes on to ask in what way it is used. Two different cases are outlined, which depend on the amount of information available to the perceiver. In the first case the attributor has information from multiple sources and can perceive the covariation of an observed effect and its possible cause. For example, one knows that a light comes on when the switch is flicked 'on';

this happens all the time, and for all people. In the second case, the perceiver is faced with a single observation (e.g., a car is seen to knock down a pedestrian). Here the perceiver must take account of the 'configuration' of factors that are plausible causes for the observed effect, such as a wet road surface, whether the driver was drunk, whether the pedestrian was careless and so on.

In outlining attribution in the case of covariation, Kelley (1967) followed Heider in the use of a naive version of J.S. Mill's 'method of difference': an effect is attributed to a condition that is present when the effect is present, and absent when the effect is absent. The underlying logic of covariation, Kelley argued, was similar to that of the analysis of variance (ANOVA). Thus Kelley (following G. Kelly, 1955) highlighted the notion of 'man the scientist'.

The essence of the ANOVA model is readily conveyed by considering a widely cited study (McArthur, 1972) that set out to test the model. Subjects were asked to explain sentences such as: 'John laughs at the comedian.' This outcome could be caused by something in the 'person' (John), the 'entity' or 'stimulus' (the comedian), the 'circumstances' (e.g. the occasion on which the outcome occurred) or some combination of these factors. In the ANOVA model, the independent variables constitute the three possible ways of examing variations in effects: (1) over persons – do other people laugh at the comedian? ('consensus' information); (2) over entities – does John laugh at other comedians? ('distinctiveness' information); (3) over time/modalities – has John laughed at the same comedian in the past?/on the radio as well as television? ('consistency' information). The dependent variable is whether the effect occurs or not. The covariation principle suggests that the effect is seen as caused by the factor with which it covaries. Thus, if only John laughs at the comedian (low consensus), if he also laughs at all other comedians (low distinctiveness), and if he has done so in the past (high consistency), then the effect is seen as caused by something in the person (John). McArthur's (1972) experiment and many studies since suggest that consensus, consistency and distinctiveness do affect attributions in the way predicted by Kelley. The attributor ascribes an effect to the cause (or set of causes) with which it covaries.

Kelley (1972, 1973, 1980) acknowledges that the ANOVA model is idealized and that there are occasions on which the perceiver lacks the information, time or motivation to examine multiple observations. In these cases of incomplete data, attributions are made on the basis of a single observation, using causal schemata. These schemata are beliefs concerning how certain kinds of causes interact to produce a specific kind of effect. They can be conceived as incomplete patterns of data in the analysis of variance framework. In the above-mentioned example, people may believe that vehicle drivers are the main cause of road accidents, but that pedestrian carelessness is also a necessary factor.

One of the simplest causal schemata is the Multiple Sufficient Cause (MSC) schema (Kelley, 1972), which considers that different causes (e.g. adverse home background, poor school environment and lack of individual effort) produce the same effect (e.g. exam failure). The operation of this schema is seen in studies demonstrating the 'discounting principle' (e.g. Jones et al., 1961; Thibaut and Riecken, 1955). Given that different causes produce the same effect, the role of a given cause (e.g. lack of effort) in producing the effect (failure) is discounted if other plausible causes are present (e.g. problems at home).

Causes may, however, facilitate or inhibit an effect. For example, to succeed in an exam, poor social background would be seen as an inhibiting cause. In this case the 'augmentation principle' might be used. The role of certain causes (e.g. individual effort) is augmented, because the presence of a poor social background would be seen to inhibit the effect. Thus, a student from a relatively poor background who succeeds in an exam may have his or her success attributed more to internal factors (such as effort and ability) than would a student from a well-off home.

There are many other kinds of causal schemata, ranging from simple to complex, available to the lay person (Kelley, 1972). Although the exact details of how and when schemata are used remain unclear (see Surber, 1981), there is evidence that lay people sometimes make attributions *as if* they were using schemata to meet the need for fast and economical analysis. Where schemata imply that strong preconceptions are held (e.g., we expect certain causes to operate in certain contexts), these may dominate the perception of covariation (see Kassin, 1979). More research on how perceivers resolve inconsistencies between existing beliefs and new data is clearly important for a satisfactory integration of the two halves of Kelley's theory (see Ajzen, 1977; Kelley and Michela, 1980; Metalsky and Abramson, 1980). The notion of covariation applies to the rather 'pure' case and, as Ross (1977) had pointed out, involves the application of essentially logical rules. In his words, it can be carried out by a 'mere statistician'. The use of configuration concepts (i.e. schemata and principles) is far more social, demanding 'considerable insight about the nature of man' (Ross, 1977, p. 181).

Summary

While there have obviously been other significant developments (a good number of which are discussed in the following chapters), the three theories outlined above are considered the major contributions in the field. Commonalities between the theories include the following general themes (see S. E. Taylor, 1981): mediation between stimulus and response; active and constructive causal interpretation; and the perspective of the naive perceiver or lay person. Most importantly, all share a concern with common-sense explanations and answers to the question 'why?' – a common attribute emphasized by the fact that Heider's theorizing provided the foundations for both of the later theories.

SOME CRITICAL ASSESSMENTS OF ATTRIBUTION THEORY

As tends to be the case with any major theory (see Kuhn, 1962), the deluge of empirical studies on attribution has now been followed by a series of critiques. It would be inappropriate to detail all of these, as only the major parts of attribution theory have been outlined. Instead, two main lines of attack are reviewed, as they give rise to the themes running through the present volume.

How much 'thinking' does the lay attributor do?

Attribution theory is exemplary of the cognitive perspective (see Eiser, 1980; S. E. Taylor, 1981), which has held a central position in social psychology since early days (Zajonc, 1968, 1980). Eiser (1980) has summarized the foci of this approach: the active processing of information; the role of expectations and comparisons on perception; organization of experience through selection and simplification; and the functions of organization in guiding action and facilitating prediction. Despite the advantages of a cognitive orientation, such as more exact empirical analyses utilizing process models (see Smith and Miller, 1979a), it has also been the target for two major challenges to attribution theory identified by Harris and Harvey (1981). These are now examined.

Attribution theory has been considered the best example in contemporary social psychology of a Hobbesian approach which views people as rational, though not infallible, information processors. In this view, perceivers are expected to make accurate decisions, given sufficient time, unless 'distorted' by social and motivational influences. Departures from logic are, in turn, seen as errors and biases. Mounting evidence has now been collected by researchers who are pessimistic about the ability of humans to process social information in an elaborate and accurate manner. This evidence refers to work on the 'crudeness' of simplifying cognitive heuristics (see below) and the concomitant 'waste' of information, leading to errors in social judgement (see Fischhoff, 1976; Nisbett and Ross, 1980). Attribution research may be limited, in this respect, to the extent that it creates impossibly complex models of common-sense attribution, such as the ANOVA model.

The second challenge identified by Harris and Harvey appears closely allied to the first. It concerns the question of whether humans analyse social cues *at all* in their day-to-day social interactions. Langer (1978) argues that much ostensibly thoughtful action is, in fact, 'mindless'. She proposes that, most of the time, people are not consciously seeking explanations, nor are they actively engaged in monitoring new information. Especially when performing familiar activities, people rely on well-learned and general 'scripts' (Schank and Abelson, 1977). Thus, attribution theorists may have presumed too much mental activity on the part of individuals engaging in many mundane activities (cf. Thorngate, 1976, 1979). These two critical challenges converge on the idea that the naive scientist model (of social judgement in general and attribution in particular) is unrepresentative. S. E. Taylor (1981) prefers the current 'metatheory' that drives social cognitive research, that of the 'person as cognitive miser'. A perceiver with limited capacity takes short-cuts (making errors or using heuristics) to produce generally accurate, rather than scientifically exact, decisions (e.g. Nisbett and Ross, 1980; Tversky and Kahneman, 1974).

It is important at this stage to consider more closely whether the lay person's social judgements should be interpreted as errors, biases, heuristics and so on. These terms are not synonymous. Harvey, Town and Yarkin (1981) discuss this issue in relation to the so-called 'fundamental attribution error' or the tendency to give person, rather than situation, attributions (Ross, 1977). They begin by stating, correctly, that the idea of any kind of *error* presupposes criteria for accuracy. While some researchers do use normative statistical models for this purpose, there appears little justification for the use of the term 'error' in attribution research. Following Kruglanski and Ajzen (1983), the term 'bias' should be used, connoting a subjective tendency or preference for a given cognition over possible alternatives. While agreeing with this distinction, the term 'heuristic' seems yet more preferable. Heuristics are generally automatic strategies which 'reduce complex inferential tasks to simple judgmental operations' (Nisbett and Ross, 1980, p. 7). They are rules of thumb, drawn from cultural wisdom rather than statistical models (Turner and Giles, 1981), which lead to quite reasonable decisions much of the time (Ajzen and Fishbein, 1983).

This view of human social judgement as 'different' rather than 'worse' is also proposed by Wells (1981). He offers a valuable distinction between two ways in which people have come to think about causal forces in their social environment. 'Original processing' refers to the direct observation of relationships, such as the covariation between two events. This is exactly analogous to Kelley's (1967) notion of covariation and has been shown when the stimuli considered cannot be assimilated to previous knowledge (e.g. Ajzen, 1977; Hansen and Lowe, 1976). In contrast, 'socialized processing' concerns how people learn about causes, and adopt cultural hypotheses, through language-based communications. As Shweder (1982) had recently pointed out, complex causal reasoning by inhabitants of the Trobriand Islands did not have to wait for a textbook on inductive logic (cf. Hutchins, 1980). This topic of socialized processing is, however, something that attribution theorists and researchers have practically ignored.

The criticisms in this section appear timely and urgent, pressing us to question how far our methods and preconceptions have fashioned the image of the lay attributor whom we study. It is interesting to note how different today's analyses of complex cognitive processes look from Michotte's (1946) conclusion that causal interpretation was direct, subconscious and perceptual. The impact of the critiques has been quite considerable, drawing attention to the operation of cognitive heuristics and also reviving an interest in motivational and functional aspects of attribution, as will be underlined in this volume.

Has attribution been asocial?

According to several critics, attribution theory has been guilty of neglecting a variety of social factors. Thus, Apfelbaum and Herzlich (1970–71; cf. DaGloria and Pagès, 1974–75; Deschamps, 1973–74) criticized a number of early studies for neglecting the social beliefs of perceivers, their personal involvement in experiments and their relationships with other participants. They argued that Jones and Davis's (1965) theory placed too much emphasis on what is personal and differentiates an actor from others, and too little emphasis on the social characteristics that an actor shares with others. This, they propose, may mask the importance of attributions that refer to an individual's group membership and that explain behaviour in terms of group stereotypes. Thereafter, Kelley's (1967) theory was criticized for treating the lay person as a statistician, and for focusing too narrowly on the perceiver's search for an 'objective' view of the world.

Apfelbaum and Herzlich's article was indeed a polemic, backed up with no empirical data. They do not appear to have considered the value of studying attribution as an intra-personal cognitive process. A more reasoned evaluation was provided by Steiner, who conveyed both the strengths and shortcomings of attribution theories in calling for a revival of the question, 'How do attributions affect the collective enterprise that is our way of life?' (Steiner, 1974, p. 103). Polemics may none the less have a value in provoking close consideration of key issues, as seen in the interchange between Semin (1980) and Harvey (1981). Semin claimed that the distinction between personal and social causality had led to a disregard for the social context. Harvey's reply drew attention to three main strands of work that address the question of whether attribution theory and research have been asocial.

The first is the study of 'accounts', initiated by Scott and Lyman (1968) and outlined at length in a later book (Lyman and Scott, 1970). Accounts are 'statements made to explain untoward behaviour and bridge the gap between actions and expectations' (Scott and Lyman, 1968, p. 46). This approach is very much a social one because it underlines *to whom* an explanation is given, and with respect to what background expectancies an explanation is necessary. Thus, social relationships and social knowledge are key issues. These authors also considered how accounts may be made to manage the impressions of an 'audience', an issue considered below. Second, Harvey considers some of the interpersonal work, such as that of Orvis, Kelley and Butler (1976) on attributions in close relationships. This research has been relevant and important to the day-to-day living of people in a social world (see also Harvey, Wells and Alvarez, 1978; Horai, 1977; Sillars, 1981). Thus attribution work cannot be said to have completely ignored the interpersonal social context. Finally, Harvey points to current work which is integrating Heider's attributional analysis and Mead's (1934) symbolic interactionism (see Stryker and Gottlieb, 1981; Zito and Jacobs, 1979).

Harvey's rejoinder would seem to scotch the claim that attribution theory and research are asocial. There is still, however, much room for expansion, especially at the level of intergroup, societal and cultural explanations. Thus the present volume has taken social extensions as one of its major themes.

INTEGRATIVE THEMES

Social extensions

This section summarizes some attempts to explore wider social dimensions of attribution. These reflect some of the great strengths of attribution theory, forging links with the study of intergroup relations and social influence, and pave the way for chapters in the present volume that explore attribution in novel frameworks or extend previous work.

Preceding the present volume, my own starting-point was the claim that attribution theory had been rather individualistic in its concern with explaining the behaviour of individuals, rather than examining attributions at the intergroup level. As outlined previously (Deschamps, 1983;

Hewstone, 1981; Hewstone and Jaspars, 1982a, 1983b), research at this level would examine how members of different social groups explain the behaviour of members of their own and other social groups (cf. Tajfel and Turner, 1979). Studies in this vein consider the attributions offered by individuals acting as group members (e.g. Duncan, 1976; Greenberg and Rosenfield, 1979; D. M. Taylor and Jaggi, 1974) and the patterns of attribution offered by different groups (e.g. Deaux and Emswiller, 1974; Hewstone and Jaspars, 1982b). Many such studies have drawn attention to a group-based equivalent of individual self-serving biases in attribution. Thus, while a tendency has been found for individuals to explain events in ways that favour themselves and enhance their personal identity (e.g. Bradley, 1978), group members too tend to make dispositional attributions for positive acts (and situational attributions for negative acts) of ingroup members (see Pettigrew, 1979). In this sense, at least, one can extrapolate from interpersonal to intergroup attributions.

A second extension was to explore attributions in some of the contexts suggested by the social influence literature. Thus, group polarization research was extended to consider the effect of group discussion on attributions. As this literature suggests (e.g. Myers and Lamm, 1976), the effect of group discussion on attributions was to enhance the initial response tendencies. Hewstone and Jaspars (1982b) reported that, while black and white adolescents both blamed racial discrimination more on the system than on dispositions of young blacks, more extreme judgements (but in the same direction) were generated by both groups following discussion. Current work on self-presentation suggests another way in which to look at the context of attributions, as shown in the work on self-serving attributions in public and private settings (see Bradley, 1978; Tedeschi and Reiss, 1981).

Research can also be enriched by examination of the social nature of what is to be explained. Specifically, attributions in more social contexts may involve a shift from explaining individual behaviour to the explanation of economic and social differences between groups (cf. Furnham, 1982a, 1982b, 1983). Hewstone, Bond and Wan (1983) investigated the explanations offered for ingroup-favouring and outgroup-favouring social facts in a field study in Hong Kong. For example, students from the two universities there had to explain why the alumni of the older, higher-status institution were placed more highly in the Hong Kong workforce. The results showed that explanations offered by members of high- and low-status groups could be used to provide respondents with a positive image of the ingroup, in comparison with the outgroup. Irrespective of whether a fact favoured the in- or outgroup, respondents made attributions that served their own group's interests. In this way, unwelcome facts were avoided (or explained away) by an appropriate choice of attribution. Thus members of one group explained the occupational superiority of the other group in terms of the former's network of business connections.

A final social extension looks to the shared beliefs that underlie attributions common to members of a group or society. It would seem that an analysis in terms of such beliefs could make a major contribution to attribution theory and research, especially in relation to the genesis of such attributions (Pepitone, 1981). A beginning has been made by a study on how schoolboys from private and state schools in England explained the academic success and failure of members of their own and the other group (Hewstone, Jaspars and Lalljee, 1982). The results showed a familiar pattern of group-serving attributions (although these were limited to certain dimensions of Weiner's (1979) model), but in addition revealed a strong correspondence between each group's attributions and the beliefs that members of the two groups shared about group membership, the school system and occupational opportunities. Pupils from private schools held beliefs about their academic superiority and differentiated between the groups in terms of 'effort' and 'ability'. For state school pupils, who were keenly aware of inequities in the school system, 'luck' was the most important dimension for intergroup differentiation.

The work completed so far has raised a number of interesting issues and opened new avenues. One obvious development should be towards the very broadest of social dimensions – the cultural foundations of attribution. Semin (1980) has made the point that the ANOVA model may be of very little relevance to the attributions of someone from a different cultural background, and Agar (1981) has argued persuasively for an integration of ethnographic and attributional positions. Rich examples of 'primitive' forms of causal attribution occur throughout the writings of ethnographers. Thus Lévy-Bruhl (1925) reports that the natives of Motumotu in New Guinea ascribed a kind of pleurisy epidemic to, in turn, the presence of a missionary, his sheep, two goats and, finally, a portrait of Queen Victoria. Such examples are interesting, but Jahoda (1979) is quite correct to insist that they do not bear directly on the psychological processes or behavioural consequences derived directly from any part of attribution theory. He argues that concepts drawn from theories that originate from within a particular culture cannot necessarily be operationalized in different cultures. An example is the Zande 'theory' of dual causation, where 'witchcraft' (as a distant cause) often operates in connection with a common-sense explanation (as an immediate cause) (see Evans-Pritchard, 1937). For these people, Jahoda says, the distinction between internal and external attributions would make little sense. As we shall see later, it may be more fruitful to consider such explanations in terms of their functions.

Despite Jahoda's rational pessimism, the cross-cultural extension of attribution theory is pregnant with possibilities for giving us a richer approach to the study of common-sense explanations. It could very usefully contribute a novel analysis in terms of the interpretation of the world by members of the group or culture under study (see Agar, 1981; Freedle, 1981; Geertz, 1973). However, what little work has so far been reported has been disparate and in need of collation. Selby (1975; cf. McDermott and Pratt, 1976) reported some interesting findings on the Zapotec Indians of Mexico. This culture seems to question the validity of personal attributions and emphasizes instead social roles and social categories (an apparent reversal of the picture gleaned from Western societies). However, this failure to find personality attributions seems hardly to justify Selby's conclusion, that attribution theory is not universally valid. There is no need to question his findings, but rather to underline that a broader kind of attribution theory – one that dealt more with social roles (see V. L. Hamilton, 1978) and with the kind of witchcraft explanations encountered – should encompass such phenomena.

Thus, some gains of a more social approach are already apparent, while others hold great potential. We seem to know quite a lost about interpersonal attributions, somewhat less about attributions in intergroup contexts, and precious little about societal foundations of explanations. Chapters in the present volume extend this social theme in a number of ways. They propose more detailed analyses of the social knowledge underlying explanations; the perspectives of persons and others; the origins of common sense; the functions of explanations; and the cultural dimension of attribution. These contributions are highlighted below, after an exposition of the second theme permeating the book.

Functional extensions

Most social scientists sensibly pause for thought before opening the Pandora's box of any discussion of functions and functionalism. As Cancian (1968) has stated, few concepts in modern social science have promoted quite the same amount of discussion. While the gains of functional analysis have been championed by some, others have dubbed it illogical and value-laden, insisting that it cannot explain everything. *Caveat emptor*!

One of the problems with considering a functional analysis is that this topic has excited debate and controversy in sociology and anthropology far more than in psychology. It is also somewhat difficult to reconcile the approaches from other disciplines (e.g. Cancian, 1968) with those from psychology (e.g. Heidbreder, 1973). To cut short some of the more esoteric issues, it may be helpful to propose 'strong' and 'weak' forms of functionalism.[3] The strong form would propose that any individual or social pattern is explained by the effects and consequences of the pattern. These consequences are seen as necessary to proper functioning, and specific patterns are limited to (or explained by) specific needs. Thus it might be claimed that a pattern of attribution (e.g. making internal attributions for one's own success) is explained by its function in maintaining self-esteem.

Before adopting this form of analysis, one would have to counter the traditional arguments used to discredit functional analysis. The most important of these is that it is vacuous; this relates to the dictum that 'a theory which explains everything, explains nothing.' Second, there is the danger inherent in this general approach, that patterns become seen as essential and thus unchangeable, or at least dangerous to change. This is the claim that functional analysis is 'Panglossian' in its focus on utility, harmony, integration, coherence and so on (Vayda, 1967). It takes its name from Dr Pangloss (the character in Voltaire's *Candide*), who held the excessively optimistic view that 'All is for the best in this best of all possible worlds.' These criticisms might be seen as particularly problematic (or, paradoxically less so) in the light of the criticism that attribution theory's absence of a formal structure already blesses it with an embarrassing power to explain almost everything (S. E. Taylor, 1981). In addition to these points, there is the danger that merely pointing to functions is sometimes interpreted as if it constituted an explanation of the phenomenon, a lapse that hinders the development of theory by implying that the task of explanation has been at least partially accomplished.[4]

These arguments are much less telling for the weak form of functional analysis, which holds that theory and research may gain from a more detailed consideration of the possible functions fulfilled by common-sense explanations. This is the form of functionalism espoused in this volume and, as was the case with the earlier discussion of social dimensions of attribution, the present work builds on previous research.

Numerous writers have suggested that attributions serve psychological and social functions, and the current attraction of this view may lie, in part, in its potential for 'humanizing' the kind of creature studied by a predominantly cognitive social psychology (see S. E. Taylor, 1981). It is not, of course, alone in providing this service, and the integration of social cognition and affect is also a worthy undertaking (see Fiske, 1981).

As S. E. Taylor (1981) relates, the rise of cognitive social psychology came as a movement away from motivation-based models of attitudes and behaviour. Thus it is not surprising to find that the original theories of attribution acknowledge motivational factors in discussing the perceiver's needs and purposes (see Heider, 1958, p. 296; Jones and Davis, 1965, p. 220; Kelley, 1967, p. 193). These first soundings have now become echoes as the pendulum swings back towards more systematic treatments of the functions of attributions. The progress so far can be conveyed by distinguishing three primary attributional functions (following Forsyth, 1980, and Tetlock and Levi, 1982).

1 *The control function*   The motivation to achieve a degree of control over the physical and social world – especially understanding the causes of behaviour and events – is dealt with in a number of relatively early psychological writings (e.g. Kelly, 1955; White, 1959) and continues to be an important theme. Forsyth (1980) subdivides this function into explanation and prediction, referring to the central role of Heider's (1958) and Kelley's (1967, 1971) work. Thus, common-sense explanations provide cognitive control for past and present events, as well as anticipating future occurrences (see Wortman, 1976). Numerous illustrations are provided by Bains (chapter 7 below), and this function helps us to understand why, for example, parents may blame themselves when their children contract leukaemia, or why cancer victims may attribute their disease to past misconduct.

2 *The self-esteem function*   Few psychologists would disagree that positive self-esteem is essential to emotional well-being, and this function is exemplified in people's need to protect, validate or enhance their feelings of personal worth and effectiveness (see Greenwald, 1980). Evidence comes mostly from studies that have compared self-attributions for failure and success. The motivational perspective holds that people protect their self-esteem by making internal attributions for success and external attributions for failure (e.g. Weary, 1981; Zuckerman, 1979).

3 *The self-presentation function*   Actors can potentially control the view that others have of them by communicating attributions that are designed, consciously or unconsciously, to gain public approval and to avoid embarrassment (see Baumeister, 1982; Tedeschi and Reiss, 1981). This function has been discussed in relation to the work of Scott and Lyman (1968) and has also been supported by a number of experimental studies which examined self-enhancing and self-effacing attributions in public and private settings (e.g. Arkin et al., 1980; Bradley, 1978). Thus attributions tend to present a positive self-image after public, not private, outcomes.

There appear, then, to be convincing claims for motivational or functional bases to attribution, and we have the beginnings of a taxonomy of such features. However, while some authors accept that attributions fulfil multiple functions (e.g. Bradley, 1978; Miller and Ross, 1975), others argue that motivational–functional explanations for these tendencies are indistinguishable from cognitive–informational ones (Tetlock and Levi, 1982). The latter authors maintain that it is possible to put forward information-processing explanations for most of the so-called motivational tendencies; equally, they admit that motivational approaches can make much the same predictions as the information-processing perspective. Thus for the present it appears impossible, or at least premature, to choose between the cognitive and motivational–functional perspectives.

The functional viewpoint does provide a valuable orientation, although it is not claimed that attributions invariably fulfil functions, or that these are always readily identifiable. Providing answers to these questions should be a topic for a fully fledged functional theory; some of the issues that require clarification are dealt with by Tetlock and Levi (1982). In this volume the approach is simply to argue for a re-direction of the research spotlight so that individual and social functions of attribution are not relegated to the background by a purely cognitive approach, and where functions are not limited by the boundaries of the previous, largely inter-personal, work. Most attribution researchers are concerned with how and why attributions are made, and often with how to explain departures from rational or normative statistical models. The weak form of the functional approach should form a legitimate part of research on these questions. Its use does not necessitate any confrontation with the cognitive approach, which is, instead, seen as vital and complementary. The use to which functional, and social, extensions are put is now considered by outlining the subsequent chapters.

OVERVIEWS OF THE CHAPTERS

Although two broad themes have been described, it would probably be unrealistic to expect a volume of contributed chapters to take a completely consistent theoretical position. The chapters reflect the breadth of an attributional approach, but all share the view that attribution theory is still a viable framework for the study of social understanding. The points of overlap between chapters are cross-referenced throughout, but are most easily highlighted now within the three parts of the book.

All the chapters in Part I deal with 'Principles of attribution'. They examine central assumptions made in some of the original theories and argue for new foci of research in the form of processes or organizing principles underlying attribution. In chapter 2 Jos Jaspars presents results of his research on the process of causal attribution in common-sense. His approach is premised on the view that, until we better understand causal and non-causal reasoning in controlled laboratory experiments, it is premature to grapple with the complex pattern of common-sense explanations in everyday life. Jaspars begins by outlining a formal model of causal attribution which, like Kelley's, proposes that information is processed by considering for each possible attribution (person, stimulus etc.) whether it is present when the effect is present, and absent when the effect is absent. This logical model suggests that attributors might determine which condition is necessary and sufficient for the behaviour to occur, and it gives a fair account of the experimental data. Shortcomings of this model then serve as the stimulus to a new process model.

From tests of the model it seems that the process of causal attribution is derived from rather different premises than those envisaged by Kelley's model. Single events are explored primarily at a superficial and low level of generality – for example, in terms of the interaction of certain conditions – rather than in terms of main factors. Thus, common-sense explanations seem to be quite different from scientific explanations and the process underlying such judgements is not as had previously been thought. Moreover, Jaspars contends that differences between scientific and common-sense explanations are likely to be more pronounced when inferences serve specific functions.

Robert Farr and Tony Anderson (chapter 3) are concerned with attributions and differences in perspective. They point to various limitations of the Jones and Nisbett (1971) hypothesis, that actors and observers make different attributions for the same phenomenon. The differing perspectives of self and other are contrasted with those of actors and observers. These authors propose an analysis of the role of perspective in freely occurring and dynamic social exchanges, such as conversations, which would consider the significance of language in relation to attribution theory. It would also go beyond Jones and Nisbett's limited notion of divergent perspectives in the visual modality.

The latter part of the chapter traces the origins of actor–observer differences beyond the work of Jones and Nisbett. This includes a discussion of Ichheiser's (1949) work, which reveals that the tendency to overestimate personal factors in making attributions must be considered in relation to society's 'collective representation' of a person (cf. Moscovici and Hewstone, chapter 6 below). The roots of the actor–observer distinction can also be traced to historical developments in psychology, notably the impact of Gestalt ideas and the rise of behaviourism. Finally, some consequences of this less cognitive and more social approach are outlined, focusing on speaker–listener differences and the importance of a shared perspective for efficient communication.

In chapter 4 Mansur Lalljee and Robert Abelson are concerned with three broad issues: (1) Is there some underlying order to the different explanations offered for different types of events? (2) How, if at all, are explanations for a particular event organized? and (3) Can one compare explanations for different types of events? They begin by discussing the existing work that has tackled these questions, but then propose an approach based on real-world knowledge. This 'knowledge structure' approach, based on the work of Schank and Abelson (1977), deals with goal-based explanation, focusing on the use of 'scripts' – stereotyped sequences of action in a particular setting. A script (or the goals it serves) may convey an explanation in itself or guide the perceiver towards a general statement of what events are worthy of explanation. This approach stresses the importance of context (in calling forth or ruling out particular explanations) and emphasizes how much explanation relies on social knowledge. While the authors have no illusions about the scope and difficulty of their task – to reconstruct where explanations come from – it is none the less one the pursuit of which should render attribution theory less idealized and more social.

The final chapter of this first section (chapter 5, by Arie Kruglanski, Mark Baldwin and Shelagh Towson) integrates attribution theory with other major parts of social cognition. It unifies approaches within attribution theory by seeing them as parts of a larger epistemic, or knowledge-seeking, process. The lay–epistemic theory assumes that all knowledge is made up of propositions or beliefs, which are validated through deductive logic and via evidence concerning specified events. But there is an infinite number of hypotheses to explain any pattern of evidence, and thus the process of hypothesis generation must be 'frozen'. The lay–epistemic analysis of attribution is based on the identification of a general principle: lay causal inferences are seen to be deduced from propositions that the attributor holds to be true. The general principle is that of 'deducibility', the central and invariant process of attribution, in contrast to the varying and domain-specific content of different attribution theories.

These authors also extend their analysis to the area of 'biases and errors' in judgement, predicting when perceivers will use certain statistical and non-statistical notions. The chapter argues for an essential similarity between the processes of naive and scientific knowledge acquisition (for a rather different view see chapter 6), but also accepts that the latter may be fallible too. This ambitious attempt to integrate the principles of various parts of attribution theory provides a suitable conclusion to the first part of the book.

The three chapters in Part II are concerned with 'Social foundations of attribution'. Serge Moscovici and Miles Hewstone (chapter 6) open this section by examining attributions in relation to common-sense ideas shared throughout societies, or groups within societies. The notion of a 'social representation' is the backbone of this chapter; it deals with how technical and scientific knowledge is transformed into common-sense knowledge. Ordinary people often incorporate scientific notions (from genetics, biochemistry, psychology, etc.) into their explanations for every-day events. This chapter suggests that many people treat science as a hobby and avidly read popularized science journals. The notion of man as a 'naive scientist' is rejected and the term 'amateur scientist' used instead.

The aim of a social representations approach is to specify more clearly how common-sense 'theories' evolve from science. The chapter deals with both 'external' processes of transformation (how unfamiliar scientific ideas are given substance and made familiar) and 'internal' processes of trans-formation (whereby common sense uses scientific theories to describe, classify and explain events). These shared representations classify and sort information, indicating when and where an explanation is required. Finally, consistent with this volume's general themes, some social func-tions of explanation are considered. The chapter indicates how common sense can be made part of a social psychological analysis, and how the notion of a social representation is central to a social psychology of explanations.

In chapter 7 Gurnek Bains examines the role of control as an organizing principle for the understanding of explanations. The first two sections provide evidence for this function by looking at how people attempt to maintain control in their understanding of events such as everyday acci-dents, disasters and unemployment. The latter half of the chapter explores the evidence for control motivation in intergroup phenomena and societal events. This deals, briefly, with stereotyping and with theories of supers-tition shared throughout societies. The final section considers individual differences in the tendency to make controllable explanations and whether the control motive has individual or cultural–ideological origins. Thus Bains's work brings attribution theory through the gamut of intrapersonal, interpersonal, intergroup and societal levels of analysis, to provide compelling evidence for a vital control function of common-sense explanations.

Bains concludes his chapter with the suggestion that different cultures may vary in the extent to which they value control. This cultural dimen-sion of attribution is then taken up in more detail by Michael Bond in chapter 8. The three central aims of cross-cultural psychology might be considered as follows: (1) striving to find universals; (2) cataloguing failures to replicate; and, consequently, (3) revising theory where necess-ary. These aims are illustrated in the chapter with some examples of how cross-cultural studies have proceeded. Despite the potential gains of such work, practical and methodological difficulties have restricted attribution studies in this vein. Bond advocates the use of unobtrusive techniques to examine when people make attributions, and he advises strongly against the unthinking export of Western attribution categories.

Referring to studies on self-serving attribution in India, Hong Kong and the USA, Bond reveals how carefully the experimental context should be chosen in order to confront the issues of real interest to the researcher. Attributions in private/anonymous settings will yield comparative data on underlying cognitive processes, whereas judgements made in public/ interpersonal situations will address the question of interpersonal norms across cultures. This chapter takes the social dimension of attribution to one logical extreme, a potential development which can only be fruitful. It is, however, still only potential, because Bond's chapter is cautiously entitled a 'proposal' for cross-cultural studies. His contribution is to plant some signposts for future research and to give social psychologists a much-needed prod in the cross-cultural direction.

Part III of the book deals with some of the 'Applications of attribution theory'. These have grown in recent years, in response to the popularity of the basic theories, and have been the subject of at least one book (Frieze et al., 1979). However, the topic deserves further treatment in the present volume for two main reasons. First, previous work has been rather limited in its preoccupation with applications of Weiner's (1979) theory, at the expense of others. Second, the present contributors have been chosen with an eye to emphasizing the functional aspects of attribution when examined in applied contexts.

The field of applications is inevitably yoked to the issue of relating attributions to behaviour. Failure to bridge the gap between cognition and behaviour has been called the 'most serious failing of modern cognitive psychology' (Nisbett and Ross, 1980, p. 11; cf. Schuman and Johnson, 1976) and some writers voice the fear that too much hope may be held out for the crucial mediating role of attributions (see S. E. Taylor, 1981). Richard Eiser (chapter 9) is concerned with this neglected link between attributions and behaviour. Before researchers make too much of the relation, three important issues require clarification. First, Eiser argues that the study of when people ask 'why' questions in various realistic contexts should be an important part of the application of attribution theory. The second issue concerns expectancy and prediction. Eiser contends that the notion of expectancy should link attribution research with social cognition research on probabilistic reasoning, thus relating prediction and causal attribution more precisely. The third issue deals with the relations between attributions, learning and behaviour. Eiser maintains that the separation of theories of social cognition from theories of behaviour is no longer tenable – they must be integrated.

Eiser concludes that cognitive social psychologists should pay more attention to the adaptive functions served by making inferences, and he states why attributions must be considered in relation to other cognitions, motivations and behavioural processes. This chapter is critical, but constructive. Those who really believe that attribution theory can be applied, and that attributions have significant behavioural consequences, should take heed of these criticisms. None the less, research relating attributions and behaviour is growing, as shown by the two other chapters in this section.

Jennifer King (chapter 10) draws attention to the behavioural consequences of certain explanations in the area of health and illness. King advocates an attributional extension of the Health Belief Model (HBM), an approach that sees the patient's perceptions of illness as crucial. In this way she aims to predict compliance, clinic-attendance and so on from individuals' perceptions and explanations of illness. The integration is clearly symbiotic, improving knowledge of the determinants of perceived risk and vulnerability, linking attributions and their consequences, and emphasizing the functional significance of common-sense explanations in a practical setting. Some of the predictions suggested by this integration are followed up in the author's studies. The first deals with beliefs about and explanations of heart disease, showing that health beliefs are related to causal explanations, and that perceived risk seems to be especially influenced by attributions. The second study relates explanations of high blood pressure to predictions of which patients will attend a screening for high blood pressure. Both studies yield encouraging results and, although this synthesis is still preliminary, the prospects are exciting.

Frank Fincham (chapter 11) begins with a critical look at how firm the foundations are for clinical applications of attribution theory. The first organizing principle for his review refers to attempts to elicit external, rather than internal, attributions for individuals' current maladaptive behaviour. The second organizing principle concerns attempts to engender internal, rather than external, attributions for adaptive behavioural change. Fincham offers a more cautious specification of the conditions under which attribution theory has clinical implications and he advocates closer links between the *theory*, rather than loose and general notions, and its clinical applications.

Fincham is more sanguine about the genuine applications in the field of close, interpersonal relationships. In these more social settings the functional role of attributions becomes more obvious and more crucial. For example, the therapist may be faced with the difficult problem of replacing an attribution that is functional for one partner, but clearly damaging for a relationship. This chapter also examines how certain types of attribution may prevent overt conflict and suggests possible interventions.

These overviews reveal that the present volume includes chapters that continue to puzzle over the processes of attribution in rather artificial settings, as well as examining explanations in more social and realistic contexts. It should also be underscored that the knowledge accrued about how attributions are used in the 'real world' may alter our starting assumptions, thus testifying to the crucial interplay between theoretical and applied work.

CONCLUSIONS

This introductory chapter has outlined the major theories of attribution and some pertinent criticisms of the original work. It has also spelled out the two themes or extensions running through the book and has integrated the contributions herein. Having looked at the past and the present, it seems appropriate to conclude by casting an eye to the future. To this end, a personal view of two potential developments is offered.

Different contributors to this volume will obviously have different views of what the future should hold, and some of their empirical goals and priorities are stated. This is as it should be, and these goals include greater use of process models and more naturalistic stimuli; analyses of the social knowledge from which attributions are generated; and closer consideration of the relationship between attributions and behaviour. There is and always has been a great diversity among attributional approaches (Harvey, 1981), but one major vision which several of the contributors share is that we should move towards a common-sense psychology of the type Heider (1958) envisaged. To borrow a phrase from Scott and Lyman (1968), attribution theory 'may not yet have forgotten its founders, but it may still have forgotten why it was founded'. It *was* founded as part of a common-sense psychology. In Heider's words, 'scientific psychology has a good deal to learn from common-sense psychology' (1958, p. 5). Common sense has been defined as: 'the source or system of those very general beliefs about the world which are universally and unquestioningly taken to be true in everyday life',[5] but this seems a rather far cry from the subject matter of most attribution studies. The results amassed from the multitude of studies constitute an impressive empirical yield, but future research should take a less restricted view. It is a vast and optimistic project, but perhaps in ten years' time we will be able to report on large-scale studies of common sense in domains such as the law, health and illness, prejudice and economics, which will paint a rather different picture of lay understanding and explanation. This is not to decry laboratory studies, nor to ignore what has been learned about human causal reasoning, but simply to supplement the existing work with a richer approach to social knowledge and one that would return us to the Heiderian fold from which we seem to have strayed.

What is 'common' sense will, of course, vary between groups, societies and cultures. Hence the second proposed development is for a fuller, multi- and inter-disciplinary orientation, embracing sociology, anthropology, ethnography and other social sciences. Disciplinary parochialism has, in fact, been less characteristic of attribution theory than of other areas of research. Attributions and explanations are fundamental phenomena; thus they bring together scholars from many disciplines – such as sociology (e.g. Scott and Lyman, 1968), philosophy (e.g. Sabini and Silver, 1980), jurisprudence (e.g. Lloyd-Bostock, 1983) and anthropology (e.g. Selby, 1975). As Harvey (1981) has insisted, attribution theorists lay no special claim to comprehending reality and cooperation between disciplines is a 'must' (see Antaki, 1981).

To the question of when both these developments should proceed, the answer is now. Heider (1976) relates how long it took for his work on social perception to be taken up. His vision of a common-sense psychology has yet to be fulfilled, the present volume included. This collection of papers does, however, contribute towards a more complete attribution theory by elucidating social and functional extensions of previous work. The aim of this book is therefore to strengthen the status of attribution theory. Like other highly popular approaches before it (e.g. balance theory and cognitive dissonance), the narrowly cognitive version of attribution theory will inevitably fall from grace. Indeed, cognitive psychologists themselves have become aware of the limitations of too narrow a view (compare Neisser, 1966 and 1976).

The view contained in this volume is that an emphasis on social and functional aspects of attribution will locate the study of common-sense explanations firmly in the social world. In turn, more common-sense analysis and more mutli- and inter-disciplinary work will help us to understand the origins, uses and consequences of socialized processing. This is a vital counterweight to the unflattering view of the lay person as an imperfect scientist. As this happens, attribution theory will be less susceptible to the ebb and flow of research fashions in social psychology, for our discipline can never afford to stop studying realistic and meaningful common-sense explanations of social events.

ACKNOWLEDGEMENTS
The author gratefully acknowledges the help of Michael Bond, Frank Fincham, Howard Giles and Penny Turner in commenting on an earlier draft of this chapter.

NOTES

1   Wegman (1979) has considered Freud (1893–95) as the progenitor of attribution theory, through the latter's notion of *falsche Verknüpfungen* (literally, 'wrong connections' between an effect and its perceived cause).

2   See Quattrone (1982) for evidence relating to the opposite tendency.

3   The interested reader might consult Cancian's (1968) comparison of 'nondistinctive', 'traditional' and 'formal' variants of functional analysis; and Heidbreder's (1973) treatment of functions as 'activities' and 'utilities'.

4   Cancian (1968) spells out that the construction of a functional theory would involve elaboration of 'functional equivalents' of the observed pattern, specification of when and why any particular pattern occurs, and the placing of this against a yardstick of 'functional prerequisites' (i.e. a list of functions that are to be fulfilled). Without these restrictions, the search for any pattern's functions is limited only by the imagination and ingenuity of an investigator. Thus, proponents of the strong form of functional analysis are provided with a set of stringent criteria.

5   The definition is given by A. Quinton in the *Fontana Dictionary of Modern Thought* (Fontana/Collins, 1977).

PART I
Principles of Attribution

2 The Process of Causal Attribution in Common Sense

Jos Jaspars

INTRODUCTION

Research in attribution theory has been concerned extensively with informational, motivational and belief determinants of causal explanations, but relatively little attention has been paid to the mental *processes* involved in making causal inferences. In none of the classical contributions (Heider, 1944, 1958; Jones and Davis, 1965; Kelley, 1967) is there an indication of how the information on which causal inferences are based is encoded, nor is it clear how such inferences are related to subsequent behaviour. The only explicit suggestion in these original publications is that the processes of causal attribution are similar to the analysis of experimental data in science. Although no one has actually suggested that common-sense causal reasoning resembles in detail a mental calculus akin to analysis of variance, terms like 'the ANOVA model' or Kelley's 'cube' have become common parlance in social psychology and appear to imply a greater similarity to scientific analysis then seems plausible on intuitive grounds. Recent studies of causal attribution processes have cast serious doubt upon the ANOVA model of causal explanations in common sense. As Smith and Miller (1979a, 1979b) and Druian and Omessi (1982) have pointed out, the ANOVA model predicts the same response time for all types of attributions. However, their studies show that response times are not the same for different kinds of explanations. The significance of these findings will be discussed below.

The aim of this chapter is, first to present and test a formal model of causal attribution that is true to the original conception of attribution theory as formulated by Kelley (1967), specifying precisely how information might be encoded. In doing so it will become clear that the model has certain limitations, in that (1) there are systematic deviations from the predictions made by the model, and (2) there appear to be conditions for which the model is not able to offer any prediction at all. It is this second observation that has prompted the search for an alternative model based on the notion of a subjective scaling process. However, even such a model does not indicate precisely how and where any biases that appear to exist in common-sense causal reasoning might emerge, as compared with John Stuart Mill's System of Logic. The second aim of this chapter is to show that cognitive inference processes involved in causal attributions are the exact reverse of the computational procedures that constitute a scientific analysis of observed covariation. This is not merely a technical matter of how to proceed in discovering the causes of observed variations in behaviour. The results of the experiment, which will be reported in the last part of this chapter, suggest that people in everyday life have a radically different conception of what counts as a satisfactory explanation. Single events are predominantly explained at the 'superficial', low level of generality, and explanations in terms of main factors, such as the person, the instigating stimulus or the circumstances, are offered only after, or in conjunction with, such superficial simple main effect or interactional explanations. A scientific analysis, of course, looks for just the opposite kind of explanation, by first decomposing observed variations in behaviour in terms of general or main factors and then considering interactions of such factors as residual effects.

A LOGICAL MODEL OF CAUSAL ATTRIBUTION

Kelley has suggested that an 'effect is attributed to that condition which is present when the effect is present and which is absent when the effect is absent' (1967, p. 194). He also suggested that for many problems in social psychology the relevant causal factors are persons, stimuli, times and modalities of interaction with stimuli (see Hewstone, chapter 1 above). The model's principal implication is that certain *patterns* of information, which can be described in terms of consensus, consistency and distinctiveness, lead to certain attributions. It is curious that these suggestions have not led to a test of the model that is in agreement with Kelley's original conception of causality. McArthur (1972) tested for a number of informational patterns but did not make specific predictions for many of them. In virtually all other studies (see Kelley and Michela, 1980) researchers have not even bothered to investigate the effect of various patterns of information as suggested by the model, but have focused on the main effects of consensus, consistency and distinctiveness for which the model does not give any predictions. However, Kelley has always emphasized patterns of information, suggesting that some of these have a prototypical quality and that causal attributions for other patterns are affected by the similarity between these patterns and the prototypical ones (Orvis et al., 1975).

In opposition to these versions of the ANOVA model, a logical model has been developed, which is directly related to the original covariational definition of causality. This model also suggests a way in which information, as presented in attributional vignettes, might be coded such that causal inferences can be derived from the encoded information. As the model has been presented in full elsewhere (Jaspars, Hewstone and Fincham, 1983a) only a brief description will be given here.

A formal representation of a vignette can be obtained by coding subject, verb and object of each sentence for presence and absence of the actor, the stimulus and the circumstances mentioned in the initial sentence. If this is done one can establish for the vignette as a whole whether the presence of any of these three determinants (or any combination of these determinants) is a necessary and/or sufficient condition for the behaviour to be mentioned in conjunction with it. If a behaviour is indeed attributed to that condition that is present when the behaviour is present and absent when the behaviour is absent, the model makes unique predictions for each of the eight combinations of consensus, consistency and distinctiveness. The predictions can be easily derived from the pattern of these informational determinants when one realizes that they can be interpreted as degrees of generalization over actors, circumstances and stimuli (see Hewstone and Jaspars, 1983a). Lack of consensus indicates that behaviour does not generalize over actors and the person becomes a necessary condition for the behaviour. If the actor is the only necessary condition, because the behaviour generalizes over circumstances and stimuli, he or she is also a sufficient condition for the behaviour to occur in the vignette and can therefore be interpreted as the cause of the behaviour. The same argument holds for lack of consistency, which indicates a circumstance attribution and distinctiveness (lack of stimulus generalization) that makes the entity a necessary condition. These rules of causal inference are in fact relatively simple for vignettes of the McArthur type because the subject only has to verify which determinants are absent when the behaviour is absent in order to determine the cause of the behaviour. The predictions that can be derived in this way are presented in table 1 together with the results of a replication of McArthur's experiment.

As can be seen in table 1, the largest proportion of attributions is always made to the conditions (causal locus) that is predicted by the model. Chi-square analyses show that the predicted attributions occur significantly more often than is to be expected on the basis of chance.

Although the predictions derived from the logical model are confirmed

TABLE 1 Proportion of attributions made to each causal locus as a function of consensus, distinctiveness and consistency*

Locus of causality	Informational pattern †‡							
	CsD̄Cy	CsDCy	ĈsD̄Cy	CsD̄Ĉy	ĈsDĈy	CsDĈy	ĈsD̄Ĉy	ĈsD̄Ĉy
Stimulus	0.20	**0.45**	0.08	0.11	0.22	0.14	0.06	0.13
Person	0.23	0.00	**0.48**	0.02	0.05	0.05	0.11	0.00
Circumstance	0.03	0.08	0.03	**0.22**	0.03	0.20	0.06	0.19
Stimulus × person	0.27	0.16	0.17	0.20	**0.44**	0.03	0.17	0.11
Stimulus × circumstance	0.06	0.11	0.05	0.13	0.02	**0.22**	0.02	0.14
Person × circumstance	0.13	0.06	0.06	0.16	0.09	0.14	**0.39**	0.11
Person × stimulus × circumstance	0.08	0.14	0.13	0.17	0.16	0.22	0.19	**0.33**

* Total number of attributions in each condition is 64.
† Cs = high consensus
  Ĉs = low consensus
  D = high distinctiveness
  D̄ = low distinctiveness
  Cy = high consistency
  Ĉy = low consistency
‡ Predicted loci of causality are set in bold type.

to a very large extent in the present experiment, one can not be entirely happy with the model for at least two reasons.

In the first place, it is obvious that many attributions are made to conditions that are not predicted by the model. Table 1 shows that, although the highest number of attributions is always made to the predicted locus of causality, this number never amounts to more than 50 per cent of all attributions. The majority of attributions are made to other loci of causality taken together. These deviations from the predictions made by the logical model appear to be systematic in the sense that *stimuli* seem to be regarded as a cause when they are *necessary and sufficient* conditions for the behaviour to occur, whereas *people* are regarded as causes when they are seen as *sufficient* conditions and *circumstances* are more likely to be interpreted as a cause when they are *necessary* conditions. It appears therefore that the notion of causality entertained in common sense is a rather flexible one which varies to some extent with the nature of the cause. Sufficiency and necessity of conditions are not always weighted equally, but their importance appears to depend upon the condition that is considered.

More critical for the logical model however is the fact that subjects appear to make attributions when the informational pattern does not allow for any prediction on the basis of covariation. In the first column of table 1 the behaviour that is described in the vignette occurs universally. The actor shows the same behaviour in the past with respect to other stimuli, and everyone else also shows the behaviour with respect to the same stimulus under the present circumstances. Thus, the described behaviour does not covary with any of the conditions mentioned, and still subjects show a clear preference for certain explanations in this case. Although this deviation from the logical inference model again could be accommodated by assuming that it results mainly from the response format used or prior expectations of the subjects, it seems more reasonable to consider an alternative model which could deal with these exceptions as an intrinsic part of the model itself.

It is suggested that the causal 'inference' process resembles more the construction of a mental model in the sense of Johnson-Laird (1980).

A SUBJECTIVE SCALING MODEL OF CAUSAL ATTRIBUTIONS

The first suggestion that the construction of a mental model might play a role in making causal attributions emerged from a study of success and failure in four-year-old children conducted by Löchel (1983). In this study the children performed a number of masculine and feminine tasks in which they were sometimes made to fail or to succeed. Afterwards they were asked, for each of their performances, why they could or could not do the particular task. In quite a few instances the children would give as an explanation an answer like: 'My hands are a bit too warm' 'too stiff' in order to explain why they could not loosen a bolt. Or, in another case, 'A bit difficult for me. . . can do the next one.' What these answers apparently suggest is that the children, in giving answers to the question 'why', are making a subjective comparison between their own ability to do the particular task and the ability required for a successful completion of the task. If they succeed, their own ability surpasses the required ability; if they fail, the task is too difficult because it requires greater ability than they possess at the moment. In other words, the children sometimes appear to give as an explanation of their own success, or failure, a comparative observation which can be interpreted as an interactive or simple main effect attribution. It is in a way the most direct explanation one can give, because it is restricted to the particular event and does not seem to imply a generalization across tasks, time or actors. It holds only for the particular actor at a particular moment and for a specific task.

In the experiment conducted by Löchel the children were not allowed to observe the performance of other children, nor were they given the same task more than once, so that it was impossible for them to generalize on the basis of the available information. In the replication of the McArthur experiment, however, which was discussed in the previous section, such information was varied systematically, allowing the subjects to construct a more complete mental model of the relationships between actors, stimuli and circumstances.

In order not to complicate matters too much from the start, let us consider a simple example which is related to the experiment conducted by Löchel and to performance vignettes as used in the McArthur replication. Let us further neglect for a moment the circumstances (i.e. consistency information) and focus on the effect of consensus and distinctiveness in making causal attributions of achievement behaviour.

The subjective scaling model of causal attribution proposed here suggests that subjects do *not* encode the information contained in a vignette in the way presented above, but instead interpret the consensus and distinctiveness information as *relations* between persons and stimuli which can be represented in the form of a subjective scale. Thus, when the subject is told that a person succeeds in (a) particular task(s), this information is interpreted as indicating that P's ability is at least equal to the ability required for successful completion of the task(s). Thus P dominates S, or $P \geqslant S$.

If the subject is told in addition that P did not succeed in another task S_i

(distinctiveness information), this information can be interpreted as S_i dominating P, or $S_i \geqslant P$. Finally, the subject might be given the information that another person, P_i did not successfully complete the task(s), and hence this information would be interpreted as S dominating P_i or $S \geqslant P_i$.

Obviously, as more information is added, the various relations can be combined in an overall representation, which in our example forms a complete rank order of personal abilities and task difficulties. Thus $S_i \geqslant P \geqslant S \geqslant P_i$.

In figure 1 this rank order has been represented in the customary form of a scale. If we assume that subjects treat these dominance relations as transitive (Coombs, 1964), it follows immediately from the subjective scale we have constructed that P is more able than P_i and S_i is more difficult than S, although this information is not presented to the subjects. In other words it is suggested that subjects construct a scale that represents the relative ability of the actor and the comparative difficulty of the task. In figure 1 such scales have also been constructed for other conditions than the one used in our example. The principles of construction are simple. Consensus information indicates that all persons dominate S, indistinctiveness indicates that the actor P dominates all tasks. Lack of consensus indicates that P dominates S and S dominates other persons, whereas distinctiveness is represented by P dominating S and all other tasks (S_i) dominating P.

It is now easy to see how the subjects might answer the question, 'Why does P succeed at S?', given that they have constructed such scales as presented in figure 1. An immediate answer would be to restate the information that is contained in the question or the description of the event one is asked to explain. In all four conditions of figure 1 P dominates S (i.e. in the figure P is shown above S), and hence an answer like 'P is good at S' would constitute a satisfactory explanation, although at a low level of generality. In condition (d) in the figure no other explanation is immediately evident from the constructed scale. In conditions (b) and (c) the positions of P and S suggest however an immediate generalization, because P is obviously seen as very able in condition (b) and the task S can be interpreted as easy in condition (c); hence the subjective scaling model would suggest that, in addition to the specific explantion already mentioned, subjects explain condition (b) by stating that the success is due to the ability of P and condition (c) by referring to the fact that S is easy. In condition (a) both interpretations are obviously possible and the model would therefore suggest that subjects will mention either P or S or both as the cause of success.

The data presented in table 1 strongly support the subjective scaling

Information patterns

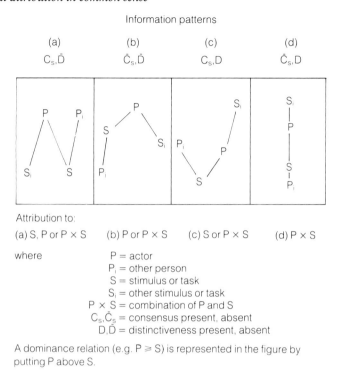

Attribution to:

(a) S, P or P × S   (b) P or P × S   (c) S or P × S   (d) P × S

where

P = actor
P$_i$ = other person
S = stimulus or task
S$_i$ = other stimulus or task
P × S = combination of P and S
C$_s$,Ĉ$_s$ = consensus present, absent
D,Đ = distinctiveness present, absent

A dominance relation (e.g. P ⩾ S) is represented in the figure by
putting P above S.

*FIGURE 1 Partial rank-orders representing dominance relations between consti-
tuent elements of hypothetical vignettes*

model. This can easily be seen if one averages the results for the high- and
low-consistency conditions and disregards attributions to the circumstances. High consensus and low distinctiveness leads primarily to P × S
attributions but also to P and S attributions separately. Low consensus
and low distinctiveness gives rise to person attributions but also to a
substantial number of P × S attributions. High consensus and high
distinctiveness strongly implies attributions to the stimulus, but P × S
attributions are also given relatively often. Finally, low consensus and
high distinctiveness (condition (d) in the figure) produces mainly P × S
explanations although stimulus explanations are also presented to some
extent.

The evidence presented here in support of the subjective scaling model
cannot, of course, be regarded as decisive, since both the logical model
and the subjective scaling model predict the results equally well if it is
assumed in the logical model that a cause in common sense can either be a
sufficient or a necessary condition. One test that might *differentiate*

between the two models could perhaps be realized by finding out whether subjects in fact construct a partial or simple order of the elements presented to them in a story. If they do, they should be able to answer questions about the relative ability of the persons involved in the story, and the degree of difficulty of the tasks, when we are considering achievement-oriented behaviour. It should even be possible to test for information that has not been given, but can be inferred from the data presented and the assumption of transitivity. If the actor in the story succeeds in a particular task in which almost every one else fails, do subjects infer from this information that the actor is more able than the other persons in the story?

One might also assume, as suggested by Johnson-Laird (1980; pp. 103–106) that the order of presentation of information affects the accuracy of the representation. One might argue, for example, that it would be more difficult for subjects to construct a subjective scale when they are given the information in a sequence that does not allow them to construct a scale, step by step, but requires that some information is kept separately in memory until it can be combined with other information that is presented later. Ruble and Feldman (1976) have reported informational order effects in causal attribution, which is compatible with the prediction made here.

Over and above such more or less direct tests of a subjective scaling model, it would be interesting to explore the mental representations more extensively by studying how much processing time various conditions take. The logical model presented above does not make any differential predictions, because it requires the subject to go through the same process irrespective of the informational condition, whereas differences in response times could easily be encompassed in a subjective scaling model. One would suspect, for example, that if local or interactional explanations have priority over explanations that require generalization over stimuli, persons and or occasions, response times should be faster for such explanations than for main factor explanations. Recent studies by Smith and Miller (1979a, 1979b) and Druian and Omessi (1982) show that this is indeed the case. The remainder of this chapter offers additional evidence that attempts to answer, at least in part, some of these questions.

COMMON-SENSE EXPLANATIONS OF FAILURE IN EXAMINATIONS

One of the limitations of many causal attribution studies is that the subjects are presented not only with a fixed and restricted response format, but also with 'second-hand' stimulus material in which they are simply informed about the degree of consensus, consistency and distinctiveness of a particular kind of behaviour. They are not required to observe the covariation of conditions and behaviour as it occurs. Since it is well known that observers are not very good at detecting covariation (Nisbett and Ross, 1980) it is tempting to conclude that the principle of covariation underlying the ANOVA model 'should be qualified as applying to perceived covariation' (Kelley and Michela, 1980, p. 462). However, this does not exclude the possibility that, in addition to biases in inferring consensus, consistency and distinctiveness from observed covariation, subjects may be using a different information-processing rule than is suggested by the ANOVA model. In order to find out whether all erroneous attributions are due to 'misperception' of consensus, consistency and distinctiveness or are the result of a different causal inference process, we would have to conduct an experiment in which covariation can actually be observed by the subjects and the response format allows for a differentiation of the two phases of the inference process. A study was conducted in which parents of high school pupils were presented with four cases of individual pupils who had failed their Advanced-level examination in one or more subjects. Three types of information were presented to the parents:

(1) the A-level results of a whole sixth form;
(2) the class list of the subject for all pupils taking that subject over the last three examinations before taking A levels; and
(3) the report cards of a particular pupil for the same three examinations.

These types of information form the naturalistic counterparts of the abstract attributional categories of consensus, consistency and distinctiveness.
Four informational patterns were used:

(1) low consensus, low distinctiveness and high consistency, which should lead to a person attribution;
(2) high consensus, high distinctiveness and high consistency, which should lead to a stimulus attribution;
(3) high consensus, low distinctiveness and low consistency, which should lead to a circumstance attribution;
(4) low consensus, high distinctiveness and low consistency, which should produce a person, circumstance and stimulus interactional attribution.

After the parents had been given ample time to inspect the various results that were spread out in front of them, they were asked why they thought a particular pupil had failed an A-level examination in a specific subject. After they had finished they were prompted to think of possible other reasons, and were then given a structured question which had exactly the same response format as the one used by McArthur. The complete response was tape-recorded and later transcribed.

An elaborate coding scheme for analysing the replies was developed and subsequently applied by at least two independent judges. The scheme itself consisted of a refinement of both Kelley's informational categories of consensus, consistency and distinctiveness and his classification of causes in terms of person, stimulus and circumstances. In addition, all the replies were also coded for 'location' to establish which information the subjects paid attention to and to determine whether the information was in fact perceived correctly. These three types of coding were applied both to the smallest meaningful units in the transcripts (where units usually consisted of simple declarative sentences containing information about one or more pupils and their performance in particular subjects at a specific time), and to the replies as a whole. The results that were obtained with the global coding of the explanations are presented first, followed by a discussion of how the parents arrived at the overall or final attributions made.

The results presented in table 2 appear to confirm the predictions made by the logical model in the sense that, exactly in those conditions where a factor or combination of factors is both *necessary and sufficient*, more attributions are made than would be expected on the basis of chance. The one clear exception is the attribution to the circumstances. To the extent that predictions are not exactly confirmed, it should be pointed out that these 'wrong' attributions almost always include the predicted locus of causality. In the case of low consensus, low distinctiveness and high

TABLE 2 Final attributions for A-level failures

| Locus of causality | | Informational patterns*† | | | | Total |
		$\hat{C}s\bar{D}Cy$	$CsDCy$	$Cs\bar{D}\hat{C}y$	$\bar{C}sD\tilde{C}y$	
Person	P	**22**	0	0	0	22
Stimulus	S	0	**14**	3	0	17
Circumstance	C	0	0	**0**	0	0
Stimulus × person	PS	6	16	0	7	29
Stimulus × circumstance	SC	0	1	13	1	15
Person × circumstance	PC	2	0	8	1	11
Person × stimulus × circumstance	PSC	2	1	8	**23**	34

* For explanation of symbols used see table 1.
† Predicted attributions are set in bold type.

consistency, for example, all attributions include 'something about the person' and never just the stimulus or the circumstances or both. Whether one wants to accept this as a confirmation of the logical attribution model or not, one is still left with the problem that certain subjects in the end settle for an explanation that is not in accordance with the precise prediction made by the theory. In order to see how these 'off-diagonal' attributions develop, it is important to attempt to follow the attribution process in its various stages to see how the final attribution is reached.

First of all, we have to consider whether the subjects did in fact notice all the information they were given. We cannot, of course, be sure that those subjects who failed to mention a particular piece of information paid no attention to it. However, taken over all conditions, it appears that the parents almost always (99 per cent of the time) mentioned the performance of the pupil in the particular subject in the past, whereas they almost never mentioned the performance of other pupils in other subjects in the A-level examination. All other information was mentioned in about 50 to 70 per cent of the cases. The over-emphasis of the pupil's performance in the subject in the past may be due to the fact that this information was in fact presented twice, once in the form of the marks on the class list and once on the report cards of the pupil. Similarly information concerning the performance of other pupils in other examinations was less salient, because it had to be selected from the overall list of A-level results, which was the same for all four conditions that a parent had to judge. These shortcomings in the experimental design could explain the preponderance of person-by-subject explanations in the experiment, but this defect cannot explain the differences between conditions.

More important, however, than these general deviations from the expected pattern is the fact that most of the information was noticed by only slightly more than half of the subjects. One wonders, therefore, whether the differences between the subjects in the information they noticed was related to the attributions they made. In fact, it appeared that there was no significant relationship between information mentioned in the reply and attribution made for any of the conditions. This surprising result seemed to warrant a closer inspection of the information perceived in the various experimental conditions. There was found to be only a 7 per cent overlap between the descriptions of the information by the subjects in the various experimental conditions. Combined with the finding that the differences in description of the information within conditions are not related to the attributions given, one is tempted to conclude that the subjects did notice the information correctly, but used different rules of causal inference. The suggestion that has been made in the past (Kelley and Michela, 1980), that deviations in attributions from the predictions that follow from the ANOVA model are due to biases in the perception of information, is clearly not tenable in the light of the present findings.

What, then, can explain why the subjects so often do not make the attribution they should make, if they performed a logical analysis as suggested above? A possible answer to this question can be found in considering in greater detail the free responses that the subjects gave to the first question. In their replies the subjects did not give just one explanation, but considered various possibilities. These multiple occurrences allow us to analyse the combinations and the sequences of the multiple explanations. To illustrate this point let us consider first the sequences of attributions that were given in the condition that should lead to a stimulus attribution. The sequential contingencies for the main response categories are presented in table 3. As can be seen, the most likely explanation to be given at first instance is not a stimulus explanation but an interactional explanation mentioning both the actor and the school subject. This interactional explanation can take many forms: for example 'he just wasn't suitable material for the history course' or 'he found physics difficult' or 'he didn't get on with the teacher.' Usually this first explanation was followed by either another interactional explanation of the same kind or by a more general stimulus explanation like 'the history course was hard.' A similar explanation might or might not be added, but that usually completed the reply to the first question. The subjects appear to start with a more specific or local explanation and either leave it at that, or go on to give a more general explanation. Clearly, the subjects do not seem to

TABLE 3 Sequence of multiple attributions for Cs, Cy, D condition*

| | | Attributions in position (t + 1) | | | | | | | Last |
		P	S	C	P×S	P×C	S×C	P×S×C	φ
Attributions	P	4	1		5		1		3
in position	S	1	13		2		1		12
t	C								
	P×S	2	8		16		1	2	12
	P×C								
	S×C	1	1		1		1		2
	P×S×C							1	2
First	φ	6	4		19		2		1

* Cell values indicate how often a particular attribution is followed by the same or another attribution. The last row indicates the attributions that were mentioned first; the final column indicates the attributions that were mentioned last. For explanations of symbols see table 1.

follow a sequence that one would expect on the basis of an ANOVA model. If they had done so they would have had to conclude, first, that there was a main effect of the stimulus (school subject) factor in this particular condition and then that there was in fact no need to specify that the subject was difficult only for this particular pupil.

A similar result emerges for the person attributions. Very few person explanations (6 per cent) refer to a general ability of the person. Most person attributions are made to abilities or powers of the pupil that are relevant to examinations: 'he just wasn't good at exams.'

Nevertheless, the parents did not always start with such a relatively specific explanation. In about 20 per cent of the explanations they started off with a general remark that the failure had something to do with the pupil, without indicating whether they were thinking of a general or a specific characteristic. Such vague explanations would normally be followed by an interactional explanation, relating the characteristic of the pupil either to the subject in which he failed or to exams. They rarely continued the generalization process to make an attribution to a general ability like intelligence, although the information pattern quite clearly showed that the pupil had failed before and was failing in other subjects whereas other pupils did quite well in the subject in other examinations.

CONCLUSIONS

It would seem that the results of these studies strongly suggest that the cognitive processes involved in making causal attributions are different from what one would expect on the basis of an ANOVA model. Any *process* model of causal explanations would have to include a description of the encoding and representation of the available information. At first it was suggested that this process might take the form of registering the presence and absence of the behaviour that is to be explained in conjunction with the presence and absence of the covarying conditions suggested by Kelley. The rules of inductive logic as formulated by John Stuart Mill then lead to unique causal inferences for the conditions that can be generated by varying systematically the consensus,consistency and distinctiveness of the observed behaviour. Such a model is quite successful in predicting the attributions made by subjects except for the fact that there are certain systematic deviations that would require a number of additional assumptions. One of these is that the notion of causality in common sense, as utilized by subjects in these experiments, is much less strict than the one underlying the ANOVA model. Subjects sometimes regard a necessary condition as a cause, and in other cases a sufficient condition is apparently treated as a cause. The latter interpretation seems to be regarded as more appropriate for personal causality, whereas the former is applied more often when physical causality is considered. Given that this is the case, certain behaviours that elicit a situational explanation are more likely to receive a causal explanation in terms of necessary conditions, whereas other acts, which ask for an explanation in terms of qualities of the person, presuppose the notion of causality as a sufficient condition. Although this assumption improves the predictive power of the inductive logic model of causal attribution, it is still not satisfactory because it cannot explain the preponderance of certain interactional explanations, especially when there is in fact no covariation to be observed.

This finding suggested that the process of making a causal attribution is more like the construction of a mental model, as suggested by Johnson-Laird, than a logical inference process. One possibility is that subjects may construct a subjective scale which represents the relationships between the constituent informational elements. Such a way of representing information does allow for the making of inferences in the case where there is no covariation, but it also has various other interesting implications, one of which was pursued further in this chapter. A representation of information in the form of a simple or partially ordered scale suggests that interactional configurations do allow for less generalization over actors, stimuli or circumstances than patterns of information that, according to the inductive logic model, should lead to attributions to the person, the stimulus or the circumstances. Assuming that generalization cannot occur unless one has observed the particular events, it would seem that subjects can always give a specific or local explanation that does not claim any generality, and that such a local explanation can be generalized when the information allows for it; but it does not follow that subjects always do this. If the process does indeed go from the specific to the general, one would expect to find a preponderance of local or interactional explanations because general explanations are arrived at via a process of generalization from particular instances.

This idea was tested in the last experiment, which showed that subjects by and large correctly perceived the information presented to them, but nevertheless do not draw the conclusions one should expect on the basis of a logical inference process. They appear to start with local explanations and continue sometimes with more general explanations, but this is by no means always the case. The process of generalization or induction often remains incomplete and leads to an abortive explanation from the point of view of a logical analysis.

These findings and their tentative explanation are potentially quite important. They suggest that any deviations from scientific explanations in common-sense reasoning are due not so much to misperception of the available information as to the consequence of the *sequence* of processing information. A scientific analysis of the kind suggested by ANOVA procedures starts with a consideration of general effects and, when necessary, adds local variations to the general rules or laws that are formulated. The process underlying common-sense causal explanations appears to start at the other end, with attributions to specific, local factors, and does not always reach the level of generality at which the ANOVA-type explanation starts.

One reason for this process difference might simply be that we have usually studied explanations of single events in common sense whereas the typical scientific question is one that asks for the explanation of a general phenomenon. If the parents in the last experiment had been asked to explain why pupils (in general) fail or succeed in school, they might have presented many more main effect explanations. It would also seem reasonable to assume that generalizations were not needed in the context of a psychological experiment, because the predictive validity of a local explanation can be just as high as that of an explanation based on a linear combination of general factors. However, if the parents had been asked to make such generalizations for a particular purpose, they might have been quite capable of doing so.

It would, therefore, be quite interesting to see how the social and psychological functions that explanations can have in everyday life may affect the process of making causal attributions. It would seem reasonable to assume that informational determinants might become relatively unimportant when social and functional requirements predominate, as is to be expected in any real-life circumstances. If one of the primary purposes of explanations is to predict and control one's environment, it is to be expected that the inductive inference process, which appears to come rapidly to an end in experimental conditions, will be extended in a direction that serves the purpose of the explanation best. The local nature of explanations offered in experiments suggests that the main informational determinants will be given relatively little weight compared with prior expectations and motivational determinants. Consider for example actor–observer differences in explaining failure in examination owing to lack of general ability of the pupil. Pupils and parents may lack information about the performance of other students, and teachers may not have the information about the performance of a pupil in other subjects. As a consequence of the differences in availability of information, they would probably arrive at different attributions; but the logical model presented above would predict causal inferences that are at variance with the well established finding that actors attribute their behaviour more to the situation and observers more to the person. A full logical analysis would lead us to expect either no explanation or a person explanation in the case of the pupil and a person-by-subject interactionist explanation by the teacher. Since this is not what in fact seems to happen, one might assume that the causal inference process stops short in the case of the pupil who does not generalize a local explanation (e.g., not getting on with the subject teacher) whereas the teacher may in fact over-generalize since the pupil ends up at the bottom of his subjective scale. Attributional differences between actors and observers in real life may therefore be not so much a problem of selectivity of information or motivational bias, as a difference in the extent to which one is willing to generalize one's initial local explanations. Whatever the case may be, the findings presented in this chapter suggest that causal reasoning in common sense is based on cognitive processes that are quite different from the mental calculus suggested by modern methods of scientific analysis like Analysis of Variance.

ACKNOWLEDGEMENTS

I would like to thank Christine Allen, Bea Jaspars and Michael Schleifer for their help in designing, running and analysing the experiments reported in this chapter. I also wish to express my sincere gratitude to other members of the attribution research group, especially for disagreeing with me without disturbing our socio-emotional relationship. The research conducted was supported by the SSRC grant HR 7135.

3 Beyond Actor–Observer Differences in Perspective: Extensions and Applications

Robert M. Farr and Tony Anderson

INTRODUCTION

By 'perspective' we mean a point in space/time from which events are viewed. This is the usage which G. H. Mead, the Chicago philosopher and social psychologist, borrowed from Einstein via the philosophy of A. N. Whitehead (Mead, 1927). In the early development of his social psychology, Mead made much use of the idea of 'assuming the role of the other' with respect to oneself. This mutual capacity for a reciprocal exchange of roles greatly facilitates many of the purely commercial transactions of everyday life.

Towards the end of his life, Mead began to substitute 'adopting the *perspective*' of the other for his earlier usage of 'assuming the role' of the other. Man[1] is unique as a species, according to Mead, in his capacity to act towards himself as an object. This capacity developed out of man's experience of being an 'object' in the social world of other people. Man's selfhood emerges from social interaction. Initially, she is an object to others and so, as a consequence of interacting with those others, she later acquires the capacity to act towards herself as an object. Man therefore is a 'minded organism'. Mind, for Mead, was a purely natural phenomenon which had emerged in the course of human evolution. He appreciated the unique role of language in the evolution of mind (Farr, 1980). Language is a distinguishing feature of man as a species. For Heider (1958), analysing the meaning of such linguistic terms as 'persons', 'can', 'trying', 'ought', 'want', 'blame, 'responsibility', etc., shed useful light on the psychology of interpersonal relations. For both Mead and Heider, man's experience of her own selfhood is rooted in her membership of a linguistic community. Language enables one to refer to things and/or to people in their absence. Attribution theorists have yet to appreciate fully the significance of language (cf. Hewstone, 1983).

By adopting Mead's notion of 'perspective', we believe we can go 'beyond' the present stage of research on actor–observer differences in perspective. Can the divergence in perspective between 'actors' and 'observers', first noted by Jones and Nisbett (1971), be applied to speaker–listener and writer–reader differences in perspective? Heider (1958) demonstrated how O is 'represented' in the mind of P as a necessary first step to understanding the psychology of interpersonal relations. O, however, need not remain silent in the presence of P. This calls for a more dynamic model than Heider provides. If P and O engage each other in conversation they will likely change their representations of each other. Much of the current research on attribution theory fails to account for the dynamics of such freely occurring social exchanges. How does the representation of 'the other' in the mind of the actor control his or her actions? The 'actor', here, is Heider's 'P'. We need a general theory of action which includes such specific activities as speaking and writing. How speakers and writers 'represent' their listeners and readers, respectively, is vital to an understanding of their dialogue or of their writing (Sanford and Garrod, 1981).

THE DIVERGENCE IN PERSPECTIVE BETWEEN 'ACTORS' AND 'OBSERVERS': JONES AND NISBETT (1971)

There is a pervasive tendency for actors to attribute the cause of their behaviour to aspects of the situation in which they act, while observers explain the same actions in terms of the stable, dispositional characteristics of the actor. The emphasis on causal attribution is quite clear – actors conceive of themselves as being responsive to the demands of the situation, while observers locate the causes of the actor's behaviour in his or her stable dispositions (e.g. personality traits). Most subsequent experimental studies confirm Jones and Nisbett's hypothesis, as Kelley and Michela (1980) point out in their review.

Jones and Nisbett think that either cognitive or motivational factors can explain these biases. They express these distorting factors, however, in terms of the psychology of individuals, rather than of interpersonal relations. The individual's concern about self-evaluation and self-presentation is a motivational factor. There are various cognitive factors; for example the amount (and type) of information available to the observer differs from that available to the actor – observers lack information about the degree of distinctiveness and consistency in the actor's behaviour. Observers are nomothetic, while actors are idiographic, in orientation. Furthermore, they differ in their knowledge of the context of action; for example, an observer's knowledge of the actor's feeling states is always indirect. Thus, actors and observers base their judgements on *different* information.

Jones and Nisbett also think that actors and observers differ in how they process the *same* information; e.g., different aspects of the situation are salient either for actors or for observers, and this salience affects their attributions. Salience here is equivalent to attention. We find this interesting, in terms of our own, more mental, approach. Jones and Nisbett contend that these differences in attention are a consequence of the location of the sensory receptors, which, in the actor, are 'poorly located for recording the nuances of his own behaviour' (Jones and Nisbett, 1971, p. 85). Clearly, they must be referring here to the eyes, rather than to the ears. From an observer's perspective it is action that is figural and dynamic, while it is the environment that is stable and contextual. Actor and observer thus differ in their *visual perspective*. This divergence in perspective corresponds to their differing locations in space.

CRITIQUE OF THE JONES AND NISBETT 'DIVERGENT PERSPECTIVES' HYPOTHESIS

Heider's classic work concerns the perception of *other persons*. Kelley (1967) first suggested that self-perception (e.g., the work of Bem and of Schachter) might usefully be included in this classic field of person perception. Bem (1967) adopts the interesting theoretical stance that people use the same kinds of evidence, and follow the same logic, irrespective of whether they are making self-attributions or deciding about the characteristics of others. Actors are self-observers, who view their own behaviour in terms of its surrounding context. In response to questions they infer their attitudes and feelings. Where Jones and Nisbett argue for a *divergence* in perspective, Bem seems to be arguing for an *identity* of perspective. Can these two positions be reconciled?

We wish to include the differing perspectives of speakers and listeners as well as those of actors and observers. When speaker and listener are two different persons and each one alternates between speaking and listening, then we have the makings of a conversation and an exchange of views becomes possible. If the two conversants face each other, then, in addition, we have the scenario of an inter-view.

However, when speaker and listener are one and the same person, the divergence between them in perspective virtually disappears, both spatially and temporally. This self-reflexivity is the basis of the social behaviourism of G. H. Mead. The very *divergence* in perspective, to which Jones and Nisbett drew our attention, is due largely to the fact that 'the actor need not, and in some ways cannot, *observe* his behaviour very closely, (Jones and Nisbett, 1971, p. 85; emphases added). It is difficult, though not impossible, for an actor to become an 'object' in his own visual field. We can, however, and do, hear ourselves speak.

The spoken word evokes in the mind of the speaker the same response as it does in the minds of other listeners. Language makes man much more reflexive (in the sense of being self-reflexive) in the auditory, than he is in the visual, modality. The divergence in perspective between self and other is directly related to the inter-face between them. P and O are on different sides of P's face; but when P talks, P hears what O hears. We cannot, literally, see ourselves as others see us, but we do hear ourselves in a similar, though not identical, manner to how others hear us. The divergence in perspective between speaker and listener is thus not so acute as that between observer and observed. It is sufficient to note, here, that much of the evidence that Bem adduces to support his theory of self-perception is of an auditory nature; for instance, the individual recalls hearing herself make various verbal statements under conditions that she associates with telling the truth, etc. It is best to assume, with respect to visual perception, that there is a divergence in perspective between self and other while bearing in mind that this may not be so when we consider speaking and listening. Thus we would reconcile the apparent discrepancy between Bem, and Jones and Nisbett by drawing attention to the difference in modality likely to be involved (i.e. that between listening and observing).

The perspectives that Jones and Nisbett (1971) chose to contrast were those between 'actors' and 'observers' rather than between 'self' and 'other'. This is a pity. They lost, thereby, the phenomenal perspective of Heider's P. In the now quite voluminous research literature that they sparked off, the perspective of the 'actor' remains a shadowy, even a blurred, one. It is difficult, precisely, to identify the actor's perspective because the writers of that literature do not themselves adopt that perspective when they write about it but choose, instead, to describe it from their own quite different perspective as *observers* of actors. Had they retained the perspective of Heider's P we would now be clear about the actor's perspective. This is a perspective that P cannot discard, or escape from, as it is rooted in his *experience* of the world.

The contrast in perspective, in Heider, between P and O is quite stark. The contrast is an existential, rather than a cognitive, one. An *awareness* of this particular divergence in perspective is the *fons et origo* of human self-consciousness. We are here in the realm of the social psychology of mind (where the theory of G. H. Mead is highly relevant) rather than in the realm of 'cognition' *per se*: 'Perceiving is *experienced* as a direct contact with the environment; it is a means whereby objective facts enter the life space. That is why we react in a special way when we notice someone *observing* our behaviour' (Heider, 1958, pp. 15–16; italics added). Here the theoretical perspectives of both Mead and Heider are very close. We are dealing with states of awareness, and not merely with 'cognitions'. Research on the 'divergent perspectives hypothesis' has diluted the significance of Heider's contrast in perspective between P and O. Heider's contrast is between the first and the third person singular. This is transposed, in Jones and Nisbett, into a contrast between two different categories of third person singular. The literary vignette (written in the third person) replaces the P–O, or self–other, divergence in perspective. The stark contrast in Heider is between events occurring in the *mind* of P and the *behaviour* of O. To talk exclusively in terms of 'cognitions' and 'information', as Jones and Nisbett and their successors do, is to ignore the contrast between mind and behaviour. The antidote is a social psychology of both mind and behaviour rather than a non-social cognitive science.

Much attributional research depends heavily on the use of literary vignettes. P and/or O cease to be real 'live' persons and become instead caricatures. We study how 'information' is processed rather than how persons are perceived. A few studies, however, have managed to preserve *part* of the richness of Heider's original distinction. Storms (1973), for example, used video to reverse experimentally the perspectives of actors and observers. He thus allowed ample scope, in his various experimental conditions, for 'I', 'me', 'you' and 'he' to operate. Mower White (1977) asked subjects in her experiment to rate the pleasantness of different balanced and imbalanced triads (POQ) derived from Heider's original theory. In one condition person P was described as 'you' (i.e., the subject), while in the other condition P was an arbitrary boy's name. In both conditions O and Q were other arbitrary boys' names. Balance theory predictions were supported in the former but not in the latter condition. This supports our contention that P, in Heider, is equivalent to the perspective of 'self'. Nisbett and Caputo (1971), in their study, asked college students to write a brief paragraph stating why they had chosen their major field of study and why they liked the girl they dated most frequently. Their subjects were then asked to write brief paragraphs explaining why their best friends had chosen their majors and their girlfriends. Their findings supported the 'divergent perspectives' hypothesis. The contrast, here, is between the second and third person singular, rather than between the first and third person singular. This effective switch in perspective, we suggest, was mediated linguistically, i.e. from 'why do *you?*' to 'why does *he?*' We suggest that a study should be made of the role of personal pronouns in mediating switches in perspective. This is one of our reasons for wishing to go beyond the original Jones and Nisbett distinction which arose within the visual modality.

In Heider's quite distinct notation, 'O' stands for 'Other' (Heider, 1958). O is thus a purely *relational* term. O is O only in relation to P, the Perceiver. O can only be *other* in relation to self or to P. This was an entirely appropriate strategy for Heider to adopt in writing a volume that he intended as a prologue to the study of a psychology of interpersonal *relations*. By transposing Heider's P–O or self–other distinction into a divergence in perspective between actors and observers in general, the relational, as well as the particular, nature of Heider's original distinction is lost. Not only has the distinct perspective of P been lost in the subsequent laboratory experimentation, but some contemporary researchers in attribution theory even use O to stand for 'observer' rather than for 'other' and P to stand for 'person' rather than for 'perceiver' (e.g. Harris and Harvey, 1981, p. 64). This latter twist actually manages to *reverse* Heider's original notation.

By separating P and O, and by treating them as independent individuals, subsequent researchers have fragmented the relational unity of Heider's original conception. Heider is quite clear concerning the *perspective* of P. His whole book portrays just that perspective. This is the perspective of P both as an actor in the social scene and as an observer of the behaviour of others. To separate these two perspectives, and then to locate them in two different individuals, is to shatter the unity of the self that Heider had been careful to preserve. For both Mead and Heider, the self is to be thought of in purely relational terms. Heider, rightly, distinguishes between P and O. If Mead were correct, however, P can 'adopt the perspective' of O (i.e., the other) and thus become an object to himself; i.e., P then becomes self-conscious. P can anticipate, at least in his imagination, how his actions might be read by someone occupying the perspective of O. Mead, rather than Heider, gave us a better idea of how this might come about.

To act intentionally one must be able to anticipate the effects on others of one's actions. To be an effective speaker or writer one must hear oneself speak and be able to monitor (or read) what one writes. Man's effectiveness as an agent is thus highly contingent on the facility with which she can alternate, in her mind, between the competing perspectives of self and of other. Thus, the development of the higher cognitive processes in man depends critically on her capacity for self-reflexion. This capacity, in turn, is rooted in social experience. This account of the self-reflexive nature of man as a species is derived from the social behaviourism of the philosopher G. H. Mead. The dialogue between the 'I' and the 'me' constitutes, for Mead, the activity of thinking. Man's capacity for interacting with herself lies at the heart of her ability to think. Research on attribution theory has, so far, singularly failed to approximate this degree of mental complexity.

For Heider, P and O are to be considered in relation to each other. Most of the research on actor/observer differences in perspective fails to do this. The awareness, on the part of P, that, from the perspective of O, considered as a perceiver, he (i.e. P) is an O, enables him to become conscious of himself as an object, i.e. to be self-conscious. This is the state of awareness that Mead characterized as 'awareness-of-self-as-object'. M. J. Rosenberg's (1969) state of 'evaluation apprehension' is just one facet of this reflexive self-awareness. Another facet is the state of awareness that Duval and Wicklund (1972) refer to as 'objective self-awareness'. These latter two states of awareness, however, are tinged with negativity or apprehension. 'Awareness-of-self-as-object' does not have to involve apprehension or negative self-evaluation; it can, for example, include empathy or inter-subjectivity. We are dealing here with an alternation in the states of awareness of a single individual, rather than with a divergence in cognition between two *different* individuals.

There are two broad options for studying divergences in perspectives if we take them as points in space/time from which events are viewed. We can take an event occurring at a particular point in time and obtain records and/or accounts of it from different locations in space. These might be oral accounts elicited from persons differently located in space with respect to the event in question (or occupying different roles within that particular social setting). One of the 'accounts' might even be a film record obtained from a camera located at a particular spot. The camera thus supplies a perspective from a specific location in space/time. Whether the event is seen 'live' or from a recording, is a temporal variation in perspective. This is the alternative option for experimentally varying perspective. An 'actress', at a later point in time, can view a video recording of her earlier 'live' performance. She then becomes an 'observer' of her own previous performance. This technique was used by Storms (1973) in testing the 'divergent perspectives' hypothesis and is standard practice in the use of self-confrontation in social skills training programmes (Nielsen, 1962).

'Actors' and 'observers', however, are frequently mere roles that attribution theorists assign to individuals. The individuals themselves are often purely fictitious. Literary vignettes comprise far too high a proportion of the stimulus material used in research on attribution theory. Real 'live', flesh-and-blood individuals, of course, have to function both as actors and as observers. The 'divergence in perspective' is then likely to correspond to alternative states of awareness or consciousness. Can we identify, then, the precise mechanisms whereby an experimenter can switch an individual out of one state of awareness into the other? These mechanisms are likely to be simple linguistic devices hidden in the experimental instructions that control and direct the attention of subjects. They are probably so prosaic and common that we scarcely notice them.

The alternative state of awareness to 'awareness-of-self-as-object' is 'awareness-of-self-as-subject (or agent, or actor).' This latter state of awareness is likely to encompass the perspective of the actor. The subject, in this state, is so task-oriented, or engrossed, that he or she is completely un-self-conscious. This contrasts quite sharply with the previously discussed state of 'awareness-of-self-as-object.' Duval and Wicklund (1972) and Wicklund (1975) have identified the experimental arrangements that are most conducive to the production of an 'awareness-of-self-as-object', i.e. the use of mirrors, tape-recorders, seeing oneself on a video monitor, etc. Milgram's conception of the 'agentic state' is probably as good an initial characterization of the alternate state of consciousness as there is available at present (Milgram, 1974; Farr, 1978). It should be possible to identify techniques or devices for switching an individual from one of these states of awareness to the other and this could be an interesting topic for future research.

Jones and Nisbett (1971) tacitly theorize in the language of visual perception. They subtitled their article, '*Perceiving* the *causes* of *behaviour*'. 'Perceiving' here refers to vision, while 'causes' betrays the orientation of the natural scientist and 'behaviour' is descriptive of that which is visible from the perspective of the observer. Their stance is behavioural, while their language is cognitive. The ratio of space devoted to describing the perspectives of 'observers' and 'actors' is that of 5:2 respectively. They even manage to equate the perspective of the actor with that of a behaviourist! Jones is later more explicit: 'Whereas the actor *sees* behaviour primarily as a *a response to* the situation in which he finds himself the observer attributes the same behaviour to the actor's dispositional characteristics' (Jones, 1976, p. 300; emphases added). While 'sees', here, is clearly metaphorical rather than literal, the words 'behaviour' and 'a response to' betray a behavioural bias that is scarcely that of Heider's P. From the perspective of P it is the behaviour of O and not that of P that is figural. In his article on Mead, Blumer better captures the true perspective of the actor: 'The actor acts towards the world on the basis of how he sees it and not on the basis of how that world appears to the outside observer' (Blumer, 1966, p. 540).

One could translate '*perceiving* the *causes* of *behaviour*' into a different theoretical language, e.g. *'understanding* the *reasons* for *actions'*. The context is now one of 'actors' who may be called upon to 'account' for their actions if *others* fail to understand them. The individual, or, more properly speaking, the 'person', is here firmly rooted in his or her membership of a linguistic community. If the two perspectives (e.g. those of 'actor' and of 'observer') are so radically different then we should not be surprised if we need a change in language to express the nature of this difference.

In his critique of attribution theory Buss (1978) distinguished between 'causes' (i.e. that which brings about a change) and 'reasons' (i.e. that for which a change is brought about). He thought it wrong to use the term 'actor' in connection with non-intentional behaviours and argued that actors explain actions (intentional behaviours) in terms of reasons, while observers explain the same actions in terms of causes and/or reasons. Kruglanski (1979), however, challenged this view, arguing that reasons and causes are not to be regarded as two equivalent explanatory types of special significance. 'Rather, reason is seen to represent a particular type of explanation, whereas cause is seen to represent explanation in general or non reason-type explanation in general' (p. 1450). He argues that there are 'an infinity of explanatory types of which teleological explanation is but one' (p. 1450). Kruglanski also attacks Buss's notion of actors explaining actions in terms of reasons and contends that Buss's objection to the linkage of the 'actor' term with non-intentional behaviour is fair only if 'actor' is interpreted narrowly to mean producer of intentional behaviours. Kruglanski takes 'actor' in the broader sense of 'a target person whose responses (voluntary or not) are being explained' (p. 1452) and concludes that 'the cause-reason distinction is not particularly relevant to the paradigm of Jones and Nisbett' (p. 1452). The actor–observer difference is one of non-teleological explanations of the actor's, or target person's behaviour – both situational and dispositional explanations are non-teleological.

Jones and Nisbett's basic error was to adopt the language of 'cognition'. It is insufficiently subtle, we believe, to capture the nuances of the distinction they drew between actors and observers. We also believe that Kelley (1967) was at fault when he sought to integrate self-attributions and other-attributions within a single theoretical framework, rather than choosing to contrast them. The *writer* (of cognitive vignettes, for example), may find it convenient, however, to adopt the third person singular in describing both P and O. This is easier than having to change languages when he switches perspectives. The psychologist, in her role as a scientist, faces a similar problem. How does one integrate the record of O's behaviour, as seen, visually, by P (i.e. the observer), with the oral 'account' that O (the 'actor') might give concerning the 'reasons' for his 'actions'? One should recognize the change in modality here between 'seeing' and 'listening' and hence one should expect a corresponding heterogeneity in the languages involved. One is here face-to-face with the problem of the cross-modal integration of 'information' *in the mind of the research scientist.* This is the classic problem, in the history of social psychology, as to whether or not 'attitudes' (i.e. self-reports) predict behaviour. As an observer of others, the psychologist might well ask questions in order to establish that there are perspectives on events *other than his or her own.* This is standard research practice in participant observation. It is also equivalent, as a research technique, to what one of us, elsewhere, refers to as the social psychology of the inter-view (Farr, 1982a). Here the divergent perspectives of both actor (or participant) and observer are retained within the one methodology.

In a recent article Harris and Harvey (1981) experienced some difficulty in trying to integrate the 'ethogenic' approach of Harré with the classic work in attribution theory. It is easy to understand their difficulty, though some sort of translation ought to be possible. The classic themes in attribution theory originate in the analysis of visual experience (e.g. the 'apparent behaviour' of the Heider and Simmel (1944) film; studies of *phenomenal* causality and of person perception; etc.), while Harré is more concerned with an analysis of rhetoric. It is the problem of trying to relate the language of visual observation to that of speech. When behaviourism became the driving force in American psychology, it led to the rejection of the verbal reports that had been the basis of the experimental psychology of the Leipzig laboratory. The espousal of behaviourism, in the historical development of psychology as a science, was equivalent to adopting the perspective of the observer. This is a theme to which we shall return in the next section.

Harré and Secord (1972) attacked the norms of behavioural orthodoxy, which then prevailed in psychology, regarding acceptable methods of research. They adopted as their own touchstone Strawson's criteria of a 'person' as someone who could monitor his or her own behaviour and give an 'account' of it. This, surely, is the model of the 'actor'. It is certainly a model of a self-reflexive agent. The methodology that flows from this comprises the elicitation and collection of 'accounts'. In essence, the approach of Harré and Secord entailed treating one's informant in a research context as a 'person'. Broadly speaking, their initiative was to switch from the perspective of the observer to that of the actor. It is best, however, to be able to alternate between these two rival perspectives in one's research strategy, rather than to depend exclusively on either the one or the other. Both the orthodoxy and the challenge to it represent partial truths. It would be unwise to hail either as being the full truth. The challenge is in knowing how to fit together the evidence that derives from two such divergent perspectives.

HISTORICAL ANTECEDENTS OF THE JONES AND NISBETT DISTINCTION

Ichheiser (1949) and the sociology of misunderstandings in human relations

Ichheiser (1943, 1949) is an important figure, as he is quoted with approval both by Heider (1958) and by Goffman (1969) and is the acknowledged source of the distinction that Jones and Nisbett drew between the divergent perspectives of actors and of observers. Ichheiser refers to 'the tendency to overestimate the personal and to underestimate the situational factors' (1949, p. 27). His monograph was, in its time, an important contribution to the sociology of knowledge. He identified many of the unconscious errors and biases that enter into social perception. He hoped, by identifying the principles underlying social perception, to be able to explain misunderstandings in much the same way that psychologists can explain visual illusions.

Collective representations

Ichheiser's approach to undertstanding interpersonal relations is firmly rooted in the Durkheimian study of 'collective representations' (see Farr and Moscovici, 1983, Moscovici and Hewstone, chapter 6 below). Heider was much influenced by Ichheiser's original discussion of 'success' and 'failure': 'the misinterpretations which consist in underestimating the importance of situational and in overestimating the importance of personal factors, do not arise by change.' They are the product of the collective experience of Europeans and Americans during the nineteenth century. The dominant ideology in both these continents during this period held the individual to be responsible for his own actions. This was the collective representation of a person (see also Lukes, 1973). It is not an exclusively cognitive bias on the part of the *individual* observer – which is how Jones and Nisbett portray it. The social dimension is missing in the Jones and Nisbett version. The restoration of the social dimension of attributions is part of the theme of this whole volume.

This collective representation of the individual may continue to operate even when it is clearly no longer appropriate. Ichheiser's observations in America, in the aftermath of the Depression, today have an uncannily modern ring about them: 'With millions of people suffering the shocks of continued unemployment, with business failures one after the other, banks closing, etc., it was vividly revealed to the man in the street that he was not, as he had been led to believe, the master of his fate, because

clearly his fate depended upon forces over which he had no control'
(Ichheiser, 1949, p. 62).

Expression, impression and meaning in social contexts

Ichheiser (1949) suggested that it was important to distinguish between
'expression' and 'impression'. It was best to assume that they were different. The distinction corresponds, in part, to that between actor and
observer. Actors express themselves and impressions form in the minds of
observing others. Ichheiser is primarily concerned, in his monograph,
with the study of 'impressions'. Here we have the origin of research on
'impression formation' and 'person perception'. Ichheiser's appreciation
of the importance of this field was highly original. It was not enough, he
argued, to study personality 'in itself'. The impressions that others form of
an individual have important consequences for that person. Therefore,
they are a worthy topic of study. Many of the early studies of 'impression
formation' in social psychology, however, lacked the social significance
that Ichheiser had envisaged because they were impressions of non-
existent individuals. Much of the contemporary research in this field is
still concerned with an information-processing approach to adjectival
checklists (e.g. Anderson, 1965).

Ichheiser's advice was that we should assume that there is little or no
relation between *expression* and *impression*. This means that misunderstandings in human relations are the norm and understanding is the
exception. This is bold advice. It is a strong advocacy of a discrepancy in
perspective between the actor (i.e. the expressive behaviour of P) and the
observer (i.e. the impression of P that forms in the mind of O). Ichheiser
was well able to handle this interface between mind and behaviour. So also
was Heider. The starkness of this contrast between mind and behaviour,
however, is lost in the purely cognitive approach of Jones and Nisbett.

The model of man as actor

Ichheiser's creative suggestion that 'expression' and 'impression' should
be treated separately raises the intriguing problem as to how they could
ever be interrelated. The individual might so present herself (i.e. so
express herself) as to control, or 'manage', the impressions that form in the
minds of observing others. This is the social psychology of Goffman
(1969). He presents a theory of action in relation to an observing and
attentive audience. While the forms of expression that Darwin (1872)
studied were largely involuntary, those that were of greatest interest to
Mead and to Goffman were largely voluntary in nature. The accomplished
'actor' or 'actress' actually 'manages' the impressions that form in the
minds of others with whom he or she interacts socially. Some forms of

expression are still involuntary – so that impressions are 'given off' as well as managed. Goffman writes in terms of 'performances' that are 'intended' for particular audiences. He thus presents a dynamic theory of action which explicitly recognizes the divergence in perspective between actors and observers. We need this sort of model of man as actor in contemporary psychology. At present it is regarded as sociology and not as psychology. It is time for theories of action to play a more central role in modern psychology. Goffman was inspired both by Mead and by Ichheiser.

Gestalt psychology and the origins of social psychology

So far we have looked at the antecedents, in the sociology of Ichheiser, of Jones and Nisbett's distinction. Divergent perspectives between actors and observers, however, have been with us for some time in the short history of psychology. Consider the following dramatic account taken from Koffka's *Principles of Gestalt Psychology* (1936):

> On a winter evening amidst a driving snowstorm a man on horseback arrived at an inn, happy to have reached a shelter after hours of riding over the wind-swept plain on which the blanket of snow had covered all paths and landmarks. The landlord who came to the door viewed the stranger with surprise and asked him whence he came. The man pointed in the direction straight away from the inn, whereupon the landlord, in a tone of awe and wonder, said: 'Do you know that you have ridden across the Lake of Constance?' At which the rider dropped stone dead at his feet. [Koffka, 1936, pp. 27–28]

Koffka then went on to ask the following interesting question: 'In what environment, then, did the behaviour of the stranger take place?' That the horseman galloped across a frozen lake is not in dispute. To explain his behaviour, however, it is necessary to understand the environment *as he believed it to be*. 'The actor acts towards the world on the basis of how he sees it and not on the basis of how that world appears to the outside observer' (Blumer, 1966, p. 540). This is clearly the same divergence in perspective between actor (the rider on horseback) and observer (the innkeeper) that Jones and Nisbett were later to portray. A comparable divergence in perspective exists between an experimenter and those who participate in his research as subjects (Farr, 1976, 1978). There are important links, of a historical nature, between Gestalt psychology and the development of social psychology in America. In the study of attitudes, for example, Campbell (1963) has demonstrated how the 'view of the world' approach to their study came to prevail over the 'consistency of response' approach. These divergent approaches represent the contrasting perspectives of actors and of observers, respectively. The 'view of the world' approach is the phenomenological perspective of the Gestalt psychologists.

The real contrast, in the history of psychology, is probably that between Lewin and Skinner. Lewin was so phenomenological in his approach that he collapsed the perspective of P into that of O; i.e., he put himself in the place of the person whose behaviour he was interested in explaining. He did not retain his own separate perspective or identity; in other words, there was no *divergence* in perspective between P and O. P tried, empathically, to enter the phenomenal world of O. Skinner, on the other hand, adopted the perspective of P on O and described what it was that he observed from that perspective, namely, the *behaviour* of O. He did not seek to elicit from O (by asking questions, for example) any perspective that might be divergent from his own. The theoretical orientations of both Lewin and Skinner are non-social. By adopting Heider's more social notation, it becomes possible to construct a bridge between these otherwise separate, and unrelated, perspectives. Separately, one deals with 'mind' while the other deals with 'behaviour'. Only Heider can handle the interface between mind and behaviour. To translate Heider into the language of cognitive science, as Jones and Nisbett did, is to lose the sharpness of the contrast he set out to sketch. The contrast in perspectives has been with us for some time in the history of modern psychology, e.g. the contrast between phenomenology and behaviourism as alternative bases for modern psychology (Wann, 1964). To be more precise, the contrast is between focusing on P's *experience* of the world (the perspective outlined by Heider) and what it is that P observes from that perspective, i.e., the behaviour of others. Lewin and Skinner give partial accounts – but only a psychology of interpersonal relations can cope with both of these partial insights.

Behaviourism as the perspective of the observer of others

Watson sought to make psychology a branch of natural science by declaring it to be the science of behaviour. Behaviourism was a systematic programme for ridding psychology of mentalistic concepts. With behaviourism there came into psychology the concept of the 'empty organism' and the 'black box'. Speculation as to what might be going on 'inside' the organism or the black box was ruled out in the interests of methodological rigour. This was part of the programmatic attempt to eliminate from psychology all reference to 'consciousness' or 'mind'. One of the early behaviourist texts was intriguingly entitled *The Psychology of the Other-One* M. F. Meyer, 1921). Meyer set out, in writing his text, to provide Robinson Crusoe, on his desert island, with the one book in psychology that would enable him to figure out what sort of man Man Friday was and what he was, and was not, capable of doing. The advice to the methodological purist is to approach the 'other' (whether machine, plant, animal or human) as though 'it' were a total stranger. This thoroughly 'objective' stance was necessary if psychology were to become a branch of natural science. Meyer believed that, in the past, we had a psychology of self – this was part of the inheritance from philosophy. Now, he felt, it was time to develop the psychology of the 'other-one' (i.e., what we now recognize as behaviourism). 'There is a special fact which has greatly retarded the advancement of the psychology of the Other-One – the fact that the psychology of the Self appears so much easier, so much more promising' (M. F. Meyer, 1921, p. 4).

Behaviourism is a *stance*. It is, thus, quite explicitly a 'perspective' in the full sense of Mead's usage of that term; i.e., it reflects what is to be seen from a particular point in space/time. This is the perspective of the observer. In the behaviourist crusade, it was necessary not only to avoid all reference to the 'minds' of others, but also to keep a tight rein on the development of theoretical ideas in the mind of the observer (i.e. in the mind of P, to adopt Heider's notation). In the radical behaviourism of B. F. Skinner one is admonished *not to go beyond the evidence* available to the senses. There is, thus, in behaviourism a certain theoretical impoverishment. This stems from a deliberate decision to avoid all reference either to the minds of others, or to events (such as inferences) occurring in the minds of the observers of those others. Hence there is, here, a head-on conflict between Skinner and Heider.

Attribution theory is directly concerned with the rules of inference whereby the observer does go beyond the evidence available to him (which is the behaviour of O as visually observed by P) when he reads the minds of others (Farr, 1982b). The original Jones and Nisbett (1971) article was a valuable contribution to the debate that Mischel (1968) sparked off concerning the existence of personality 'traits'. 'Traits' may exist as 'biases' or 'inferences' in the mind of the observer rather than corresponding to the characteristics of actors. Ichheiser had already anticipated Mischel's point in his discussion of 'impressions'.

Many researchers have taken up, and greatly amplified, this theme of biases in the mind of the observer (e.g. Nisbett and Ross, 1980). This confirms us in our belief that the hidden perspective in Jones and Nisbett is that of the observer. Frequently the biases that are noted are those of the layman. The canons of orthodoxy from which the layman departs are those of the statistician or the professional scientist. Needless to say, the layman comes off worst in most of these comparisons.

The original concerns of Heider have here undergone a subtle transformation. Heider was interested in taking stock of what it was that the layman knew about his fellow man. What the layman and the psychologist share in common is not a commitment to science, but an interest in explaining the behaviour of others. In the present debate the psychologist comes off best and the layman worst because the psychologist is the better scientist. However, the layman might be better than the scientist in being a better psychologist. Hence it might be worth taking stock of his ideas before setting out to improve on them. This was Heider's original intention.

Part of the conflict between Heider and Skinner concerned the *content* of psychology. For Skinner, psychology is the science of behaviour. Heider was concerned with the inferences in the mind of P concerning the behaviour of O. He was not concerned with P's perception of the *causes* of behaviour – which was the subtitle of Jones and Nisbett's article. Heider, and the Gestalt theorists generally, were as opposed to behaviourism in America as they had been to the experimental psychology of Leipzig when they were in Germany. What is it about O that P knows? The answer is – the mind of O. Psychology is a mental science rather than the science of mere behaviour. The current preoccupation with cognition is but a first step on the road back from behaviourism. It is not yet a full social psychology of mind.

CONSEQUENCES

We have taken some preliminary steps in this chapter to clear the ground for dealing with speaker/listener and writer/reader divergences in perspectives as well as the actor/observer one. There have been some studies conducted within the framework of attribution theory investigating language and attribution (e.g. Peeters's (1971) consideration of attributions as a function of intermessage semantic relations). We have not, however, been able to locate any studies that directly address this question of speaker/listener differences in perspective within the framework of attribution theory.

Rommetveit's (1979) emphasis on the contractual aspects of language is highly relevant to such further studies. He is particularly interested in what he terms 'states of inter-subjectivity', which are set up when the private worlds of two individuals are transcended in an act of communication. He is interested in how two individuals, through communication, come to share a particular sub-domain of the social world. Rommetveit argues that speech is continuously *listener-oriented*: the speaker monitors his speech in accordance with his assumptions about the extent of the overlap between himself and his listener in their common knowledge of the social world to which their conversation refers. Conversely, listening is *speaker-oriented*, i.e. is aimed at a reconstruction of what the speaker *intends* to make known. As Rommetveit puts it, the speaker must monitor what he says on the premisses of the listener, and the listener must listen on the premisses of the speaker. Both of them, moreover, must continually relate what is said at any particular stage of their dialogue to whatever, at that stage, has been jointly presupposed. Inter-subjectivity is based on mutual faith in a shared social world, and to some extent has to be taken for granted to be achieved. Decentration in both interactants is a necessary basis for intersubjectivity. 'What George Herbert Mead coined "taking the attitude of the other" (Mead, 1934) constitutes such a basic and pervading feature of normal social interaction that it remains entirely inaccessible to the reflective consciousness (of both participants)' (Rommetveit, 1979, p. 96). Thus, speech is guided by a representation of the listener, and is based on a capacity to adopt the listener's perspective.

Blakar (1973), one of Rommetveit's colleagues, described an experimental task with which one can measure a subject's capacity to take the perspective of the Other. The task investigates communication efficiency in dyads, and involves one subject explaining a route through a map to the other subject, who also has a copy of the map. In one condition the task is simple in that the maps are identical. In the experimental condition, however, the maps are different, with the follower's map having one more street than the explainer's. This violates one of the most basic preconditions for successful communication, that of the participants having 'a shared social reality', a common here-and-now within which an exchange of messages can take place (Rommetveit, 1974).

The difference between the maps induces a situation of conflict in communication which the subjects have to resolve by identifying the error in the maps; if the task is not solved within a fixed time span (40 minutes) the task is terminated. Sølvberg and Blakar (1975) demonstrated that parents of schizophrenic patients failed to solve the complex task within the prescribed time limit on four out of five occasions, while all of the control dyads (matched parents without pathological offspring) solved the complex task.

An example of non-decentrated speech would be where, in giving route directions, a subject produced an utterance like: 'and then you go up there'. The exact meaning of such utterances as 'here' and 'there' could not be known to the other subject and would constitute an example of non-decentrated speech. Sølvberg and Blakar (1975, p. 531) noted that such non-decentrated utterances were observed frequently in the group S (schizophrenic patients' parents) dyads.

Sanford and Garrod (1981) present arguments concerning writers and readers that are very similar to some of the points argued by Rommetveit. As Sanford and Garrod put it, when a writer writes she has to tailor her words to her audience. Furthermore, for a piece of writing to be intelligible and coherent the writer has to elicit in the mind of the reader a package (or packages) of background information (situational knowledge from the reader's long-term memory) which will provide pragmatic cohesion between successive sentences. To be successful in this, the writer must operate within the constraints imposed by the reader. Text cohesion and comprehensibility rely on the appropriate use of devices (such as anaphoric and pronominal references[2]) in a way that takes into account the reader's limitations of memory and processing. Thus, a representation of the reader enters into the writing process at least to some extent, and encoding has to involve anticipatory decoding for coherence to result.

Additional evidence in support of the notion that one aspect of language use involves the successful induction of a shared perspective in dialogue comes from the area of artificial intelligence. In her paper, 'Focusing in Dialog', Grosz (1978) explicates the notion of *focus*, i.e. the tendency of conversants to concentrate their attention on a sub-domain of their knowledge.

> When two people talk, they focus their attention on only a small portion of what each of them knows or believes. Not only do they concentrate on particular events (objects or relationships), but they do so using particular perspectives on those entities. *In choosing a particular set of words with which to describe an entity, a speaker indicates a perspective on that entity. The hearer is led, then, to see the entity more as one kind of thing than as another.* [Grosz, 1978; emphasis added]

This suggests that the sharing of perspectives, at least in the auditory modality, is something of an automatic process. Grosz, however, does point out the possibility of perspective differences arising in dialogue, albeit comparatively subtle ones. She cites the example of a dialogue between an expert and an apprentice working on a task, namely the dis-assembly of an air compressor. The expert's orientation is functional, i.e. knowing how the machine works. The apprentice's orientation is shape-based. Problems can arise when the two individuals refer to the same entity in different ways. What the apprentice calls 'little ribby things', the expert calls 'cooling fins'. The problem is overcome by working towards a shared view: in this instance, this is achieved by checking that they have established a common referent, and hence a common focus. This involves one participant (the expert) using the other participant's terminology. It is an implicit goal in a dialogue, according to Grosz, to establish this sort of commonality of perspective.

It may be easy to establish a common referent when we are discussing a joint task with respect to a piece of apparatus, as in Grosz's example. When the expert is commenting on some aspect of the actor's performance we are back again with Jones and Nisbett. This might be the relation, for example, between coach and athlete. The psychology of sport is a burgeoning area of research interest. Someone should review the literature on coaching in the light of the Jones and Nisbett paper. The coach obviously 'sees' the athlete's performance differently from how the athlete sees it. This is the divergence in perspective between actor and observer. The coaching relationship is obviously a good example of how change might be effected by using this divergence in perspective. The therapeutic relationship is another (see Farr, 1982a).

CONCLUSIONS

The contrast in perspective between actors and observers first identified by Jones and Nisbett (1971) is much less *existential* and less *social* than Heider's (1958) original treatment of P(erceiver) and O(ther). We have suggested that the perspective of P is that of self in relation to other. In Heider's formulation, the perceiver's perspective is both that of an actor in the social scene and that of an observer of the behaviour of others. Furthermore, Perceiver and Other are to be considered *in relation to each* other. By contrast, researchers working in the area of attribution theory, following on from the Jones and Nisbett distinction, treat P and O as separate, independent individuals rather than in relation to one another. They also treat the actor/observer difference as a difference in the cognitive information available to two different individuals, rather than thinking of the distinction as a possible basis for differing states of awareness which might alternate within the one individual.

We are particularly critical of the use of the literary vignette in attribution studies. While this is obviously a conveniently simple methodology, we would argue that its non-social nature is not in the spirit of Heider's original formulations.

We argue that man, as a species, is more self-reflexive in the auditory than in the visual modality and that differences in perspective are therefore more profound in the visual than in the auditory modality. We have considered evidence from various sources which suggests that the sharing of perspectives is an integral part both of speaking and of listening. Conversation is a way of discovering the initial divergence in perspective between conversants, and it is also the means whereby a common perspective can be subsequently negotiated. Attribution theory does not yet take sufficiently serious notice of language. Our paper is a first tentative step *beyond* the original divergence in perspective first noted by Jones and Nisbett (1971) in the direction of studying the social psychology of conversations.

NOTES

1 'Man' in this paper refers to the species and not to the gender.
2 *Anaphora*: 'the use of a word such as a pronoun to avoid repetition of a word or words, as for example *one* in "He offered me a drink but I didn't want one" ' (Collins English Dictionary).

4 The Organization of Explanations

Mansur Lalljee and Robert P. Abelson

Events can be explained in a variety of different ways and the content of the explanations for different types of event is systematically different. Thus, for instance, in the domain of achievement behaviour, success and failure are frequently explained in terms of the actor's intelligence or effort or interest in the subject. With reference to other domains, other explanations are relevant, and the explanations for success and failure on an academic task may be very different from the explanations for the success or failure of a marriage. These may be very different from the explanations for why a person steals or behaves altruistically. But is there some order underlying these differences? Is there some organization of explanations for a particular event, and is it possible to compare explanations for different types of event? This chapter explores different ideas about how explanations are organized. The first three sections examine some of the main distinctions that have been made in attribution theory; the fourth and fifth sections explore an alternative, knowledge-structure approach to understanding explanations.

THE PERSON–SITUATION DISTINCTION

For Heider (1958), it is of vital importance for people to explain what has occurred because the explanation gives meaning to the event, thus assisting one's orientation towards the world. An explanation may clarify whether the event in question is likely to recur, and may assist in our control over its outcome (see Bains, chapter 7 below). An explanation may mediate moral responsibility, may help us decide who is to blame, and what rewards or punishments they should receive. Explaining involves assigning transient events to relatively stable aspects of the world.

Foremost among these invariances, says Heider, are the motives of other people.

In his chapter on 'The Naive Analysis of Action' (see Heider, 1958), Heider drew a distinction that was to become central in the study of attibution processes:

> In common-sense psychology (as in scientific psychology) the result of an action is felt to depend on two sets of conditions, namely, factors within the person and factors within the environment. Naive psychology also has different terms to express the contributions of these factors. Consider the example of a person rowing a boat across a lake. The following is but a sample of expressions used to refer to factors that are significant to the action outcome. We say, 'He is *trying* to row the boat across the lake', 'He has the *ability* to row the boat across the lake', 'He *can* row the boat across the lake', 'He *wants* to row the boat across the lake', 'It is *difficult* to row the boat across the lake', 'Today is a good *opportunity* for him to row the boat across the lake', 'It is sheer *luck* that he succeeded in rowing the boat across the lake'. These varying descriptive statements have reference to personal factors on the one hand and to environmental factors on the other. [Heider, 1958, p. 82]

The distinction between attribution to personal or to situational forces has become enshrined in much of the work on attribution processes. In spite of the heterogeneity of person and situation explanations (see Lalljee, 1981), researchers frequently elicit judgements on bipolar rating scales of attribution to the person or the situation. The person–situation distinction has been central to exploring the explanations for unexpected behaviour. It has been argued (see Kelley and Michela, 1980) that unexpected behaviour is explained more in terms of the person, while expected behaviour is explained more in terms of the situation. Kelley (1972) has partly explained this in terms of a 'discounting principle'. Essentially, this stated that, where there are two plausible causes for an event, the role of any one particular cause in producing that effect is discounted. When someone behaves in a way appropriate to a particular context, there are two plausible causes: the behaviour could be a true reflection of the individual's personality, or the person could be behaving in that way because it is the appropriate way to behave. The latter explanation presumably inhibits the credence given to the former. In the case where the behaviour is unexpected, the latter situational cause is irrelevant, so there is only one plausible cause.

Though the person–situation distinction has taken attribution theory along its first faltering steps towards understanding explanations, the basic model underlying this approach is inadequate. The assumption seems to be a 'hydraulic' one – that for any event a person distributes a fixed 'amount of causality' to personal or situational forces. But surely this is not the case. Some events need explaining – others do not. For some, simple explanations are adequate, while others call for complex answers. Indeed, when attributions are elicited on separate scales (one for attributions to the person, another for attributions to the situation) the correlations between these scales are usually low and very variable (see Solomon, 1978; Lalljee, Watson and White, 1982). It seems clear that attributions to the person and to the situation are not alternatives.

The inadequacy of the hydraulic conceptualization is of vital importance when considering the explanation of unexpected behaviour. In a study where subjects were asked to provide explanations in their own words, Lalljee, Watson and White (1982) have shown that unexpected behaviour is not always explained more in terms of the person. Explanations for unexpected behaviour are more complex than for expected behaviour, and are likely to involve both more person elements and more situation elements. The context in which the behaviour occurs is also crucial in its explanation. When the explainer is familiar with the context, unexpected behaviour is explained by incorporating person elements, while if the explainer is unfamiliar with the context, unexpected behaviour is explained by incorporating situation elements. Accounting for people's explanations of unexpected behaviour is a central challenge for the study of attribution processes.

Further, and this point will be taken up again in the section on covariation, the discounting principle argument may tell us that the explanation is something to do with the person – but what? The model does not tell us, and it is hardly likely that the explainer will stop at this abstract point. One would still have to draw upon one's knowledge of the world to decide which explanation is relevant. In any case, for any event there is usually a wide range of possible explanations, and the process whereby we decide there are only two is not dealt with. Let us consider the following brief narrative, which is based on an experiment by Jones et al. (1961), an experiment that is frequently cited as support for the discounting principle and the idea that unexpected behaviour is explained more in terms of the person.

'John went for an interview for the job of submariner. He knew that good submariners were supposed to be extroverts and very much team players. During the interview, John came across as being a quiet, independent sort of person.' This seems relatively unexpected. Why might he come across as being quiet and independent? There could be several plausible explanations:

> because he is an introvert;
> because he didn't want the job;

because he was not in a good mood;
because he did not get on specially well with the interviewer.

No doubt there are several more. If the last sentence of the vignette were changed to a more expected conclusion – viz., '. . . John came across as being extroverted and a good team player' – one can also think of a range of plausible explanations. The point is that in this context the experimenters presumed that two explanations (i.e., in terms of personality and in terms of behaving in a way that will get him the job) were the most important, although it is also possible that he did not want the job or that he behaved in a way that would cost him the job just because he was not in a good mood. Perhaps in this example the 'extra' explanations are not as plausible as the main two, but in general one must rely on real-world knowledge to specify which explanations are plausible. The use of real-world knowledge in arriving at explanations will be considered in the knowledge structure approach outlined in the fourth and fifth sections.

MORE DIMENSIONS

Thus it is clear that organizing explanations in terms of a person–situation (P–S) dimension is inadequate. One way of dealing with this is to suggest that the P–S dimension is only one of a number of dimensions that are important. With reference to the explanations for success and failure, Weiner proposed a two-dimensional and then a three-dimensional model (Weiner et al., 1971; Weiner, 1980). Besides a dimension referred to as 'locus', which specifies whether the cause of an event is internal or external to the person (the P–S distinction), Weiner (1980) suggests a 'control' dimension (which refers to the extent to which the cause of the event is controllable) and a 'stability' dimension (which refers to the extent to which the cause of the event is a relatively enduring factor). Weiner's main concern has been to investigate the relationship between these dimensions and other judgements. Thus, the stability dimension is related to judgements about what will occur in the future, to judgements about the predictability of the actor's behaviour; the control dimension is related to judgements of evaluation; and the locus of the cause to esteem-related affects. Research has shown that this theoretical model matches well the distinctions that people actually make when considering explanations for success and failure (Bar-Tal and Darom, 1979; J. P. Meyer, 1980; Passer, unpublished, reported by Weiner, 1980).

Note that Weiner's work suggests that explanations are organized in a particular way and that these dimensions are systematically related to other judgements as well. The possibility that there are essentially a few basic dimensions underlying the organization of explanations in all domains is certainly an exciting one, but it seems unlikely that this will be the case. Passer et al. (1978) found that the distinctions people make between explanations for negative interpersonal behaviour are different from those made in the achievement domain. Their study, which involved multidimensional analyses of similarity ratings between explanations, showed that the most important dimension was concerned with the actor's motives, and contrasted conventionally good reasons for acting in a particular way (e.g., 'Actor thought it was in the partner's best interest') with conventionally bad reasons (e.g., 'Actor does not care for partner'). Similarly Lalljee, Furnham and Jaspars (1982) have shown that the dimensions underlying the explanations for moral and immoral behaviour are also concerned with the motives of the actor.

Thus it seems that, although the dimensions of control, locus and stability may well underlie our explanations for success and failure, these dimensions may not be central in other domains. Indeed, explaining why someone succeeded or failed on an exam is very different from explaining why someone was rude to another or told a lie. In the first case the question concerns *outcomes* (as in Heider's 'rowing across the lake' example cited earlier), while in the second and third instances the question concerns *actions*. Asking 'Why was he rude to his wife?' is more like asking 'Why did he take the exam?' or 'Why did he work hard?' than asking why he did well or badly. Explanations for outcomes do not usually engage the actor's motives – explanations for actions frequently do.

A decade ago McArthur (1972) asked whether different types of event are explained in systematically different ways. The events she studied fell into four categories: actions, accomplishments (a category very like our outcome category), emotions and opinions. She found important differences between actions and accomplishments on the one hand and emotions and opinions on the other. The idea that emotions are seen as more reactive to situational forces than are actions has been well established (Hansen, 1980; Lalljee et al., 1983). However, McArthur reported that actions and accomplishments were explained in very similar ways. One reason for this may be that the dependent variables were abstract categories (such as attribution to 'the Person', 'the Situation', 'the Circumstances', etc.) rather than explanations expressed in everyday language. The use of these abstract categories may have resulted in the neglect of crucial within-category differences. Thus 'Because he didn't try hard' and 'Because he didn't want to' may well both be explanations in terms of the person, but the former refers to a causal antecedent, the latter to a motive.

Thus, the domain of success and failure, which has attracted much interest in work on attribution processes, seems to be systematically different from explanations for actions. Though an explanation of failure in terms of effort may well be important in clarifying issues of praise and blame, explaining why the person did not try hard may be even more crucial. The need for some taxonomy or principle for organizing *what is being explained* is just as important as looking for *the organizing principles of explanations*.

COVARIATION AND KELLEY'S CUBE

So far the ideas discussed about how explanations are organized have not been based on any theory about how a person arrives at an explantion in the first place. The theory about the processes involved that has domin- ated the attribution arena has been that of Kelley (1967, 1972, 1973). Two central features of Kelley's theory are: (1) detection of covariation between events; and (2) the dimensions along which covariation is sought, i.e. across people (consensus), time (consistency), and entities (distinctive- ness). Elaborating on his earlier formulation, Kelley (1973) considers the pattern of different levels of consensus, consistency and distinctiveness and relates them to patterns of attribution based on the principle of covariation. Besides attributions to the person and to the stimulus, he distinguishes attributions to the circumstances (C) and then considers how different patterns of information will lead not only to attributions to P, S and C, but also to attributions involving interactions between these – i.e., $P \times S, P \times C, S \times C$ and $P \times S \times C$ attributions. Indeed, it was this sort of system that was adopted in the McArthur study mentioned earlier. It is clear from the studies reviewed by Kelley, and from experiments that have been conducted more explicitly to test his ideas, that people can use covariation to arrive at their conclusions and that, when presented with consensus, consistency and distinctiveness information in various com- binations, they do make attributions in much the sort of way that Kelley would predict (see Hewstone, chapter 1 and Jaspars, chapter 2 above).

There are, however, two major objections to this view. First, most experiments that have explored this problem have *presented* subjects with the relevant information and examined how the information is *used* (see Lalljee, 1981). Though people can use covariation information and, indeed, information about consensus, consistency and distinctiveness in the way suggested by the theory, this does not imply that they normally do.

The second objection is similar to the one made earlier with reference to the discounting principle. Even though the theory does attempt to tell us how people arrive at a particular category of explanation (i.e., a P attribution or a P × S attribution; etc.), it does not tell us which P attribution or which P × S attribution is selected, or even how people begin to make this decision. Consider a specific example: 'John lied to Mary.' If we wanted to explain why John lied to Mary, Kelley's theory would suggest that we would want to know whether other people lied to Mary, whether John usually lied to Mary, and whether John usually lied to other people. If the answers to these questions were no, yes and no, respectively, then we would make a P × S attribution. But which P × S attribution? Is it that he thinks she will disapprove of what he has done – or that he thinks she will approve? Just as person and situation attributions are heterogeneous, the categories elaborated by Kelley also include a wide range of different explanations. The theory does not tell us how the choice between competing explanations within a particular category will be made. In order to do this we would have to call upon our knowledge about relationships and why people lie to each other. And once this point is accepted, one may wonder what part covariation analysis has to play in the process anyway.

Recent preliminary experimental work casts further doubt on whether covariation analysis is the process typically at work in attributions. Druian and Omessi (1982), for example, have shown that, upon being given various events to explain, it consistently takes subjects longer to answer the general person-versus-situation question than to choose among specific attributions. Such a result would be odd if indeed the first thing that subjects did were to resolve person-versus-situation causation, and only later try to generate a more specific attribution.

Rather than the essentially inductive approach that Kelley has adopted, Lalljee et al. (in press) have suggested that the process of arriving at an explanation involves not so much a covariation analysis as seeking specific information that will enable a person to choose between different hypotheses about why the event occurred. Thus in the lying example, our predominant hypotheses may be that either he does not like Mary or that he has done something that he thinks she will disapprove of. The person will then seek information that will facilitate a choice between these explanations. Indeed, the studies conducted by Lalljee et al. (in press) which allow subjects to seek information do suggest that this description of the process is more likely to be correct. The approach stresses the importance of the knowledge that people have of events, and it is to an approach that explores the organization of real-world knowledge that we will now turn.

THE KNOWLEDGE STRUCTURE APPROACH TO ATTRIBUTION

Kelley's approach to the processes of arriving at an explanation is essentially abstract, inductive and concerned primarily with causal explanation. The approach taken by Schank and Abelson (1977) is essentially concrete, based on the knowledge that people have of the world, and focuses primarily on goal-based explanation. Now, the difference between causes and reasons is a prickly philosophical problem, but we wish to note one central aspect. Kelley's approach stresses the antecedents of an event; Schank and Abelson stress the purpose that an action fulfils. Schank and Abelson are concerned with 'knowledge structures' or schemas (Rumelhart, 1980) that individuals and computer programs (Schank and Riesbeck, 1981) use to comprehend, remember and summarize text or conversation about everyday reality, and their approach can readily be extended to analyse people's explanations for human action. It would be surprising if the processes involved in understanding stories do not have similarities with the processes involved in understanding everyday social behaviour. In any case, since in much attribution work the stimulus material consists of written descriptions, the analogy is surely even more appropriate. Schank and Abelson (1977) considered a variety of knowledge structures of which scripts, plans and goals can be used as central concepts in organizing the layman's explanation of action. This section will deal with the nature of scripts, how they provide a framework for understanding what events are worthy of explanation, and how scripted behaviour is explained. In the next section the processes whereby unscripted action is explained will be considered.

A script is a stereotyped sequence of actions in a particular locale, serving standard goals of its actor(s). Examples are going to a restaurant, a laundromat, a doctor, a wedding, etc. The 'instantiation' of a script leads the understander to expect a particular sequence of actions. The script concept has received a good deal of recent attention in both cognitive psychology (Bellezza and Bower, 1982; Bower et al. 1979; Galambos and Rips 1982) and social psychology (Abelson, 1976, 1981).

In terms of the psychology of explanation, the important thing about scripts is their stereotypy: once the script is invoked, one can fill in its standard details. In memory experiments (Bower et al. 1979; Graesser, 1981) people in fact 'remember' the presence of such details even when they were not given. Thus, in the restaurant script discussed in detail by Schank and Abelson (1977), one expects sitting down, ordering, eating, paying and leaving to occur as part of the appropriate behaviour of that script. Further, the restaurant script is a standard way of satisfying certain goals, e.g. the goal of eating. Asking 'why' of a scripted action is an odd thing reserved for children, foreigners and social scientists. Behaving in script-appropriate ways seems explanation enough for the behaviour. Thus the question, 'Why did he take off his shoes?' can be answered by saying 'Because that's a mosque', and 'Why did he check in ?' with 'You always do for international flights.' In experimental contexts, if people are instructed to give more detail about why scripted actions take place Galambos and Black, 1981), it turns out that these explanations may take the form either of action enablement (i.e., to enable the person to perform the next action in the sequence) or at other times refer to the satisfaction of the main goal of the script. Thus the question why someone asked for the menu could be answered by 'To see what there was to eat', or in terms of the general restaurant goal of eating. In any case, seeking an explanation for the act essentially arises where the questioner does not know the relevant script, and the explanation itself may be in terms of the goals served by the script.

Besides scripts, there are a range of routine ways of satisfying goals that are generally culturally acceptable. Some acts are standard ways of fulfilling particular goals. 'Why did he lock his bike?' is a trite question if you know that people generally want to keep their possessions safe, and that locking something is a standard way of doing this. Other acts may possibly fulfil a variety of goals, and the questioner may want to know what goal is being fulfilled (e.g., 'Why did he go to the restaurant?' 'Because his friends were going'). Social life is organized in terms of a range of other structures, such as role obligations and interpersonal relations and contracts, with reference to which an explanation may be adequate. Consider the following examples:

Question: 'Why did you give him that book?'
Answer: 'Because it was his.'

Question: 'Why did you give him the money?'
Answer: 'Because he helped me when I was broke.'

Question: 'Why did you do what he told you?'
Answer: 'Because he's the boss.'

Question: 'Why did John walk two miles in the rain to see Mary?'
Answer: 'Because he loved her.'

The first two questions are not likely to be asked by someone who knew the relevant antecedent, nor are the third and fourth questions likely to be asked by someone who knew the relevant role relations. If the questioner did have that knowledge, then one would be puzzled by the question and seek a different frame in which to make the question intelligible. Barring such a complication, answers are given straightforwardly in terms of rules governing the particularities of the contents.

Traditional attribution theory formulations have little to say about what events are considered worthy of explanation. Scripts and other similar cognitive structures enable us to clarify what events are generally regarded as worthy of explanation and point the direction from which the explanation is likely to be sought. Issues also arise about the learning of scripts by young children and foreigners. The former question is already being addressed by Nelson and Gruendel (1979), and the latter would be an important advance on current research on learning how to behave in a foreign country (Bochner, 1982).

CONSTRUCTIVE VERSUS CONTRASTIVE PROCESSES

Thus far in our discussion of explanations via knowledge structures we have focused on cases in which there is reference to an available script, or other stereotypic knowledge structure. In this section we will be concerned with the explanation of unscripted behaviour. Two types of process will be outlined. In some cases, which we will call 'constructive attribution', identification of the goals of an actor are seen as central. In cases of 'contrastive attribution', we suggest that an explanation is sought by contrasting the action with a normal action, with reference to which the action is seen as in need of explanation.

At the simplest level of construction are examples in which a plan must be inferred and its steps filled in. Consider this vignette adapted from Schank and Abelson (1977):

> John knew that his wife's operation would be very expensive. There was always Uncle Harry. John reached for his book of phone numbers.

Here, the question of why John reached for the book of phone numbers is presumably answered with a plan that includes calling his Uncle Harry to achieve the goal of obtaining money for his wife's operation. This could be wrong, but it is plausible – which is all one can expect when information is fragmentary. When the explanatory structure's relevance is highly obvious, little cognitive effort is required in accessing the explanation. However, when the explanatory structure is to some extent hidden or remote, a certain amount of cognitive search is required to construct an explanation, and 'why' questions are more interesting.

Wilensky (1978) has written a computer program that is, at least in principle, capable of constructing explanations by fleshing out simple plans. Two things are very important to the program, and presumably also to human explainers: (1) there must be a great deal of concrete knowledge about the nature of plans and the functions of objects in plans; (2) the program is opportunistic in trying to use scraps of information from the context. Thus, to explain the phone book example above, the explainer should know that phone books enable phoning, which enables communication; that sudden expenses engender a need for money; that family members often help with family crises; that needing money for an operation is such a crisis; that loans provide money; and that getting a loan requires asking. Opportunism comes in, for example, in picking up on 'Uncle Harry' as a family member, providing the link that makes asking for a loan the likely method. (Imagine the example without the Uncle Harry sentence: explanation would be underdetermined and incomplete.)

This suggests a process model which claims that people create an explanation of an action by: (1) identifying the operative goal(s) in the situation; (2) identifying the plan being used to satisfy the goal(s); and (3) hooking up the action to that plan. The approach stresses that a coherent plan is inferred from bits of knowledge instantiated in the particular context. Such a scheme, which we call *constructive attribution*, would not have the abstract elegance of the covariation principle, but it would be much more plausible and complete in providing the level of detail of explanation that people actually give. Such a process model could be studied by the sort of reaction time experiments that have become widely used in cognitive psychology and have occasionally been conducted in the attribution arena (e.g. Smith and Miller, 1979a; Druian and Omessi, 1982).

Constructive attribution, of course, would run into difficulty if the explanatory plan were overly cryptic ('John went to the hardware store to get a triangular piece of corrugated metal'), or bizarre ('John put a rose in his back pocket and sat on it'), or if specialized knowledge were required to interpret the background behind certain actions ('The Jewish Defense League sent packages of matzohs to the Russian Embassy on Passover'). But any attribution model deserves to founder if the information base is too sparse.

Another class of cases arises from what might be called *contrastive attribution*. These are explanations of failures of expectation, rather than of confirmation: the focus is on why the actor did *not* do such-and-such, and the explanation is sought by contrasting it with the normal or expected action. Take for instance the event: John left his bicycle unlocked. It makes sense to ask why this occurred, because one would normally expect people to look after their possessions and keeping something locked is one way of achieving this goal. But since John did not do the normal thing, then either of these assumptions or indeed a wide range of other assumptions that would normally be made may turn out to be false. Maybe he did not have that goal, or maybe he did not have a lock, or maybe he was in a hurry. In the work on story understanding, classifications have been suggested for plan failures (Dyer, 1982) and expectation failures (Schank, 1982). A classification system should take as its point of departure the notion that people explain other people's behaviour with reference to goals attributed to them, and in order to achieve goals the person has to carry out certain plans competently, and these plans may involve certain skills and tools. Focusing on failures to complete normal plans, and using the bike example for illustration, the resultant classification system may sort explanations in terms of:

(1) *planlessness*: not even realizing that the goal is desirable (e.g., he's naive, or zonked on drugs);

(2) *planning failure*: not having the requisite means for accomplishing the goal (e.g., he didn't have a lock);

(3) *external interference*: being prevented from executing the plan (e.g., thieves took the bike before he could lock it);

(4) *goal reversal*: having the opposite goal (e.g., he did not particularly want the bike; or he was trying to get rid of it);

(5) *goal satisfied*: having the normally relevant goal satisfied in some other way (e.g., he was inside a private courtyard);

(6) *goal conflict*: pursuing some other, more important goal (e.g., he was late for an important appointment).

In broad outline, a knowledge structure model of contrastive attribution can be specified: the explainer could find a 'normal' action with which to contrast the stimulus action; embed by constructive attribution this normal action in a normal script or plan sequence; instantiate the various categories of possible failure of that normal sequence; and prioritize among these categories to select likely candidate explanations. Finally, the attributor might test the various explanations against what is known about the context to find the first (or the most) plausible explanation. This sequence of steps might vary somewhat (for instance, the context might be used to suggest rather than to test candidate explanations), but its general essence is clear. The different categories of explanation elaborated would form another basis for comparison across events. For different types of event, different types of explanation may receive priority. For questions about outcomes such as success and failure, explanations in terms of planning rather than in terms of goals are called forth. For interpersonal events, explanations in terms of goal conflict may be seen as most likely (see Fincham, chapter 11 below). Explanations of why people have particular goals (rather than why they performed a particular act) may lead to explanations in terms of higher-order goals.

Another interesting issue concerns how the explainer knows with what to contrast the given event. Lehnert (1978), in a treatment of computer programs for question-answering, discusses the problem of the *focus* of a question. Take for example the question, 'Did the waitress bring John a menu?' Here it is unclear what precisely is being asked. Is it: 'Did the *waitress* (as compared to the hostess) bring John a menu?' or 'Did the waitress bring John a *menu?*' (rather than something else). Lehnert suggests that such questions of focus can be dealt with in a number of ways, including intonation pattern and syntax. Particularly relevant for our present discussion is the importance of contextual and knowledge-based determinants. In general, it is natural to focus on the most unusual aspect implied by the question. Thus, if the question is 'Why did the cashier serve John the chateaubriand?' we do not want to say 'Because he ordered it' or 'What else was she to have done with it – thrown it at him?' We want to recognize that meals are usually served by waiters, so that we must account for the absence of a waiter in this action. Perhaps they are sick or on strike.

The availability of a relevant script is an important way in which focus is determined. Question focus attaches to the point of difference between the given event (e.g. the cashier serving the food) and the script event that is most similar to it (the waiter serving the food). In other cases, the focus falls naturally on an unusual plan. Thus the question, 'Why did John roller-skate to McDonald's?' calls for an answer in terms of his mode of locomotion (though specific knowledge about his eating habits may well lead the focus to rest on his choice of restaurant). In such cases the focus is on the manner of execution, rather than on the superordinate action sequence. Political scientist Robert Jervis (1982), in a discussion of attribution processes in the explanation of international behaviour, stresses that in many cases it is the manner of execution rather than the goal or the relationship between the plan and the goal that needs explaining. He suggests, for example, that Hitler's invasion of Czechoslovakia upset the British not so much because of the goal itself, or because of any consequent change in military power, but because of the methods used. The brutality and coercion with which the goal was achieved led to the inference that the German government could not be trusted and probably sought more far-reaching objectives.

The explanation for many unusual actions may involve both contrastive and constructive processes. The statement, 'John is lying down in the tutorial' contrasts with the normal state of sitting down during a tutorial. Sitting may generally be the most comfortable way of reading out an essay.

Maybe he did not have the goal of being comfortable, and drawing on our knowledge of lying down we may construct other explanations. It may of course be that he did have the goal of being comfortable, but that, since he had a bad back, lying was for him the most comfortable posture. But we might also wonder about the normal goal of being socially appropriate, not giving offence. Lying down might run the risk of violating this goal. How could it not do so? Perhaps John's back is so bad that he feels the risk warranted (goal conflict). More likely, he has explained his situation to his tutor, who doesn't mind (goal satisfied). Thus the attributor may move back and forth, contrasting and constructing, explaining both why the actor didn't do the normal thing and why he chose the particular alternative he did. When actions simultaneously serve multiple goals, explanations with multiple aspects may be necessary.

The knowledge structure approach also stresses the importance of context in arriving at explanations. Most attribution experiments have used as their stimulus material either a single sentence or a few sentences that describe the event to be explained. Even when the stimulus material is longer, it is not based on any particular theory of what is being included in that material, other than general considerations like evaluative neutrality. Yet in everyday life, events are perceived in context. Imagine presenting the information in the sentence, 'John left his bicycle unlocked', in a picture. You would have to show the bicycle – what sort is it? New, brightly painted and with ten speeds, or old and rusty, apparently on the verge of falling apart? And what about John? What does he look like – neat and well dressed or a bit of a mess, an apparently absent-minded type? And where does this scene take place? Is there a lock visible? Such contextual information would inevitably raise expectations that would influence which explanations appear most plausible. Thus the explanation arrived at may be crucially affected by the specific information that is available (whether in a picture or verbally). If the bike is old and rusty, then maybe he doesn't really care whether it is stolen. If the lock is visible, he obviously did not forget the lock, and so on. This fits in well with the claim by Lalljee et al. (in press) that people have specific hypotheses about why events occur and then seek specific information that will enable them to disambiguate their hypotheses.

This approach emphasizes the importance of contextual information in ruling out or rendering plausible particular explanations. It is in this way that covariation may enter the picture. In order to substantiate a particular explanation, one may call upon covariation information. When explaining the unlocked bike in terms of John's carelessness or with reference to the question of whether most people leave bikes unlocked, a covariation analysis may come in useful to test the explanations. It would not be much help to test the explanation that he left it because it was rusty, or because he had forgotten the lock. Our general sense of the matter is that covariation is not likely to be the prime attribution strategy, although it could serve as an adjunct within a knowledge structure approach.

CONCLUSIONS

In much of his writing, Heider stressed that our everyday model of individuals is that of goal-directed agents. We have attempted to show that this model of people as goal-directed agents provides the basis for understanding explanations in everyday life. By assuming that people use concepts like scripts, goals and plans, we can get further along the road to understanding understanding. This approach has been contrasted with that derived from traditional attribution theory. Though the theories put forward by Kelley are powerful abstract theories, it seems that their very abstraction leads them to be inadequate as a framework for understanding explanations. But basing explanations on specific real-world knowledge is not without its own difficulties. Increased realism brings a huge increase in the need for theoretical detail, and the need to specify the underlying structure or system is particularly urgent. Explanations in terms of scripts and other such structures are an important step in the right direction.

Scripts are a central unit for organizing our understanding of social life. The routine-stereotyped sequences of events that they represent characterize our consensual knowledge of appropriate behaviour in particular social contexts. Seeking explanations for scripted behaviour (or behaviour that is part of other routinized knowledge structures) is unusual, and normally implies lack of knowledge of the script or lack of knowledge that the relevant struture has been instantiated. For explaining unscripted actions, two types of process have been described. For some actions the explanation may be generated by specifying how the behaviour in question is linked to one of the actor's goals. For other actions the explanation may be sought by contrasting the action with the relevant expected behaviour, and explaining the action by contrast. In order to do this, the preconditions for the performance of the normal behaviour must be elaborated and the explanation sought in the failure of one of the relevant preconditions. For some events, both contrastive and constructive processes are involved. The categories of explanation involved in contrastive attribution may also serve as a basis for exploring the consequences of different types of explanation. Explanations in terms of goal conflict are likely to be related to judgements of anxiety; explanations in terms of planning failure may raise questions of carelessness and responsibility; and in either case one would have different expectations about the actor's future behaviour. Thus, besides contributing to an analysis of the processes involved in arriving at attributions, an explanation of the functions of attribution is also within the purview of the knowledge structure approach outlined in this chapter.

ACKNOWLEDGEMENTS
This paper was largely written while Mansur Lalljee was a Visiting Fellow at Yale University. He wishes to thank the Social Science Research Council, UK, and Professor Abelson for making the visit possible, and colleagues at Yale for making it stimulating.

5 The Lay-Epistemic Process in Attribution-making

Arie W. Kruglanski, Mark W. Baldwin and
Shelagh M. J. Towson

INTRODUCTION

Perhaps one of the more frustrating experiences for a student of social
psychology is to be confronted, in close succession, with the cognitive
consistency sourcebook (Abelson et al., 1968), the Harvey et al. attribution volumes (Harvey, Ickes and Kidd, 1976, 1978, 1981) and the
Nisbett and Ross (1980) exposé of inferential shortcomings. Are all the
contributing authors in these tomes actually talking about the same creature? Is it possible that human beings are rational information-processors,
rabidly self-justifying consistency maintainers and incorrigibly lazy and
inaccurate non-statisticians – and all at the same time? The present chapter represents an integrative attempt which assumes that we are studying
the same creature after all, and provides a unified structure for these
seemingly disparate views.

The theory of lay epistemology (cf. Kruglanski, 1980, Kruglanski and
Jaffe, 1983; Kruglanski and Ajzen, 1983) evolved in response to the
diverse theoretical models populating the causal attribution countryside.
A close look at these theories revealed a number of consistent themes, the
synthesis of which led to the development of a model of the epistemic, or
knowledge-seeking process in general. This lay-epistemic approach provides a perspective from which to view a number of areas of interest to
social psychologists. The present chapter focuses on implications of lay
epistemology for attribution-making and inferential shortcomings. Elsewhere (Kruglanski and Klar, 1982; Kruglanski, Baldwin and Towson,
1983) we also address, from lay-epistemic perspective, the theories of
cognitive consistency and social comparison processes.

It is well to note at the outset that the theory of lay epistemology does not represent startling new insights into the human cognitive process. Many of its ideas and contentions are, in a sense, common knowledge about how people reason and make inferences. The innovation of our theory lies, rather, in putting these ideas together in a unique fashion and in providing a rationale for taking definite stands on issues previously characterized by confusion and ambiguity. We believe that the resulting framework constitutes a rather powerful tool for re-interpreting old phenomena, with several surprising implications up its sleeve concerning previous theories and research.

THE THEORY OF LAY EPISTEMOLOGY

The theory of lay epistemology addresses the epistemic, or knowledge-seeking, process. The theory starts with the assumption that all knowledge is made up of propositions or beliefs (e.g., 'The world is round'; 'It is raining'). Beliefs have several interesting features: (1) they provide an orienting *structure* concerning some topic or issue; (2) they furnish a specific *content* or meaning for a given topic rather than other possible contents; (3) they are held to be *valid*, that is, to represent the *truth* about their particular topic.

Central to lay-epistemic theory is the tenet that beliefs are validated via deductive logic. For example, a person might subscribe to the proposition (1), 'Only if it is raining outside will I see drops of water falling from the sky and hear thunder.' Suppose now that our individual (2) sees falling drops and hears thunder. Logically speaking, premisses (1) and (2) yield the conclusion that (3) it is now raining. In other words, according to lay-epistemic theory, even 'direct' or 'perceptual' knowledge (seeing with one's own eyes that it is raining!) constitutes a belief with a logical structure and specific meaning which must be validated deductively.

Consider now a situation in which somebody whispers in our knower's ear that MGM is filming on our knower's street a re-make of *Singing in the Rain*. This knowledge might undermine our knower's faith in premiss (1) above, that water drops and thunder occur *only if* it is actually raining, and invite the alternative hypothesis, that they might also be produced by MGM's special-effects team. To decide between the two hypotheses, our knower might construct a different 'only if . . . then' proposition, such as 'Only if it is raining authentically rather than artificially will the drops and the thunder be observed also by Bob living three blocks from here.' The knowledge that it is, after all, really raining might then be deduced from Bob's confirmatory observation. In sum, our knowledge is validated deductively via premises of the 'only if x, then y' form and via evidence concerning the (x or y) events specified in the premiss.

In the same way that confidence derives from logical consistency among propositions, or their deducibility from one another, the awareness of inconsistency will result in doubt and confusion. A logical inconsistency occurs when two contradictory beliefs, 'A' and 'not A' both appear to be true. If a belief is contradicted by other beliefs, the result will be a loss of confidence. Because my understanding of rainstorms includes a number of beliefs about sky conditions and so on, I might be less certain that it is raining if I notice that the sky is perfectly clear and no one is carrying an umbrella. For probabilistic accounts of such processes see W. J. McGuire (1981) or Wyer and Srull (1979). Doubt also results from the awareness of an alternative hypothesis that is also consistent with all the available evidence. The possibility that the drops and the thunder are produced artificially is inconsistent with the supposition that they respresent a natural rain; hence it undermines confidence in the latter proposition. Inconsistency can be resolved only by denying one of the contradictory cognitions, that is, by identifying which of the contradictory pair of statements is probably false. Suppose that Mary confirmed the drops and the thunder whereas Bob, reporting from the same location, vehemently denied them. The confusion could be dispelled if Bob sounded a bit drunk on the telephone, had a reputation as a practical joker, or was known to suffer from sudden fits of pathological lying. In such a case one would probably deny the validity of Bob's report, resolving the inconsistency in Mary's favour.

Freezing and unfreezing mechanisms

For any pattern of evidence (that is, any set of believed-in propositions) there is an infinite number of possible explanatory hypotheses. Drops of water falling from the sky could, to the imaginative epistemologist, repre-sent lawn sprinklers, window washers or wet birds. As long as these hypotheses are consistent with the evidence, they remain as plausible alternatives. But even if all but one of the rival alternatives were pain-stakingly weeded out, confidence in the remaining alternative would still be precarious. For, in principle, one could always come up with other hypotheses or become aware of evidence inconsistent with an accepted belief. How then can one ever know anything for sure (or at least feel that one does)? According to lay-epistemic theory, at some point along the line the individual stops generating hypotheses and attains 'closure' on a given belief. In the language of lay epistemology, this is called *freezing*. When a belief is frozen, the individual no longer evaluates it against competing alternatives and/or inconsistent bits of evidence. With the freezing of the hypothesis generation sequence, the belief comes to be held with a greater degree of confidence, owing to the removal of alternative hypotheses. Accepting a belief as valid in this way constitutes the experience of knowledge.

Factors determining whether a belief will be frozen or unfrozen include the individual's *capacity* and *motivation* to generate alternative hypotheses on a given topic.

Capacity

Hypothesis-generating capacity depends on a person's general store of knowledge in a given domain. For instance, a person whose car has broken down in the middle of a road could be helplessly waiting for rescue or busily generating hypotheses concerning the source of the trouble, depending on his or her prior knowledge of auto-mechanics. Hypothesis-generating capacity may also depend on the momentary *availability* of ideas in a person's mind. In turn, availability may depend on the recency of usage or the linkage of notions with other momentarily salient ideas. For instance, I may be more likely than usual to employ psychoanalytic theory in interpreting a friend's behaviour if I have recently had a session with my analyst. Social and cognitive psychologists have been interested increasingly in factors determining the availability and/or salience of ideas and how these affect people's judgements (for a recent literature review, see Taylor and Thompson, 1982).

Motivation

As noted earlier, beliefs (a) provide orienting structure, (b) have a specific content, and (c) are assumed to be valid. Each of these properties of knowledge could be a source of motivation affecting the hypothesis-generation process. Specifically, lay-epistemic theory distinguishes among three epistemically relevant motivations: (1) the need for structure, (2) the need for specific conclusions, and (3) the need for validity. We consider them in turn.

Need for structure   The need for structure is the desire to have *some* guiding knowledge on a given topic – any guiding knowledge as opposed to confusion and ambiguity. If one urgently needs to act on a belief, for example, one will cling to whatever hypothesis is held with most confidence. The press of time and the need to reach a decision (e.g., when the waiter peers over one's shoulder while one is poring over the wine list) may heighten the tendency to seek cognitive closure and to refrain from critical probing and extended assessment of a given, seemingly adequate, solution to a problem (cf. Frenkel-Brunswick; 1949, Smock; 1955; Tolman, 1948).

Thus, the need for structure is assumed to effect the freezing of the epistemic process. It is assumed to reduce the inclination to generate alternative hypotheses and/or to attend to evidence inconsistent with a currently accepted hypothesis. However, when the inconsistent evidence is particularly blatant and can not be 'swept under the rug' any longer, the person with a high need for structure is more likely to experience discomfort than a person with a low need for structure.

Need for specific conclusions The need for structure involves a general desire for clarity and orientation concerning a given issue; the need for specific conclusions denotes the desire to uphold a belief with a particular content. People often need or want to maintain specific beliefs because these denote the fulfilment of their wishes. I might, for example, need very strongly to believe that I am a judicious decision-maker, that people get what they deserve, or that I won't let other people push me around. When these kinds of beliefs are threatened by logically inconsistent information, the discomfort that ensues can lead to behavioural and/or cognitive gymnastics to reduce the inconsistency. In terms of the freezing and unfreezing of hypotheses, conclusional needs can work both ways – freezing favourable beliefs and unfreezing unfavourable ones. The individual's tendency to generate alternatives to a given belief is weakened to the extent that the belief is desirable, and strengthened to the extent that it is undesirable.

Need for validity In general, no knowledge can be sustained in the face of a recognized invalidity: to know something while believing it to be false is a contradiction in terms. That is why the awareness of inconsistency (indicating possible invalidity) is upsetting to a person with a high need for structure in some domain. There may be times when one desires structure even to the point of ignoring inconsistent evidence; at other times, however, one might desire validity more strongly even if it means temporarily abandoning a comforting structure. Before agreeing to share a flat with a friend, for example, I might want to feel absolutely sure that he will be suitable, and therefore I will probably entertain a large number of hypotheses. I will consider the possibility that, although he seems friendly, he may be really grouchy at home; and that, whereas he seems carefree and fun to be with, he may be lazy when it comes to doing the washing-up. In this way, the *need for validity* will unfreeze the epistemic process, resulting in the generation of more hypotheses. This need for validity can often result from a *fear of invalidity* when the anticipated costs of a mistake are large.

Summary of lay epistemology

All knowledge is validated deductively from propositions of the general form 'only if x, then y'. Beliefs can be held with varying degrees of confidence, with increased confidence being placed in propositions that are logically consistent with other beliefs and decreased confidence resulting from the awareness of logical inconsistency. In principle, one could engender a vast number of alternate hypotheses to account for any set of data; however, if one did, one would bé forever 'buried in thought' without ever 'knowing' anything for certain. Instead, in every instance of definite knowledge a freezing of the hypothesis-generation process inevitably occurs. Factors determining whether a given belief will be frozen or unfrozen include the person's capacity and motivation to generate alternate hypotheses on a given topic. Generational capacity depends, in turn, on one's store of past knowledge and on the momentary availability of various ideas. Furthermore, hypothesis generation can be frozen because of a need for structure, unfrozen because of a need for validity, or influenced either way because of the belief's implications for a conclusional need.

The theory of lay epistemology describes the general process whereby all knowledge is acquired and modified and provides a framework for more restricted models of human inference. In the next section we undertake an epistemic re-analysis of one such model, attribution theory.

ATTRIBUTION THEORY

Since Heider's (1958) original discussion of the knower as naive scientist, major attributional formulations have addressed themselves to a wide variety of epistemic problems. In Kelley's (1967) analysis of variance (ANOVA) formulation (see Jaspars, chapter 2 above), the attributor's problem is to determine whether some effect was caused by (1) the external entity, (2) the person's unique properties, (3) the interaction modality or (4) the 'time' at which the interaction occurred. In the Jones and Davis (1965) model of correspondent inference, the perceiver must decide whether or not some act was prompted by some correspondent personality attribute. The model studied by Weiner and his associates (Weiner et al., 1971) addressed the problem of attributing one's success or failure to ability, effort, task difficulty or luck. The perceiver's problem discussed by Kruglanski (1975) is to decide whether an action was performed as an end in itself, or as a means to a further end.

These and other attributional models differ primarily in their concern with different epistemic problems. Rather than describing how people make attributions in general, each model attempts to describe how people might go about answering some specific question (about task outcomes, personality traits, etc.). This specificity would not be a liability if the authors intended to describe how a particular causal problem might be resolved. More often than not, however, the authors intended their models to explain the general *process* by which people determine causality. The resulting content–process confusion is akin to that which might be created by a learning theorist who promises to define the term 'reinforcer' in general and then proceeds to describe the characteristics and effects – of a carrot. In order to understand the processes involved in making causal attributions, it is necessary to identify a general principle used by lay perceivers in all cases of causal inference. Once such a principle has been identified, it can then be applied to any question of interest.

According to the theory of lay epistemology, causal inferences are rendered in the same way as are all inferences. They are deduced from the appropriate 'only if . . . then' propositions that the attributor accepts as true. Some such propositions could derive from what the attributor understands 'cause' to mean. Just as 'rain' is typically understood to mean 'drops of water falling from the sky', 'cause' to most of us may mean 'something that precedes the effect', and 'without which the effect would not have occurred'. The latter condition, more technically speaking, means that the cause is *covariant* with the effect: whenever the 'cause' is present so is the effect, and whenever the 'cause' is absent so is the effect.

Thus, given several different entities suspected of being the cause of some effect, the attributor might well formulate a premiss whereby 'only if one of the entities covaries with the effect while the remaining ones did not, the covariant entity is the effect's "cause".' Precisely such a premiss seems to be adopted by the attributor in Kelley's (1967) ANOVA model. According to Kelley, confident ascription of causality to the external entity, for example, occurs when the external entity is noted to covary with the effect (the distinctiveness criterion), while time, modality and person do not covary with the effect (consistency and consensus criteria). For further details of this argument see Kruglanski (1980).

While covariation can be used as a criterion for ascribing causality, it is hardly the only criterion. First, one could construct 'only if . . . then' propositions around the time precedence meaning of 'cause'. One could reason that 'only if one of the several entities precedes the effect in time while the remaining ones do not, is the former entity the effect's probable cause'. But beyond the *time* and *covariation* criteria having to do with the meaning of the term 'cause' to an attributor, our lay-epistemic framework allows that causality be derived from *any* conceivable premiss depending on the individual's idiosyncratic belief structure. For instance, members of a cult might infer causality from the epistemic authority of their guru reasoning that 'only if the guru pronounced something to be the cause of x is it then indeed the cause,' etc.

In sum, according to our theory, the general principle for ascribing causality is that of deducibility. And the 'attributional criteria' are nothing more than premises some people might generate to evaluate plausible causes for some effect.

Understanding the attribution process from this perspective can have a liberating effect. It opens the door for the development of models that describe attributions in some specific content area, without attempting to portray the attributional process in general. An investigator interested in devising a model to explain how people make attributions about political phenomena, for example, need not worry about how covariation, distinctiveness and other such constructs are represented in the particular domain of interest. All that is required is a survey of the hypotheses typically entertained for the attribution of interest, and the implicational propositions and evidence typically used to test the hypotheses (cf. Lalljee and Abelson, chapter 4 above).

The lay-epistemic framework can thus be useful in synthesizing the extant attributional models as well as generating new models in an infinite number of interesting content areas. As long as the distinction is maintained between the process of making attributions and the content of specific attributional problems, there is no reason why we should not all be attribution theorists.

As viewed from the lay-epistemic perspective, extant attributional formulations neglect the knower's *capacity* and *motivation* to pose a given causal problem. For example, attribution models tacitly imply that people universally pose the same attributional problems, such as whether an effect was caused by 'the person' or 'the environment' ('internally' or 'externally'), or whether a success or a failure was caused by 'ability', 'effort', 'luck' or 'task difficulty'. The lay-epistemic analysis, on the other hand, suggests that the attributor's formulation of a particular problem depends on various factors – for example, on the mental availability of specific causal categories and on this individual's need for orienting structure in a specific domain. Indeed, research reported by Kruglanski et al. (1978) suggests that whether people are interested in the 'internal–external' distinction between causes depends on the degree to which an answer to the internal–external problem advances their situational goals (see also Jones and Thibaut, 1958).

Attributional formulations typically are viewed as 'informational' rather than 'motivational' in nature. Yet numerous attributional writings stress the role of defensive needs in the generation of defensive attributions. (For a recent review of the relevant literature, see Zuckerman, 1979.) In lay-epistemic terms, defensive attributions reflect the workings of a particular conclusional need; the maintenance of positive self-esteem. Viewing defensive attributions in this way highlights their non-uniqueness. In other words, a person could have a variety of conclusional needs besides self-esteem; such needs could similarly bias attributions towards desirable conclusions. For instance, one may need to believe in one's physical and economic well-being or to perceive the world as a just place; either of these needs would render need-congruent conclusions more likely than less congruent ones.

The lay-epistemic analysis also points to relevant attributional problems ignored by previous formulations, such as the problem of identifying the conditions under which attributions would be more or less subject to reconsideration. In light of new evidence, those conditions may involve the freezing and unfreezing processes mentioned earlier and illustrated empirically below.

In conclusion, the lay-epistemic theory furnishes a framework within which attributional phenomena can be understood in a novel way. On applying the epistemic perspective it becomes clear that previous attributional theorizing has perpetrated a content–process confusion, which has hindered the elucidation of the general principles underlying causal judgements. It also becomes apparent that causal judgements, like all judgements, are validated via the principle of logical consistency or deducibility. Finally, it becomes clear that previous attributional theorizing has neglected several important factors relevant to causal inferences and related to the person's capacity and/or motivation to pose a given attributional problem.

The relative neglect of the motivational dimension has earned attribution theory the reputation of being 'rationalistic' and 'cold'. By contrast, the cognitive consistency paradigm that virtually ruled over social psychological research in the 1960s is generally considered (cognitively) 'hot' and 'irrationalistic'. The shift of interest from cognitive consistency to attribution theories is often thought to reflect an emergent preference on the part of social psychologists to perceive the cognitive process as basically logical rather than as predominantly motivational. From our present perspective, however, the juxtaposition of logical (or rational) versus motivational (irrational) views of human inference is ill-advised: according to the lay-epistemic theory, there is no incompatibility between logical and motivational factors. In fact, every instance of inference is in a real sense both logical and motivational at the same time. It is logical in so far as it observes the criterion of logical consistency for deducibility; and it is motivational in so far as it reflects the needs for structure, validity and conclusional contents – impinging on the epistemic process at a given moment.

It is of interest to note that, while early attributional formulations emphasized the reasonableness of human inferences, the tide has once again turned. A quick scan of the literature reveals that the sterling image of rationality has become tarnished, and we have gone right back to poking fun at the poor lay people, prone as they are to bias, error and other inferential atrocities. In the following section we examine this current irrationalistic emphasis somewhat more closely.

BIASES AND ERRORS OF JUDGEMENT

In forming beliefs about the world, the new lay-attributor is assumed to use less than completely rational information-processing short-cuts, or 'heuristics'. While these heuristics sometimes lead to valid conclusions, they often distort reality in major ways. Errors result because heuristics, like representativeness and availability, divert attention from information deemed necessary for optimal processing (often defined by reference to statistical models), such as sampling bias, selective attention and recall, anchoring and perseverance, all of which enhance the error proneness of lay-inference. As compared with the superior normative models used in scientific inference, use of heuristics leads to failings.

From a lay-epistemic perspective, use of the so-called normative models is no guarantee for the truth or even the probability of inferences. In this contention we concur with such contemporary philosophers of science as Karl Popper, Thomas Kuhn, Imre Lakatos and Paul Feyerabend (for a recent review of their positions see Weimer, 1976). From our viewpoint, normative models are simply hypotheses advanced to account for data – highly formalized and mathematicized hypotheses, to be sure, but still no more than hypotheses. Many alternative interpretations can exist for any 'normative' interpretation of a set of data with no possibility of judging in advance which of the competing interpretations is more valid. A simple example should suffice to make this point (for a more detailed discussion see Kruglanski and Ajzen, 1983). Imagine that you are a schoolteacher trying to decide why pupils who did remarkably well on last week's test scored somewhat lower this week, and pupils who failed last week did not do so poorly this week. If you have had some exposure to statistics, you might conclude that the pattern of test scores was due to the phenomenon of statistical regression (whereby extreme scorers move closer to the mean on subsequent testing). But you could be entirely wrong! It may be that last week's high-scorers took a few nights away from the books to celebrate, and last week's low-scorers studied more diligently for fear of failing the course. Or it may be the case that the high-scorers were teased for being 'teacher's pets' and so made some intentional errors, and the low-scorers were similarly abused for being 'flunkees' and so prepared for this week's examination by writing pertinent information on the soles of their tennis shoes. If this latter 'stigma' explanation is the correct one, you as the teacher might be wise to implement a procedure to keep individual test results private. Unfortunately, if you opt for the statistical explanation, you will not bother to try to remedy what might be a serious problem. In other words, the statistical notion of regression is only one of an infinite number of plausible hypotheses, and should not be considered a superior mode of inference with any *a priori* claim to validity.

One interesting application of the lay-epistemic perspective is the prediction of conditions in which people *will* use statistical notions in making judgements. As with other hypotheses, a statistical hypothesis will be considered when it is available to the individual and is perceived as relevant to the problem. In a recent study, Kruglanski et al. (1981) created conditions that made the possibility of statistical regression rather salient to the subjects. Specifically, subjects were provided with information about a basketball player who at a given game scored either well above or well below his average. Subjects' predictions of the player's score at the next game followed regression logic; those subjects told that the player had scored well above his average predicted a markedly lower score at the next game, and those told that he had scored well below his average predicted a markedly higher score. The statistical regression hypothesis, or any statistical notion, can be used by the naive knower when it is salient and seems relevant. In this respect, it is used in the same way as any other conception or hypothesis.

Another bias assumed to characterize the inferential behaviour of lay persons (but presumably avoidable via the use of normative science) results from the apparent tendency of lay beliefs to persevere despite discrediting evidence. From the lay-epistemic perspective, belief perseverance could represent a 'freezing' of the hypothesis-generation process. Of course, such an interpretation divests belief perseverance of any claims for uniqueness. All firm beliefs are in a sense frozen beliefs, including all firm scientific beliefs. In this sense, belief perseverance is not a unique feature of lay inference; rather, it is a part of scientific inference, a view cogently expounded by Kuhn (1962) in his classic work on scientific paradigms.

Perhaps more important, our lay-epistemic theory can make several suggestions concerning conditions under which 'belief perseverance' or 'freezing' may be enhanced or reduced. For example, the unfreezing of a perseverant belief should be more likely when a person's need for validity is heightened, or when the belief's content is highly undesirable. Unfreezing should be less likely under a heightened need for structure or when the belief's content is highly desirable. Finally, unfreezing should be more likely when the belief is initially weak rather than strong. These implications of the lay-epistemic model were tested in several experimental studies.

An experiment conducted by Kruglanski and Meschiany (1981) attempted to overcome belief perseverance in a paradigm developed by Ross et al. (1975). In the Ross et al. experiment subjects were falsely led to believe that they had either succeeded, failed or performed at an average level on a task involving rating the genuineness of suicide notes. They then learned that, in fact, feedback and performance had been unrelated. Even though subjects saw the experimenter's list randomly assigning them to success, failure or average-performance feedback conditions, the debriefing seemed to be totally ineffective. Subjects' later reports of their performance indicated that they still believed the false feedback.

Interpreting this phenomenon as an occurrence of epistemic freezing suggests the type of factors that might work to relax it – for example, a heightened need for validity, or a conclusional need with which the perseverant belief was inconsistent. These needs were manipulated in the Kruglanski and Meschiany (1981) experiment. First, the Ross et al. perseverance effect was successfully replicated. Subjects' evaluations of their performance on a suicide note rating task, based on the experimenter's false feedback, persisted despite a debriefing procedure. In the accuracy-set condition, subjects' need for validity was increased after debriefing by informing them that their evaluations would be publicly compared with their real scores. They were also told that accuracy in self-perception was of considerable importance to an individual and was particularly valuable for decision-making and adjustment to new situations. Subjects in this condition seemed to unfreeze their beliefs, and the perseverance effect was washed out.

To manipulate the conclusional needs construct, some subjects were told, again after debriefing, that further credits and opportunities for interesting research were conditional on their task performance. Some were told that successful subjects would receive these benefits; some were told that unsuccessful subjects would be the fortunate ones. Beliefs were generally unfrozen in the predicted situations – when the false feedback had been inconsistent with the self-image that was now desired.

Belief perseverance is one important area in which lay-epistemic constructs can make interesting suggestions about limiting conditions. A series of experiments completed recently by Kruglanski and Freund (1982) applied these same principles to such disparate phenomena as primacy effects in impression formation (cf. Luchins, 1957), ethnic stereotyping (cf. D. Hamilton, 1979) and anchorage of numerical estimates in initial values (cf. Tversky and Kahneman, 1980). All of these phenomena can be interpreted as instances of epistemic freezing. Primacy effects reflect the crystalization of impressions after scanning only the early information about a person, and remaining insensitive to later information. Similarly, stereotyping may reflect the basing of judgements on pre-existing categories and an insensitivity to fresh evidence. Finally, anchoring may reflect the persisting impact of initial estimates, and the relative inefficacy of subsequent evidence, in suggesting the need to revise those estimates.

Based on this line of reasoning, Kruglanski and Freund (1982) conducted three experiments, in each of which need for structure, manipulated via degrees of time-pressure, was orthogonally crossed with need for validity manipulated via an expected loss of face in the case of a judgemental inaccuracy. In the experiment dealing with ethnic stereotyping, for example, students at a teachers' seminary were asked to evaluate a composition supposedly written by a local fourth-former. Stereotyping was assessed as the degree to which evaluations seemed to be based on the child's ascribed ethnic background, rather than on examination of the essay. Subjects were given either a full hour (low need for structure) or only ten minutes (high need for structure) to complete their grading. In the low-need-for-validity condition, subjects were assured that the purpose of the research was not to assess in any way the correctness of their judgements, but rather to identify possible individual differences in evaluative style. In the high-need-for-validity condition, the subjects were told that they would be asked to defend their grading before a group of their peers. The results of this experiment lent strong support to the lay-epistemic analysis, with freezing being significantly stronger under high- versus low-need-for-structure conditions and significantly weaker under high- versus low-need-for-validity conditions. These results were replicated in two other experiments in which primacy effects and numerical anchoring were used as the judgemental phenomena.

Finally, a recent experiment by Chaiken and Baldwin (1981) provides indirect support for the lay-epistemic prediction that strongly believed propositions would be more resistant to unfreezing than weakly believed ones. Chaiken and Baldwin reasoned that a proposition will likely be believed in more steadfastly if it is well articulated; that is, if it is coherent, or internally consistent. By the same token, poorly articulate propositions may be believed in less steadfastly. Their study confirmed this reasoning. The experimenters found that only subjects with poorly articulated attitudes modified their attitude judgements when information regarding their past attitude-relevant behaviour was made salient. Subjects with well-articulated attitudes remained frozen in their original self-assessments, and did not shift to accommodate the salient behavioural evidence.

Rather than continuing to debate the lay person's ultimate rationality or irrationality, the present analysis suggests shifting to an analysis of the conditions under which a given judgemental bias may be more or less likely. Rather than debating whether persons are bad or good intuitive statisticians, we should be concerned with the conditions under which people utilize statistical concepts (such as regression). And rather than stressing the 'irrationality' of perseverant judgements, we should be concerned with identifying those factors that facilitate or inhibit perseverance.

CONCLUDING REMARKS

Our lay-epistemic analysis has the following general implications for attribution theory. (1) It shows how the process–content confusion in the attributional literature has obstructed progress in the area, and promoted ambiguity and uncontrolled proliferation. (2) It suggests the need to supplement attribution theory by epistemic variables unattended to heretofore. (3) It offers a view of human rationality that differs from previous conceptions in considering bias and error as inevitable aspects of all inference, including scientific inference.

The failure to distinguish between attributional contents and process has led to an unfortunate situation in which specific causal categories, themselves of no unique significance, have received a highly exaggerated attention in numerous attribution studies. At the same time, despite years of research, the process whereby all causal attributions are made has not been clearly specified. Lay-epistemic analysis draws attention to the idea that causal inferences are rendered in basically the same way as non-causal inferences: specific causal hypotheses are engendered in accordance with the knower's generative capacity affected by this person's past knowledge and the momentary availability of various ideas. The tendency to continue generating different hypotheses also depends on the individual's epistemic motivations for structure, validity and conclusional contents. Once generated, the causal hypotheses proceed to be validated in accordance with the principle of deducibility, or logical consistency.

Lay-epistemic theory further assumes the essential similarity of the processes by which both naive and scientific knowledge are acquired (cf. chapter 6 below). We do not adulate lay inference and assume it to be marvellously free of bias, error or motivational influences; rather, we downplay the glory of scientific inference and assume that it contains the very same sources of fallibility. Our approach thus implies the futility of debates concerning the ultimate rationality or irrationality of lay judgement. Such debates usually invite the comparison of lay inferences against various normative models of scientific inference, assuming, quite inappropriately we would hold, the proven superiority of the latter. Rather than engaging in 'rationality debates', we propose a re-orientation of research efforts in social–cognitive psychology towards a better understanding of conditions under which given judgemental biases are manifest.

Beyond its theoretical implications, the lay-epistemic framework is, first and foremost, a psychological theory of the knowledge-acquisition process; as such, it has a variety of researchable implications. In preceding pages we have described some of the research suggested by the epistemic analysis, research into problems of causal attribution, belief perseverance, impression formation and social stereotyping. This research illustrates the heuristic potential of the lay-epistemic model for a wide variety of phenomena of interest to the social cognitive researcher.

ACKNOWLEDGEMENTS

This chapter is based on 'Die Laien-Epistemologie von Kruglanski', to appear in D. Frey, and M. Irle (eds.), *Sozialpsychologische Theorienperspektiven* (vol. 2). Bern: Verlag Huber. The preparation of the chapter was supported by a Social Sciences and Humanities Research Council of Canada doctoral fellowship to Mark W. Baldwin.

PART II
Social Foundations of Attribution

6 Social Representations and Social Explanations: From the 'Naive' to the 'Amateur' Scientist

Serge Moscovici and Miles Hewstone

INTRODUCTION

One of the central arguments of this volume is that we need to consider the wider aspects of attribution theory. One way in which this can be done, and the theory rendered more social, is to consider explanations alongside the beliefs that are shared by large numbers of people within and between societies. The study of these beliefs brings attribution theory back to the issue of common-sense psychology and deals with the rather neglected question of *where* attributions come from.

This last question has been posed by Pepitone (1981) and Lalljee (1981), while other scholars have lamented the 'surprisingly little research on those beliefs and theories shared by the mass of people in our culture' (Nisbett and Ross, 1980, p. 30). Kassin (1981) has provided a heuristic conception of attribution principles according to the amount and complexity of information that an observer must encode in order to make an attribution. 'First-order' principles involve a single observation and 'second-order' principles concern multiple observations of cause–effect relations; both these aspects have stimulated much experimental work. But 'third-order' principles, dealing with *theories* that guide inferences about how causes combine and operate, require much closer attention. Kelley (1983) has also pointed to the neglect of 'perceived causal structures', meaning ordinary people's ideas about the temporal ordering of causes and effects. In a similar vein, he has discussed how adults learn numerous theories about 'causality at a distance' – involving agents such as bacteria, genes and atomic particles (Kelley, 1980). Yet, we still know very little about how such technical terms become part of the lay person's repertoire of explanations. Our aim in this chapter is to look at such questions in terms of more general ideas about common sense, using the notion of a social representation.

The points of departure for the social representations approach (e.g. Herzlich, 1972, 1973; Moscovici, 1961, 1981, 1983; Moscovici and Farr, 1983) are questions such as: 'What is the genesis of common-sense ideas about various scientific disciplines?' and 'What happens to a scientific discipline when it passes from specialists into society?' We take the *transformation* of scientific knowledge to be a fundamental aspect of common sense. Its importance for any theory of explanations was shown in the first social representations study (Moscovici, 1961), on how ideas about psychoanalysis had seeped into French society. Individuals assimilate such knowledge (e.g. the term 'complex') and use it as a basis for explaining their own and other people's behaviour. Thus we are now familiar with explanations such as 'He thinks he's no good – he just has an inferiority complex.'

The concept of a social representation concerns phenomena and topics that lie at the crossroads of anthropology, sociology and psychology. This gives it a certain generality and complexity, because it touches on a variety of contents and levels of cognitive elaboration. We are concerned with the way knowledge is represented in a society and shared by its members. The social representation has some similarities with the notions of attitude, opinion and stereotype, but it goes beyond them to consider knowledge in the form of common-sense 'theories' about all aspects of life and society. This whole is also seen as greater than the sum of the parts, and thus irreducible to a collection of individual representations (see Durkheim, 1898).[1] For example, we may study the ideas about health and illness that are shared throughout a society (see Herzlich, 1973), rather than individual perceptions and explanations (cf. King, chapter 10 below).

In the following pages we use this notion to underline the relationship between science and common sense, seeing this as the disembarkation point for a common-sense psychology. This leads us to view the lay person as an 'amateur scientist' – consuming, digesting and transforming ever-developing scientific knowledge – in contrast to the rather pejorative term, 'naive scientist', as used by Heider (1958) and thereafter. The invidious comparison of lay person with scientist is eschewed and we concentrate instead on the processes by which professional science knowledge becomes amateur science knowledge. Thus we consider there to be two forms of common-sense knowledge: a residue of widely shared knowledge, which may be systematized by science; and a transformation of *new* scientific knowledge into everyday language.

The link between representations and explanations is illustrated by considering the former as frames of reference, classifying and selecting information before suggesting suitable explanations. As St Augustine noted, 'No-one, indeed, believes anything unless he previously knows it to be believable.' While such explanations may often appear bizarre or 'irrational', our emphasis on shared social beliefs underlines their societal foundations, rather than showing them as errors and biases in cognitive information-processing. Finally, the functions of social explanations are considered briefly, with special reference to scapegoating and conspiracy theories.

Thus our chapter deals with what Wells (1981) has called 'socialized processing' or 'taking advantage of language-based communication channels to adopt cultural and parental hypotheses' (p. 320).[2] We draw attention to the social foundations and functions of attribution, advocating the development of a true common-sense psychology.

THE ABSURD AND THE REASONABLE BEING

In considering common-sense and lay explanations, we are dealing with a paradox. In spite of certain doubts, we consider that people are generally reasonable, as witness science and logic. Moreover, these latter disciplines place at our disposal methods or models that forewarn us against all possible deviation towards error. With their help, each one of us *could* and *should* think and behave according to reason. And yet a mass of prejudices, superstitions and common illusions reveals how much lay people base their existence on ideas that are totally lacking in reason. What is more, if one examines in detail the manner in which they choose a piece of information, predict an action or think out a problem, one can see that most people act like very unskilled scientists. This is the paradox that has merited the attention of anthropologists studying Africa or Asia (e.g. Lévy-Bruhl, 1922; Lévi-Strauss, 1962) and of Western psychologists (e.g. Heider, 1958; Nisbett and Ross, 1980). The French philosopher Bergson captured this in the phrase, used as a heading for this section, 'De l'absurdité chez l'être raisonnable' ('The absurd and the reasonable being').

In order to understand this paradox, one asks questions of the following type: 'Why do people think the way they do?' 'How do people think?' 'How do people understand their world?' 'How do they account for other people's actions and their own?' and 'How do people use the information conveyed by science or common experience?' One tries to explain the nature of the gap between the ideal of reason and the reality of thought in the social world. This explanation takes into account the concept of social representation, the study of which was suggested by a collection of factors. Everything is conspiring to make science part and parcel of our daily life; it is inseparable from the intellectual life of a group and from social intercourse. The ascent of research has been rapid, as has its diffusion through the media and the educational system, while our respect for its development is fuelled by natural curiosity. As a consequence, our ideologies, on a grand scale, and our so-called common sense, on a lesser one, are full of ideas, images, words and rules drawn from the fields of physics, medicine, psychology, economics and so on.

Scientists do not want to know, and philosophers of science are not in a position to understand, that, all the while they are fighting in people's minds against accepted forms of language and thinking, they are imposing new perspectives on the lay person. Ordinary people consume developing scientific knowledge and use it in their everyday communication and behaviour. But they do not simply process this knowledge; they turn it into a game of 'science as a hobby', a modern version of common sense. This hobby is encouraged by magazines such as *Science Digest*, *Popular Science* and *Psychology Today*, to name but a few. From its inception, the notion of social representation was conceived in order to study how the game of science becomes part of the game of common sense. Whether this has been done successfully so far is another story.

THE BIFURCATED MIND

In talking of science and common sense, or in other words of scientific and lay epistemology, each of us immediately understands what it is about. We are dealing with a very old opposition, described many times before. Man, at least Western man, has the curious privilege of being a citizen in two worlds of thinking. Ordinary people enjoy in constant alternation two kinds of intellectual experience: the professional and the casual one, the disciplined and the spontaneous one, each of which has it own logic, limits and attributes. Rational thought has on its side rigour and predictability, but it is very limited in its possibilities for exploration. In its field we only have to deal, in theory, with competent people and discrete information. Its counterpart, on the other hand, offers the chance of intercourse, however ephemeral, with anybody – friends or neighbours as well as strangers – whatever their training or interests. We could conceive of it as a 'Citizen Band' science, on the fringe of official channels, dealing with a kind of science digest – but science turned into more palatable fare, just one more item off the shelf of consumer goods. Here as everywhere tastes may differ. Hence it is no wonder that people are so reluctant to choose and ascribe superiority to either of these worlds of thinking.

This leads to a bifurcation, to a radical divergence between two worlds of knowing or acquiring knowledge, the standard and the non-standard one. Several labels have been used to describe it – logic and myth; 'domestic' and 'savage' thought (Lévi-Strauss, 1962); 'logical' and 'pre-logical' mentality (Lévy-Bruhl, 1922); 'critical' and 'automatic' thought (Moscovici, 1981, 1983) – but the nature of these opposites remains the same. On the one hand, standard thinking seeks and finds out the truth. It is a reflective mode of thought, which controls and formulates certain criteria to negate or confirm its reasoning. The mind trained to follow its rules supposes that to every question there is one, and only one, answer. The rule leading to correct conclusions, for all authentic problems, is logical in character; and, finally, conclusions and reasonings are valid for all people, places and times.

In contrast, non-standard thinking corresponds to a more 'natural' form of thinking, a native one which is acquired directly without any special training. People express and use such knowledge in their workaday activities and are not concerned exclusively with its scientific validity. This thinking is chiefly influenced by prior beliefs or social stereotypes, not by precise and objective collection of data.

Today, scientific epistemology is obviously the epistemology of standard thinking and lay epistemology, that of non-standard thinking. The question that remains in contemporary social psychology is simple: are they opposite or complementary? This bifurcation is, however, a consequence not only of a division of thought, but also of a division in society. Everyone is aware of the vast differentiation within modern culture. This is manifested in the splitting of science, technology and even art. In one respect these types of knowledge are made 'sacred', and knowing them to be devised by specialists makes them autonomous. This has led to the creation of a culture of experts, ensconced in their institutions and disciplines. Alternatively, what might be called 'profane' knowledge has been relinquished, fragmented and wrung out in mass culture. This has led to a bifurcated society: a minority of specialists and a majority of lay people, consumers of knowledge that is sucked through the straw of a brief education and the omnipresent media. The opposition between standard and non-standard thinking, between the informed mind of the scientist and the naive mind of the lay person, is less part of a logical or organic order than of a social order. Unfortunately, social psychologists rarely debate the social reasons for this *philosophia plebeia*, and they take even less account of it.

COMMON SENSE: FROM FIRST- TO SECOND-HAND KNOWLEDGE

A lay epistemology has as its object the study of a particular type of knowledge: that is to say, common sense. Thus it must first describe this type of knowledge and who is the 'knower'. The description obviously depends on the point of view one favours: ours is based on the social representations approach. We are not in a position to draw a line, to say where and when common sense or naive thinking begins and ends. However, we can grasp it in contrast with science, in the same way that we can compare 'new' with 'old'.

Having images and making mental connections is our most general working tool. The crucial element of human intelligence is to visualize and to forge links. It can thus go beyond the given (Bruner, 1957) to discriminate patterns, hierarchies and so forth. Common sense comprises the images, mental connections and metaphors that are used and talked about by everyone when trying to explain familiar problems or predict their outcome. It is a corpus of knowledge based on shared traditions and enriched by thousands of well-practised 'experiments' and 'observations'. Things are named, individuals are classified, spontaneous conjectures are made in the course of action or ordinary communication. All this is stored in the language and in the minds of the members of society. It is this knowledge that gives to such images and mental connections the character of irrefutable evidence, of consensus around which 'everybody knows'.

We therefore see in common sense a body of knowledge that is accepted by 'everyone'. Moreover, it seems to be a specific characteristic of people with pure and innocent – such is the meaning of 'naive' – minds; that is, of people whose understanding has not been corrupted by education, philosophical speculation or professional rules. This supposition concerning their naivety leads to another: that is that, using their common sense, people see things as they are. In this sense, too, we are talking about first-hand knowledge. Sciences seem merely to refine and sift the ordinary materials delivered by common sense. In this progress towards clarity and simplicity, contradictions are exposed, that have remained buried for thousands of years. This allows us, on the one hand, to select relevant hypotheses and, on the other, to proceed to valid generalizations. In this way, for example, the ordinary idea of force, describing the effort of muscles or the activity of a machine, has been modified and transformed into a mathematical concept. What had been accumulated by tradition is transformed through reason. Thus science might be seen merely as a distillation and ordering of common sense:

What is called science is merely a systematic continuation of those activities we carry out in everyday life in order to know something. [Carnap, 1955, p. 45]

It is the work of a specialist, trained to follow and improve the rules of standard thinking. As T. H. Huxley said, 'Science is nothing but trained and organized common sense.'

Although readers might reproach us for wasting their time, bringing up such well-known things, we have done so because this is not the only relationship posited between science and common sense. Of course, most sociologists and social psychologists keep this fact in mind when they study ethnomethodology (Garfinkel, 1967), naive psychology (Heider, 1958) or lay epistemology (Kruglanski, 1980; see chapter 5 above). Indeed, in general, they do so whenever they try to analyse the methods and explanations used in people's spontaneous attempts to make sense of their everyday world. But the classic point of view, that science is born out of common sense, does *not* appear to correspond with contemporary reality. The function of present-day science is not to start from common sense, but to break with it and upset it totally; to raze to the ground the old ideas and familiar notions. Science (particularly natural science) bulldozes, destroying stone by stone the stately mansions of thought in which have been stored, through generations, the fruits of people's observations and ideas.

The revolution in communications has allowed the diffusion of images, notions and vocabularies that science keeps inventing. They become an integral part of the intellectual baggage of the lay person. Everyone today has a more or less vague notion of economic theories, unemployment, inflation, psychological conceptions of neurosis and so forth. As the philosopher Duhem remarked,

This science is constantly diffused by instruction, by conversation, by books and periodicals; it penetrates to the bottom of common sense knowledge; it awakens its attention to phenomena hitherto neglected; it teaches it to analyse notions which had remained confused. It thus enriches the patrimony of truths common for all men or, at least, for all those who have reached a certain degree of intellectual culture. [Duhem, 1962 edn, p. 261]

Nowadays, in classrooms, on television, in films, at coffee breaks and so on we can notice an avid consumption of news in scientific fields as much as, if not more than, in politics. We know something of what impels people to acquire such knowledge from empirical studies (Roqueplo, 1974) and the motivations include: the acquisition of a competence equal to that of the society in which one lives; a curiosity about 'how things work'; and the need to give meaning to and master one's life. One could consider these injections of knowledge as a kind of addiction. They become a drug for the lay person just as they may do for the researcher. This is why some call science the new religion of the people, and others call it the Valium of the people.[3]

The motivation to transform scientific knowledge is a powerful one. It comes from the pure thirst for knowledge and the desire to take part, however modestly, in this great adventure of our times. People, knowledgeable or not, want to consume, digest and share science. In the process, these bits of knowledge become more and more detached from a method or a system, and more mixed up with one another than they really are. For specialists there are *sciences*; for their public there is *science*, and this difference changes everything.

This development marks a kind of 'dethroning' of common sense (see Gregory, 1981). Common sense is seen as a catch-all of popular science, continually transformed as science advances or changes. It is no longer seen as a font of natural wisdom. Thus the new common sense, derived from science and marked by reason, is held as second-hand knowledge, and for the most part we place our confidence in the authority of science.

To reiterate, what we call 'common sense' appears in two different ways. First, it appears as a corpus of knowledge, based on tradition and consensus, spontaneously produced by the members of a group. It is a first-hand knowledge that gave birth to and reared science. Second, it appears as a sum total of mental images and links of scientific origin. It is a second-hand knowledge that spreads and steadily builds a new consensus around recent discoveries and theories. The old common sense is still prevalent in the spoken word, that of conversation and rumour. The new common sense is diffused through the media. It can be split into as many folk, naive or lay sciences as there are professional sciences: lay psychology, lay anthropology and so on. This development reflects the division between two spheres of human thought, and it must have far-reaching consequences; but few researchers seem to have had the curiosity to analyse or even describe them.

The retooling of science as common sense provides a different picture of the latter. It supplies also a rationale for phrasing the questions that social psychology must ask itself on the subject. If we examine scientific epistemology, we notice that the main question concerns the passage from ordinary knowledge to a systematic knowledge, from the proto- (or pseudo-) science to natural science. In the words of the philosopher Frank, 'The essential problem in the philosophy of science is how to get from common-sense statements to general scientific principles' (Frank, 1957, p. 2).

However, we could say that the problem for social psychology is exactly the reverse. After all, what is presented to people for their consideration is not the objective world of persons and things, information as it may be supposed to exist independently of human collective life. It is from the outset a theory, an image – in short, an interpretation to which science contributes its share. This passage from science to common sense involves two aspects. There is the *socialization* of science, its diffusion and its adaptation by every member of society, and the *rationalization* of all realms of our society. When researchers presume that the lay person ought to follow the rational model of scientific enquiry (Nisbett and Ross, 1980), they consider this process as having reached its conclusion. However, when they find that, in fact, the ordinary person fails to use formal rules or uses them incorrectly (or in the wrong place, or at the wrong time), there is often no obvious explanation to account for this failing. This is simply because the assumption is not verified, nor is the passage from science to common sense analysed in its own right. The lay person's laws of thinking are thereby incriminated, in a peculiar way, as if he or she had a different brain from that of the scientist, lived in another society or belonged to a particular species of primate, separate and distinct from the human race.

In reality, there are two steps in this passage from science to common sense. It begins with the retooling of science as common sense, the transformation of standard into non-standard thinking. Yet it does not stop there. People want to know in order to come to terms with the physical and social world. This is why they use this derived common sense to give meaning to phenomena, understand their relationships with other people and explain events in the social world. We propose that this picture of a new common sense and the question of its origin necessitates an authentically social psychological approach. Everthing touching on the life of social minds still remains a riddle; but it is a puzzle that fascinates and seduces – at least, when we envisage it tackling vernacular realities instead of academic ones.

PEOPLE WITH SCIENCE FOR A HOBBY

The first research on social representations concerned common sense or popular psychology (Moscovici, 1961). The same is true for research on social cognition (Heider, 1958). Together they started from a similar hypothesis, which Heider stated clearly:

> since common-sense psychology guides our behaviour toward other people, it is an essential part of the phenomena in which we are interested. In everyday life we form ideas about other people and about social situations. We interpret other people's actions and we predict what they will do under certain circumstances. Though these ideas are usually not formulated, they often function adequately. [Heider, 1958, p. 5]

In both approaches the lay person is regarded as a scientist, but the expression is too general for the time being. Let us define precisely who is the knower involved when someone speaks of common-sense psychology, physics, sociology and so on. This knower is often called a 'naive', 'intuitive' or 'lay' scientist. If one takes into account the observations made above, one can understand that these appellations are inappropriate for two reasons.

First, in considering man as a naive scientist, we are turning him into a sort of Adam on the day of his creation, with no prejudices, no scheme of things – a pre-social individual opening his untutored eyes on a world of pure sense impressions, not yet coordinated in any conceptual structure. Even if we acknowledge that he has a background knowledge or an implicit framework, we can nevertheless suppose three things: first, an innocent outlook; next, neutrality towards the world; and last, the clearness of information with which he deals. If one of these suppositions is infringed, we accuse the lay scientist of being biased; of being unduly influenced by prior theories; and of generalizing erroneously on the basis of distorted samples of events or behaviours. In other words, lay people are said to be irrational. But, in the event of their being truly naive, how could they have reasoned in a logical way? Everyone knows that drawing inferences from observations is not so much a natural gift as a long, difficult process. Lay people are not able to do so following scientific rules. So there is not much to be gained by keeping up the notion of a naive or intuitive scientist, as opposed to a scientist in the real sense of the word. This is even more true in that the latter has the same intellectual capabilities, yet often makes analogous mistakes and is subject to similar biases (Kuhn, 1962).

Second, from another perspective, to qualify the ordinary knower in these ways does not correspond with any socio-cultural reality. There are no people whose activity can be studied as naive, intuitive and so forth. It is a fiction, a left-over from the days when one believed in 'savage' philosophers, 'natural man' and 'primitive society'. The lay person was then assimilated to the child and the primitive; all three were deprived of the enlightenment of science and of civilized, adult thought.

Taking these reasons into account, and the nature of the new common sense, the lay person can be considered as an *amateur scientist* (Moscovici, 1976). This title still confers a difference from professional scientists, but it avoids various connotations of the term 'naive'. It also reminds us that professional scientists are nearly always amateur scientists outside their specialized fields. Every one of us, and particularly those who have received an advanced education, has a tendency to be an amateur scientist. We are readers of the number of books aimed at the public's interest in science. This public is a consumer of discovered scientific notions, an assiduous reader of popular magazines or books and a passionate follower of scientific news. Such knowledge is gained from contacts with physicians, psychologists and technologists, or information is gleaned from politicians' speeches about economic and social problems. This mode of information search and acquisition must remain our model. Certainly, one would be wrong to suppose that the cultural background of the lay scientist was a *tabula rasa*. On the contrary, he or she has too much culture, and it is often confused.

Normally, we consider the common-sense psychology, thanks to which we can explain the behaviour of our neighbours, as having been formed during past action and experience – before, or independently of, the scientific study of the phenomena in question. But it is more realistic to think, for example, that numerous members of our Western society (having undergone personal therapy, taken part in group analysis and so on) have themselves practically become experts. One can envisage very easily how such experiences would have an impact on attributions made in inter-personal relationships. To neglect such influences is to risk attributing to the 'natural psyche' what, in reality, is a cultural consequence. That *would* be an attribution error! Academic psychologists who ignore this point will study as a proven fact, in their laboratory subjects, what is really the result of the work done by practising psychologists or those who popularize the discipline.

For us, the archetypal example of the amateur scientist is provided by the novelist Flaubert. He used and immortalized this category of person in his novel, *Buvard et Pécuchet*. The two title-heroes illustrate perfectly the image of the knower implied by the social representations approach. The novelist depicts them in an era when science was a wide-spread hobby. Amateur scientists were swarming. They tried to understand nature, mind or society for their own amusement and excitement. Everybody 'did' science, without thinking of it as a career or profession, just by collecting specimens, experimenting with chemical materials, building microscopes, telescopes and other apparatus. Although some of the 'hobbyists' became famous, most of them were untrained in the specific sense. They wrote no dissertations, no polished articles and often nothing at all.

Buvard and Pécuchet (their very names suggest plodding cattle) join up with the goal of studying various sciences, scrutinizing their theories and transposing them into their familiar world. What they do together is quite obvious – they copy and reproduce. Thereby the contents of every book they read become metamorphosed. The novelist gives a subtle analysis of the cognitive labour through which concepts of anatomy, chemistry and medicine become unrecognizable in the hands of his characters. Once their work is over, they experiment and produce information to validate their representations of theories, and what they have understood. Moreover, theory and information come to pervade communication and social relationships in the village where Buvard and Pécuchet live.

This deserves to be pointed out. For while the picture of the 'naive scientist' bears the stamp of an individual and anonymous person, that of the 'amateur scientist' can immediately be placed within the framework of society and culture. Buvard and Pécuchet are two associated and complementary individuals. Their whole lives are impregnated with communication and sociability: they comment on what they read, they talk about scientific subjects and write letters to learned men. The knowledge they have acquired gives them a certain prestige and position in the village. Amateur scientists in almost every field, they even become amateur psychologists – discussing the then-popular phrenology of Gall.

Buvard and Pécuchet are therefore the cultural archetypes of all those who make science their hobby or, if not a hobby, consume it to sate their curiosity. It is for this reason that we have painted in some detail the portrait of the knower associated with the new common sense. It has enabled us to depict the amateur scientist in relief, against the images and portraits that have come to predominate in social psychology's picture gallery.

RETOOLING SCIENCE AS COMMON SENSE

The evolution of theories

In the foregoing example we have described the amateur scientist more precisely as the prototype of the ordinary knower. The first question we should now face is this: how does the amateur scientist achieve his or her aim? In other words, how is science used to produce practical common-sense knowledge? The task is to pierce the depths of the amateur scientist's mind and analyse its cognitive activity. This is not an easy task, however, or one to which we can find a simple solution.

Cognition, such is the current paradigm, is in principle founded on information; that is to say, on physical and social data, ready to be inspected and explained. What does this imply? Simply that individuals acquire knowledge by recognition and by sorting the bits of information that reach them from the outside world. In trying to straighten things out and to obtain a stable view of the world, each individual makes inferences, allowing him or her to attribute causes and make predictions. Lacking a proper training, one is vulnerable to systematic biases and errors, and the source of these shortcomings can be found in the implicit theories, schemata and other conceptual systems that guide the flow of information-processing. All this is too well known for further development to be of any immediate use. Theories concerning the epistemology of naive science, causal attribution or social cognition are all based on this view of cognitive activity.

It is however possible to construct many arguments against this position. First, we should emphasize that cognitive elements never appear in their raw state. They gain importance only in conjunction with a theory, an idea that varies from individual to individual, from group to group. It is thus very necessary to understand how these theories or conceptual systems have evolved in society – such is the goal of a theory of social representations. It is much less crucial to know how information is processed and how people draw inferences from it. As the holy Francis of Assisi once put it, 'What we are looking for is what is looking.'

Informative and transformative processes

In examining these theories, an important distinction can be made between the human capacity to *learn* and the capacity to *represent*. The one defines the mental work aimed at storing and ordering, by habit or otherwise, knowledge gained by the senses from the external world; the other concerns the activities by which one reproduces, by substitution of one modality for another (words by images; drawings by ideas; emotions by concepts; and so on) the various pieces of knowledge culled from the physical world. But it is also a question of the reproduction of absent, fictitious or foreign objects in the form of present, factual or familiar objects. Thus cause and intention, atoms and wavelengths (to name a few things that are by definition invisible) are made visible by imagery, models or other means. Both capacities are important, of course, but it is evident that from a cognitive point of view we can learn mainly what we are able to represent.

These remarks lead us to the difference between *informative* and *transformative* processes. The former concerns the organization and stabilization of existing data. More precisely, it concerns the reduction of sensory events and perceptual observations to some cognition or habit. The transformative processes express literally a restructuring of some initial experience or idea. It is always a journey with maps. No transformation can be described as regular, since each one is as unique as a fingerprint. But there are stages, and the passage from one to the other is surprisingly typical. We shall consider this point further below, for we are touching one of the essential features of cognitive activity as used in common sense. Representations are related to transformative rather than informative processes. Such is the first conclusion that we want to convey. This means that fundamental representations of a stable and widely diffused kind are not resolvable into, or derivable from, observations and rules of inference. They are to be found in the amateur scientist's mental work, and also in the end-products generated by this activity.

Transformation: external processes

Both transformative and informative processes will be examined and illustrated. But first, let us visualize again the situation of our lay scientist faced with science and reality. The former, in its objective fashion, generates continually surprising data about human nature and the nature of things. It describes excitingly the dream world of those who have strained to see past and throw off the blunders of common intelligence. It relates thrilling stories of stars, oceans, physical phenomena and universes that are beyond our usual imaginings. There is a much-quoted remark of the English biologist J. B. S. Haldane, that 'reality is not only stranger than we conceive, but stranger than we *can* conceive.'

While amateur scientists are attracted by this dream world, and away from the factual one, they attempt at the same time to make it familiar. We have often observed people making just such an attempt, when creating a representation for themselves. Studies in this vein (Herzlich, 1973; Jodelet, 1980; Moscovici, 1976) remind us of *Flatland* (Abbott, 1926), a Victorian fantasy whose characters are assorted geometric shapes living in a two-dimensional world. The narrator, a middle-aged square, first dreams of visiting Lineland, a frustrating country whose inhabitants can only move from point to point. Then his grandson, a hexagon, suggests the possibility of a third dimension, of a realm in which you move up and down as well as from side to side. The square angrily contradicts this foolish notion. But that very night he has an encounter with a sphere, an inhabitant of Spaceland. This shatters all his previous notions. And when he shrieks aloud: 'Either this is madness or it is Hell,' the sphere calmly answers: 'It is neither, it is Knowledge; it is Three Dimensions. Open your eyes once again and try to look steadily.'

The fable illustrates perfectly the nature of relations between people with different representations. Each describes the other's view as biased or mistaken, as scientists do. Furthermore, we can witness what happens when new scientific discoveries are transposed to the existing order of ideas. It is not the information given, but the change of perspective, the way in which the information is represented, that stays in the mind.

From this example we now wish to specify the transformation process. Some simplification can be achieved by distinguishing between the external and internal processes. The external processes describe the changes that scientific theories have undergone at the common-sense level to become social representations. The internal processes concern the transformations that register at the core of these representations. We will begin with the external processes, which can be treated in three stages.

(1) The *personification* of knowledge and phenomena is the first and most noteworthy stage. This is obvious inasmuch as each theory or science is associated with an individual, designated by name, who becomes the symbol of that theory, science or approach: Freud and psychoanalysis; Einstein and relativity; Pavlov and conditioning. This is what gives theory a concrete existence and allows it to be treated as if it were a tangible social reality or, even better, as if it were a well-defined personage. Theories may, moreover, become associated with a particular social group – psychoanalysis with psychoanalysts; conditioning with Soviet Russians; behaviourism with Americans – which renders the link that much stronger.

(2) *Figuration* refers to the substitution, or the superposition, of images and concepts. As scientific notions become part of common sense, they become almost metaphorical diagrams and images. They become almost visible. As a rule these pictures prevail over the remote or abstract images or ideas. For example, certain images disseminated in the context of the European Economic Community – milk and wine 'lakes'; sugar and butter 'mountains'; lamb and cod 'wars' – come to predominate over the, admittedly palid, underlying economic concepts. In this way our most advanced intellectual adventures in abstract thinking can be carried beyond the boundaries of logical understanding, into the realms of figurative thinking. The vividness of most reasonings and notions of common sense (Moscovici, 1983; Nisbett and Ross, 1980) is the most obvious consequence of all this.

(3) Lastly, the movement from the scientific to the commonsensical would seem to go hand in hand with an '*ontologizing*' of logical and empirical relations. By this we mean that, whereas personification assimilates the idea to a person and figuration turns it into an image, 'ontologizing' gives the notion some sense of being. We well know that the logic of science is the same logic as that of relationships – as far as possible, it avoids all personification of the results of analysis. Certain physicists go so far as to hesitate in their belief in the reality of material phenomena such as 'wavelengths', 'particles', 'fields' and 'black holes'. Representation has a propensity to make qualities and forces correspond to ideas or words – stated baldly, to give ontological life to something that is no more than a logical, even verbal, 'being'. This process has been illustrated elsewhere (Moscovici, 1976) for the psychoanalytic notion of a 'complex'. For a relatively large number of people it signifies neither a relationship between parents and children nor an abstract idea in a theory. On the contrary, for

lay people it refers to a psychic object, or even to a quasi-biological organ.

The reader might possibly ask why we have not chosen an existing word (e.g. 'reify', 'substantialize', 'hypostatize') to designate this stage, instead of the barbaric 'ontologizing'. The answer is that these more familiar words, having been created to indicate different propensities of the thought process, seem to produce a rather distorted image of the process. We are simply referring to a tendency to prolong an image, to give it breadth and depth, and to create a place for it in the ontology of common sense. We mean to convey only that this process is a useful intermediary for an intangible concept. This transformation is above all of cognitive importance. On the one hand, it integrates new notions into nature, society or a body; on the other hand, by 'ontologizing' them, it transforms the intellectual representation and makes it a part of common sense.

Drawing together these three stages, it is easy to see that they separate the contents from an original form and have obvious functional significance. They extract a notion from its specific context only to re-introduce it in a general context, thereby facilitating its assimilation. The result of these external processes of transformation is that a science, having infiltrated the society in which we all live, takes on a different structure, rationality and impact than it had in the world of the scientist. The alert reader will note that we use these same external processes in this chapter in trying to give some substance to the notion of a social representation.

Transformation: internal processes

In order to understand the internal processes, it must be remembered that representations are, or play the role of, theories; as such, they must show 'how things work'. In other words, their task is first to describe, then to classify, and finally to explain. Science warns against any hasty move towards an explanation. However, lay people tend to overestimate the certainty and consistency of science. On this basis they are inclined to pass easily from the 'what' to the 'how', and thence to the 'why'.

Taking account of this singular characteristic, it is understandable that Heider (1958) should have reserved the central role of common-sense psychology for causality; and that sociologists (e.g. Windisch, 1978) should grant it a major role in their study of ideology. It is thus clear that the internal process is interpreted by the almost automatic passage from description to explanation. This gives it a force: it seems to have a reply for everything, to be ready to saturate any aspect of reality. In science it is the descriptive factor that tends to predominate, the factor closest to observation; while in common sense it is the explanatory factor that seems most powerful.

More specifically, we could say that a representation plays the three roles of a theory simultaneously. This can be illustrated with an example. Research by neuroscientists has postulated a lateralization of brain functions. The left hemisphere would seem to control verbal and analytical knowledge, while the right hemisphere is the seat of global and perceptual knowledge. However, researchers acknowledge that the specialization of each half of the brain is not an all-or-nothing affair; rather, it falls along a continuum (Springer and Deutsch, 1981). When looked at from a logical point of view, this theory is totally descriptive; but for reasons that deserve elucidation, it has been widely diffused to an appreciative audience of amateur scientists. A common-sense neuroscience has been born. The remarkable part of all this is that the two halves of the brain (or mind) have become two brains (or minds) corresponding to two seperate modes of thought, feeling and behaviour. In fact, it is a localization of everybody's favourite pair of opposites: rational–intuitive; conscious–unconscious; masculine–feminine; logical–mystical; and so on. It is a strong representation, both from the point of view of the image that replaces the concept and from the point of view of its ontological character. Let us now look at how an American scientific journalist, Maralyn Ferguson, author of *The Aquarian Conspiracy* (1978), shapes and changes it. In this way the book becomes a kind of treatise on common-sense neuroscience, aimed at folk scientists.

What began as a descriptive theory ends up by accentuating the right–left dichotomy and pushing it to an extreme. All distinction becomes contrast, all relation exclusion. The brain has been 'ontologized'; not only are the contents of each hemisphere differentiated, but the single brain is replaced by two. By extending the domain in which this idea is prevalent to include people and situations, it becomes a method of classification. Through this device individuals are organized into categories. Thus left-brained people are distinguished from right-brained people. Each category has certain characteristics, and it is possible to discern certain well-known types.

At the third stage, moving beyond description and classification, the representation is complete. It explains several modes of behaviour and certain social situations. For example, the rich are seen as gifted with one sort of brain and the poor with another; hence they achieve unequal results in their respective undertakings. This proposition, as well as others, obviously goes far beyond the scientific data.

Thus, the use of a descriptive theory in folk neuroscience has changed its nature. It has been turned into a classificatory and explanatory representation of people and their behaviour. It illustrates the propensity with which one can pass from 'what' to 'how' to 'why' in quick succession – and with deep-rooted consequences.

Informative and representative thought

The internal and external processes of transforming the scientific into common sense are what we believe one sees happening in the amateur scientist. It is a question of the transformation of informative thought into representative thought. Each of these alternatives has its own rationality and can be contrasted with regard to the other's dominant, but not exclusive, characteristics. For example, informative thought is character- ized by the use of concepts and signs; a focus on empirical validity, and is dominated by the 'how'. Representative thought uses images and symbols, is based on consensual validity and is dominated by the 'why'.

All representations of scientific theory constitute profound alterations, not only of the content, but also of the cognitive structure. And once provided with a representation of what things can or must be, individuals look for them. Or rather, they create them in order to make valid their predictions or explanations (e.g. Snyder and Swann, 1978). We propose, in general, that social information is created to fit into a pre-existing common-sense framework (although, of course, one must always allow for the development and innovation of social thought). Informative cognitions are transformed into representative cognitions, and descriptive contents into explanatory contents. Our task is to study the way a concept becomes an image, an abstract being a reality, and an objective theory a conven- tional representation – and all this in a remarkably short time. This change is due to the fact that people do not try to play the game of science. They want to change it in order to take it up in their favourite game, the game of common sense.

ON REPRESENTATIONS THAT ARE SOCIAL

To arrive at a definition of social representations does not require much more discussion. After all that we have just said, they would appear to be cognitive matrices co-ordinating ideas, words, images and perceptions that are all interlinked. They are common-sense 'theories' about key aspects of society.

The inner core of our representations is difficult to discover. For example, when dealing with the question of racialism it is possible to note the presence of certain stereotypes – a Jew's love of money; the violent disposition of blacks; the North African's promiscuity. One might also remark on the 'statements' referring to the intellectual superiority or inferiority of these groups, supported by statistics or by citation of scien- tific authorities (Eysenck, Jensen and others). Often, people who sub- scribe to such views will act in a certain way: they avoid areas where members of these groups live; they won't allow their children to attend mixed schools; and so on. Such attitudes and actions appear to be superficial, and it is often thought that, by becoming aware of prejudice, by changing language, it is possible to tear up such racism by its roots. But if, in talking with people, one searches out the bases of their thoughts and actions, one often discovers a representation of human nature, including ideas on the hereditary factor in national character or the blood relationship between individuals. One may also find a clear view of what is a 'normal' individual, and an explanation of the differences between individuals or groups. It is surprising to note how many biological, psychological and even religious elements go to complete the representation. These ideas constitute the deep-seated inner core that is rarely touched upon.

This example was chosen to reveal an indisputable fact: that is to say, beyond stereotypes and attitudes, there is an implicit body of images and ideas that gives birth to the explicit manifestations of racialism. In short, racialism corresponds to a particular representation which replies to questions like 'What is man?' 'What is the origin of man?' 'Why are people different, and never identical?' 'Why do some succeed and others not?' Racialists use these questions not only in forming a judgement with respect to minority groups, but also with regard to themselves, their children, and in the choice of a spouse. Thus we consider the words people use, the attitudes they take, the kind of information they look for, the behaviour they enact, the relationships they engage in or the meaning they give to an object or person, all as symptoms of a social representation.

Hence social representations are related to a wide class of cognitions that are shared by broad categories of people. The sharing in itself is important (see Jaspars, in press), inasmuch as it leads to distinctions from other categories and establishes a group identity (Tajfel, 1978). It is probable that some advanced group would formulate these representations more consistently, and express them more concisely, than would the wider public. For this reason it would not be fair to say, as is sometimes said, that they are always an oversimplification, an impenetrable prison to the unique views of individuals. On the contrary, all those who have studied such representations are fascinated by their flexibility and their multifarious interpretations of a relatively limited situation. This is why they must not be confused with stereotypes, which are both simple and rigid, or with narrowly-defined social perceptions or cognitions.

Having stated the case so far, we can now go on to define the social nature of such representations. The cognitive act can be described by a binary concept: subject pole and object pole. The subject pole is the idea that will be represented. The object pole is the knowledge itself, the material upon which the mind will set to work. Inside the individual is consciousness, thoughts and values stored for reflective analysis. Outside there is the physical or social reality, the data of sense perception ready for inspection or explanation.

But the individual also has relations with others. The knower locates a source that provides him or her with a certain number of cognitive elements; these can be combined with elements within the knower. On the other hand, the knower turns to reality to integrate what is known with what is seen. Thus, when people uphold some view about a person or group, and explain their view, we can be sure that they are not simply giving an interpretation of the observed facts. They are at the same time comparing this interpretation with some others made by a real or imaginary partner (cf. Mead, 1934). All representations are then triangular – subject, object and third person. But the third person may vary, and the 'audience' for a representation may change, in which case different forms of language will be used to verbalize the ideas.

When a representation is born from and for the good of a relationship, one can say that it is 'conventional' in contrast to 'valid' knowledge. This conventional knowledge is seen in the prevalence of representations in collective thought (Lévi-Strauss, 1962), and their power lies in the fusing of disparate cognitions from the most abstract to the most concrete. Having introduced the triangular notion, the relation with others, we can now consider briefly some of the social functions of representations. These have been dealt with elsewhere (Moscovici, 1976, 1983) and are merely highlighted here, as a preamble to the more pressing issue (in this volume) of an explanatory function.

First, representations permit communication between individuals or groups. Whatever the motivation, people communicate first in order to come to an agreement about a view of reality and then to maintain an identity with their partners or group members. During conversation, scientific data are interpreted, combined with other knowledge, added to by imagery and translated into everyday language. The representations resulting from this process then function to allow members of a group to confront each other with their perceptions and judgements, and perceive similarities. Thus, representations are food for thought and food for talk.

A second function is to guide social action. Empirical work confirms that, when people share a representation, they interpret their own conduct and that of others in the light of this knowledge. A series of studies has shown the importance of where individuals locate the cause of mental health problems. Farina et al. (1978) showed that individuals holding a 'disease' representation saw mental health problems as more like an illness than did individuals with a 'behaviour/social learning' orientation. The former also believed more firmly that one could do little oneself about such problems, a representation the effects of which carried over into therapy sessions. These results were followed up in a more realistic study by Fisher and Farina (1979), which showed that individuals sharing a 'social learning' representation of mental illness are more inclined to turn to a therapist to alleviate their difficulties than are individuals whose representation is 'biosocial'.

A third function involves the socialization of individuals. Every member of a group, by birth or otherwise, has the group's representation impressed on him or her. In this way representations infiltrate to the core of the individual's personality. They restrain one's attitudes and perceptions, and one's attachments or repulsions with regard to objects. Anthropology has dealt most ably with this kind of phenomenon, studying how a representation materializes in the mind of the individual, as it is passed from generation to generation by a tacit apprenticeship.

Certainly, social representations – as the raw material of common sense – help us to comprehend and predict. They are, in this way, analogous to a science, although comprehension and prediction are not their predominant functions. They also function in the practical social order, and social representations of Marxism, psychoanalysis, racialism, or health all convey the distance between science and a common-sense representation. Unfortunately, however, the richness of representations is not noticeable in the laboratory. Our experimental procedures seem often to force certain kinds of thinking or responding, and subjects tend to leave their culture at the door.

SOCIAL REPRESENTATIONS AND COMMON-SENSE EXPLANATIONS

We have now arrived at the point where we can explore how social representations shape most common-sense explanations. They do this, in part, by defining the degree of reality of things or behaviour. It is all very logical: people define what is real before asking themselves why something happens the way it happens.

In fact, one of the roles of social representations is to reduce ambiguity and to make information unequivocal, just as attributions were accorded this same role by Heider (1958). Representations grade and classify information, and one such major classification appears to be between 'matters of fact' and 'matters of opinion'. The former possess an external referent, which the latter do not. This idea can be put into a more concrete form by using a familiar analogy. Imagine someone who complains of pain and suffering without any apparent physical reason. What do we do when presented with this person? If we have an organic representation of illness, we assert that we are dealing with a hypochondriac and an imaginary illness. We decide not to pay too much attention to this person, maintaining that only 'physiological' illnesses express real ill health and merit appropriate treatment (see Herzlich, 1973). On the other hand, if we have a psychological representation of illness, we will judge the pain and suffering to be real. We will ask the sick person for further information and attempt to lessen his or her anguish.

The same processes of selection and classification are illustrated in recent work on the socialization of obesity-prone behaviour (Woody and Costanzo, 1981). Although there is very little empirical justification for a theory-based expectation of sex-differences in factors relating to obesity, parents appear to view the concomitants (causes?) of the condition very differently in boys and girls. The obesity of boys is perceived to be associated with, for example, less exercise, less emotional excitability and less peer involvement. But the pattern for girls is quite different – greater influence of moods on eating, more parental restraint on eating, and emotionality and displeasure with the self.

Other examples could be given, but these are clear. Here, as in analogous cases, information is not ignored, but filtered. We are led, by our representations, to classify facts differently, and those that do not correspond to the representations are seen as less real than those that do. More accurately, some of them are supposed to come from the internal world and others from the external world. The former are 'matters of opinion', the latter, 'matters of fact'. When we classify in this way, the former information remains arbitrary and we enjoy a certain amount of freedom in this respect. The latter information forces itself upon us with all the weight of facticity. We are in the position of a scientist who, according to the paradigm in force, can easily dismiss unwelcome observations as accidents or spurious phenomena. In contrast, this scientist must take into great consideration all the regularities and all the phenomena that this paradigm foresees, in order to decide whether it modifies the hypothesis or not. Classifying information in this way prepares for future explanations. Implicitly, these categories indicate where to find the effects and where to choose the causes; what must be explained and what explains.

These remarks can now be applied to a well-known problem. Research on causal attribution has endeavoured to ascertain under what circumstances people attribute the cause of a certain outcome in terms of the person involved, or in terms of the situation. To many people's surprise, despite the information provided, the results show that most people attribute the outcome to the person and not, as they should, to the situation (Nisbett and Ross, 1980; but see Quattrone, 1982). The conclusion drawn from this is that there exists a 'fundamental attribution error' in the processing of this information (Ross, 1977). Situational information is apparently ignored or poorly judged.

Starting from a social representations approach, one offers a rather different, but no less plausible, interpretation. Information that refers to the person is seen as more real because of a dominant cultural representation tainted by individualism (see Bond, chapter 8 below). Even Nisbett and Ross (1980) acknowledge that the dispositionalist theory is 'thoroughly woven into the fabric of our culture' (p. 31). Ichheiser (1943) saw this dispositionalist 'misinterpretation' as a collective phenonomenon (see Farr and Anderson, chapter 3 above), and a consequence of the nineteenth-century ideology of individualism – an ideology entrenched in such concepts as merit and blame, success and failure, responsibility and irresponsibility. In stark contrast to some current thinking, he did not see such misinterpretations as 'errors', but rather as 'an indispensable part of the working system of a given culture and society' (p. 148). Indeed, he maintained that culture and society could not function without such misinterpretations.

Many other 'biases' and misunderstandings in social or interpersonal relationships could be interpreted in similar fashion, as due to different representations leading people to classify in different ways and weight information accordingly. Thus, information does not have the same factual force for everyone.

EXPLANATIONS WITH AND WITHOUT A CAUSE

The above examples express clearly the difference between explanations in science and those in common-sense, or social, representations. Briefly stated, in science the question determines the reply and in common sense the reply determines the question. It is as if science were an art of asking why or how, and social representations were mainly an art of answering 'because'. People believe that they know in advance the way events are going to turn out, they know the outcome of the questions they meet: Jews are to blame because . . .; the poor are exploited because . . .; blacks are inferior because . . .

This ubiquity of answers leads us to believe that, by and large people have an answer for everything. Through this 'automatic explanation' everything becomes normal and predictable, every unexpected effect becomes the expected answer of a known and recognized cause. As the logician Stebbing wrote: 'The ordinary man is satisfied with the obvious because it always happens so' (1950, p. 235). Thus the explanations of a professional scientist are different in nature from those of the amateur scientist.

Looking more closely at attribution theory, it is legitimate to ask whether it has paid attention to such non-scientific explanations of lay people. The results consolidated in this area are impressive, but we contend that it has neutralized the context in which ordinary people deal with causes. What this neutralization consists of is easy to see from an analogy. Let us compare what happens in science. Here, in order to explain something, two elements are combined: a theory of the phenomena and a list of causes associated with them. No science or scientist could separate these two components, since the theory defines the nature of the phenomena to be explained and envisages the possible relations between causes and effects.

Now, an attribution approach separates the theory from the causes, so as to concern itself solely with the latter. In all the major theories (Heider, 1958; Jones and Davis, 1965; Kelley, 1967; Weiner, 1979) it inquires into whether the cause of a certain behaviour is internal (personal) or external (situational). In doing this, it overlooks the obvious fact that, for example, even if two people observe the same person, they can none the less describe that same individual differently – according to whether they have a 'psychic', 'organic', 'Christian', 'Buddhist' or whatever representation of the human being and behaviour. It is, then, a short step to consider that people giving such different descriptions will give equally different explanations. By dealing only with causes, this approach neutralizes the observer's background. It deals with the surface of the matter and forgets the heart, composed of common-sense theories. It is as if attribution theorists believed there to be but one common-sense psychology, whereas there are in fact several. By pulling all these remarks together, we draw the conclusion that attribution theory is often a theory of *causes without explanations*. It studies *how* explanations are made, but not *why*.

We should specify that the social representations approach, like science, associates a 'theory' (the description and classification of facts) with a set of causes and effects. But, in contrast to science, it is dominated by automatic explanations, which we mentioned above. In other words, causes are singled out and put forward before the available material has been sifted, and before the effects have been seriously examined. This means that in a great many explanations of normal events – why a child cries, why a foreign worker is poor, why someone is unemployed, etc. – people do not make inferences of the type dealt with in attribution theory. Without much exploring or thinking, they apply their representations of what is the cause and leave it at that (cf. Lalljee and Abelson, chapter 4 above on explanations of script-congruent behaviour). It even seems that each individual or group often chooses from among causes the one that plays the part of a 'supra-social' cause. Events are attributed to 'imperialism', 'complexes, 'race' and so on, 'causes' that are so vast and vague that they are almost supernatural. The ordinary person seems at such pains to establish that things do not happen by chance, that an explanation is given although a real cause is lacking. The great achievement of science was to eschew such monolithic causes, but they continue to have an irresistible hold on our common-sense thinking.

The lay person's motivation to avoid chance happenings (see Bains, chapter 7 below) is one facet of what we consider to be the 'bicausal' nature of social representations. It is intended to eliminate the contingent, searching out an explanation for accidental and extraordinary events (e.g., why a tile fell on someone's head). We may accept that such events are extraordinary, but none the less seek to avoid seeing them as mere coincidences. To be fair to lay people, or amateur scientists, we should note that explanations without a cause are sometimes found in professional science too. These are empty explanations, by which we attribute an effect to causes that we do not know. In medicine, for example, the terms 'functional' or 'psychosomatic' illness are used to 'explain' symptoms the origins of which are unknown.

The second facet of common-sense explanations is nearer to the models of attribution theory. It is aimed at making us understand why things are as they are, and not otherwise. Rather than seeking explanations for unexpected, and often transitory, events here we are concerned with explanations for enduring aspects of life and society. For example, Jodelet (1980) reported on the representation, shared by members of a village community, of illness in terms of lack of food. Poverty was seen as the source of illness, and wealth was allied to health. When the same villagers gave lodgings to a group of the mentally ill, and observed their strange behaviour, they altered slightly the old representation for ordinary illness: 'It's the nerves you know; they have to be fed', or 'It's through lack of food and care.' Some villagers also conceived of some sort of excess, going beyond the physical force that food provides, leading to similar results: 'He was over-educated, it affected his brain. . . . It was books that did for him. . . . He was too clever. It got to his nerves.'

The need to consider representations as reservoirs of available explanations is also evident from Windisch's (1978) study of xenophobia. When asked to explain why there were more strikes abroad than, in Switzerland, respondents revealed a shared representation that was neither narrowly personal nor explicitly social. They saw the French as lazy and complaining, itself an outcome of upbringing: 'The Swiss are brought up more seriously. Once a Frenchman's got his bread, wine and Boursin [cheese], well . . . . But the Swiss want Switzerland to stay proper' (translated from Windisch, 1978, p. 101). Such explanations, linking past causes (upbringing) to present causes (lazy and complaining), and thence to present effects (strikes), reiterate Kelley's (1983) claim that we should pay more attention to 'perceived causal networks'. They also illustrate how rich, varied and unpredictable common-sense explanations can be, and how necessary it may be to look in depth at social representations.

To summarize, it seems possible to identify primary and secondary explanations in common sense. The one, more primal, eliminates chance; the other, more cerebral, associates an effect with a cause. Each one translates a vernacular belief – the former, that 'there is no smoke without a fire'; the latter, that 'the invisible lurks behind the visible'.

SOCIAL FUNCTIONS OF EXPLANATION

Attributions are often made to serve explicit psychological and social functions. This fact was emphasized by Fauconnet (1928), who considered the concept of responsibility as part of a system of collective representations. He underlined that one of the major motives in responsibility attribution is to punish the cause of crime, and to prevent its return or increase. This led him to the notion of the person as a first cause, an idea that was eagerly taken up by Heider (1944).

Fauconnet also considered the *need* to find a culprit, especially when the crime is very serious – sacrilege or high treason, for example – and when it is vital for the functioning of society that someone be found and be seen to be punished. He illustrated this with the rather macabre practice, in *ancien régime* France, of meticulously carrying out penal procedures against corpses. The absurdity was obvious to all, but the concession functioned to placate religious or monarchist fanatics.[4]

Fauconnet's discussion of the functions of attribution (see his chapter 6) also included the phenomenon of scapegoating – from Nero, who blamed the Christians for the great fire of Rome, to Christians through the ages who have vented their wrath on Jews, witches and heretics (see Bains, chapter 7 below). This topic is treated at greater length by Poliakov (1980). He integrates scapegoat-type explanations with the fascination of human beings for an elementary and exhaustive causality, a 'first cause'. Evidence is presented for the operation of a pattern of thought – so-called '*causalité diabolique*' (diabolic causality) – which has been a recurrent social representation at several periods of history. The 'demons' blamed for catastrophes are, in fact, the protagonists of a 'world conspiracy'. This unfortunate lot has fallen, at times, to witches, Jews, Jesuits, freemasons and Marxists. In turn, the ills of society were ascribed to their machinations. One of the consequences of this pattern of attribution was the

proposed solution – extermination of the relevant group. Thus the attribution functioned, indirectly, to 'cleanse' society. This function was identified by Durkheim, writing at the time of the Dreyfus affair:

> When society undergoes suffering, it feels the need to find someone whom it
> can hold responsible for its sickness, on whom it can avenge its misfor-
> tunes. . . . What confirms me in this interpretation is the way in which the
> result of Dreyfus' trial was greeted in 1894. There was a surge of joy on the
> boulevards. . . . At last [people] knew whom to blame for the economic
> troubles and moral stress in which they lived. The trouble came from the
> Jews. [quoted in Lukes, 1975, p. 345]

These examples illustrate how certain explanations may function to
identify *any* cause, and to justify the scapegoating or even eradication of
that cause. But there are often social rules about what kind of explanation
is acceptable, and these function to regulate the social order. A classic
example is given by Evans-Pritchard (1937), in relating the ubiquitous
part of witchcraft in Zande life. Witchcraft is a normal aspect of this life, a
common idiom for expressing and explaining a whole variety of misfortunes, from blight affecting the groundnut crop to an unsuccessful hunt
for game. However, the Azande also have a kind of clause in the social
fabric that proscribes the explanation of certain events – lying, adultery,
stealing or disloyalty – by witchcraft. If a man murders another tribesman,
then he is put to death. Vengeance can be exacted on the man, and it is not
necessary to ascribe the outcome to witchcraft. Similarly, the notion of
witchcraft is simply not permissible in the context of offences against
authority, or when a taboo has been broken. If a child becomes sick and its
parents have had sexual relations before it was weaned, then the cause lies
in the breach of 'ritual prohibition'. When there is a history of incest,
witchcraft cannot be given as the cause of leprosy. Thus there are limits to
the use of a social representation in explaining events.

The examples given in this section illustrate some of the social functions
served by explanations. Such attributions may suggest solutions to societal
problems, while the rules concerning acceptable explanations may also
function to contain violence and control the social order. Such explanations are social in their origins and consequences, emanating from and
acting back upon society.

CONCLUSIONS

In this chapter we have begun to look at where explanations come from
and how they become part of social life. Our studies on common-sense
'psychology', 'mental health' and 'neuroscience' have led us to suggest

that, on the one hand, explanations are part of larger social representations and, on the other hand, it is the representations that give 'causes' their cognitive power. Moreover, many so-called common-sense explanations are derived and not 'first-hand'. They are the result of a transformation of scientific explanations that impose upon a society, or a particular group, at a given time. It is these explanations that determine, in part, the treatment and creation of information. From a psychological point of view, it may therefore be more important to know how social knowledge is transformed than to know how individuals process information.

Some readers may contend that our ideas about common sense, science as a hobby and social representations are too general. They may require more data and precision. And they would be perfectly right. But, in our opinion, there is now a need for a more general notion in this field, sufficiently open to cover a wider range of mental phenomena – especially ones that go beyond the individual or inter-individual level of reality. We have tried to paint several themes in broad brush strokes, rather then to focus on minutiae. But the consequent imprecision is unavoidable in discovering new knowledge (see Festinger, 1980). We believe that a richer analysis of common sense and social knowledge, going beyond the present limits of the attribution approach, is a viable extension of attribution theory. And we contend that the social representations approach provides such a valuable orientation. Without a deeper analysis of how knowledge is transformed and represented in society, where it comes from and what people 'make' of it, we shall be unable to propose an adequate theory of social explanations. Confronting the layman, we shall be left, like Lord Byron, pleading, 'I wish he would explain his explanation.'

NOTES
1 While some readers might accuse us of slipping from social psychology to sociology, it is worth noting that Durkheim (1898), who first used the term *représentation collective*, advocated a branch of sociology concerned with such representations and which he called 'social psychology' (Lukes, 1975, p. 8). In addition, Durkheim's notion is dealt with at some length in Allport's (1968) standard chapter on the historical background of modern social psychology.
2 Interestingly, Wells (1981) illustrates this point (in a footnote on p. 320) by pointing to psychodynamic interpretation as an influence on lay analyses of causal forces in the twentieth century. This, as we have noted, is exactly where the social representations approach began (Moscovici, 1961).
3 For a fictional personification of this type, see Salim the merchant in V.S. Naipaul's novel, *A Bend in the River*. This character eagerly devours 'a magazine of popular science', eking out nuggets of specialized information and dreaming of a life that might have been, in the pursuit of such knowledge.
4 Hibbert (1982) gives another example of what might be termed 'over-sanctioning'. At the height of the French Revolution there were cases of guilloting the corpses of some unfortunates who had sought to escape the mob by taking their own lives.

7 Explanations and the Need for Control

Gurnek Bains

> It is our needs that interpret the world.
>
> Nietszche

INTRODUCTION

The idea that motives can influence and distort the way we perceive events in the world is not new. It is, however, a view that attribution theory has neglected. To be sure, there has been a robust interest in errors and biases, but in the main these have tended to be interpreted in cognitive, information-processing terms. In part, this neglect of motivational influences reflects a general tendency evident in social psychology, particularly in the 1960s and 1970s. But it also arises because the attribution process has tended to be seen as an end in itself and rarely as a tool used by people for certain ends. For if it is accepted that people often have a reason other than intellectual curiosity for wanting to explain events, and that, because of these reasons, they are likely to find certain answers more satisfying than others, the objectivity and purity of the attribution process must inevitably be eroded. If 'man is a scientist', he may well be one whose desire to hold a particular view leads to a high selectivity in data collection and interpretation and the relegation of uncomfortable results to the bottom drawers of file cupboards. If such practices are not rare in science, our theories should not set naive and unrealistic standards for others.

One of the most important functions of attributional inquiry is the greater control of the environment that an understanding of causal relationships enables (Heider, 1958, 1976; Kelley, 1971; Pittman and Pittman, 1980). However, while knowledge itself is power, it is important to recognize that certain forms of knowledge imply greater power than others. That is to say that our perceptions of the controllability of events in the world is crucially dependent on the particular nature of the causal antecedents that are held to be important, and especially whether such antecedents are controllable or not. This idea has found empirical expression in Rotter's (1966) internal–external locus of control measure, which attempts to discriminate between people who have a passive world view, and who regard important events as being essentially independent of their actions, and those who believe that, in the main, such events are within their locus of control. Weiner (1974) has also recognized that explanations may differ in terms of their implications for control over the world. However, unlike Rotter, he does not conceive of such differences as being completely synonymous with an internal or external locus of causation, and he has suggested that the controllability of a causal antecedent is, theoretically at least, independent of its locus and even of its stability.

Both Rotter's and Weiner's approach has been to examine the implications that a certain world view or a particular explanation may have for control. However, it takes little imagination to suggest that there may well also be a reversal of causation, and that, given the well-documented desire for people to exert control and mastery over their environment (Adler, 1949; J. W. Brehm, 1966; De Charms, 1968; White, 1959), control motivation may actually influence and distort the way people explain events. Kelley (1971) was among the first to suggest this possibility when he argued that, in cases of ambiguity and doubt, 'controllable factors will have a high salience as candidates for causal explanations.' Since then this idea has been reiterated by several authors, finding its most complete expression in Wortman's (1976) paper on 'Causal Attributions and Personal Control'.

It is intended below to discuss the various ways in which need for control can influence explanations for events at the personal, interpersonal and societal/intergroup levels. The section on explanations at the personal level will review briefly and appraise the ideas put forward in Wortman's (1976) paper. It will be argued, however, that the influence of control on explanations may be much wider than that envisaged in her paper; that, apart from 'victim derogation', there may exist an influence on interpersonal perception in general; and that, furthermore, control motivation may be used to understand a variety of beliefs at the societal/intergroup level. Thus, control may be used as an organizing principle for undetstanding explanations in a variety of contexts. In the final section it is contended that an individual differences approach may be used to test some of the proposed influences that control motivation may have on explanations, and the results of such a test are described. It is also argued that individual differences in the motivation to cast the world in a controllable light may provide a parsimonious explanation for certain constellations of traits and beliefs that may have been found in social psychology.

EXPLANATIONS AT THE PERSONAL LEVEL

Evidence for the existence of a 'control bias' at the personal level may be found in people's implicit beliefs about the effects of their own behaviour on the environment. Much of this evidence has been reviewed by Wortman (1976) and consequently will not receive a great deal of attention here: the reader is referred to that paper for a much fuller account of this evidence. Briefly, however there seems to be a convergence of research which suggests that people frequently underestimate the role of chance on outcomes that seem fairly obviously to be randomly determined (Henslin, 1967; Langer, 1975; Wortman, 1975). Henslin found, for instance, that 'crap shooters' believe that confidence is a crucial factor in successful throwing, and that they frequently explain lack of success in terms of a failure to exercise the necessary control over the dice. Similarly distorted beliefs concerning random events are illustrated in a series of experiments on people's behaviour in chance games conducted by Wortman and Langer. Basically, these authors have found that subjects' sense of control on random tasks can be increased by having them know beforehand which outcomes they are trying to produce, by increasing their familiarity with the task, by making them physically responsible for producing the outcome, and by increasing their degree of involvement in the task. The fact that all these variables can increase notions of control, they argue, suggests that people do not usually approach random tasks as if they are purely chance phenomena.

Wortman (1976) also discusses a range of findings on people's explanations for unfortunate life events in terms of control. A number of studies suggest that individuals frequently blame themselves for accidents and illnesses to which they fall victim (see also King, chapter 10 below). Abrams and Finesinger (1953) have found, for instance, that cancer patients often attribute their disease to some past misdeed. Chodoff et al., studying a related phenomenon – parents' reactions to their children contracting leukaemia – made a similar finding;

> Sometimes it seemed as if a parent was trying to prove that she had done or failed to do something which might have been responsible for her child falling sick. The process, even if it involved the assumption of blame by the parent, brought with it a feeling of relief and the allaying of anxiety, as in the case of one mother who decided that her daughter had 'caught' leukaemia from the tumours of a pet which she herself should have removed from the household. This mother was made demonstrably uneasy by the efforts of one of her doctors to dissuade her from this explanation. [Chodoff et al., 1964, p. 246]

Here the last observation – that the mother became upset at the physician's attempts to dissuade her – is particularly interesting because it suggests that the explanation served some psychological function and did not merely represent an erroneous and ill-informed lay theory of leukaemia. Wortman argues that tendencies towards self-blame are also to be found among victims of rape, natural disasters and those who are made redundant. She suggests that one way of explaining such counter-intuitive findings may lie in the fact that, by blaming themselves for these unfortunate events, the victims reject the notion that they could occur by chance and, more importantly, preserve the view that in the future such calamities can be avoided by taking appropriate actions. The fact that such self-blame attributions tend to be made to internal and unstable causes supports this interpretation.

Before accepting a purely motivational interpretation, it is perhaps worth considering alternative explanations for the 'self-blame' and 'beliefs concerning random events' findings that Wortman discusses. On a general level, all these studies can be construed as suggesting that, either implicitly or explicitly, people do not seem to use chance as an attributional category. Wortman considers this to arise from the fact that people are motivated towards perceiving random events as being under their control. However, it is possible that people's failure to ascribe events to chance may arise from certain cognitive difficulties in actually perceiving randomness in the world. Langer (1975) has suggested that in everyday life the distinction between random and controllable events is difficult to make because most outcomes involve an element of both. However, this does not explain why errors, when they occur, almost always involve an exaggeration of control over random events and not an exaggeration of randomness over controllable outcomes. One possible explanation for the unidirectionality of this confusion may be that the perception of randomness involves a more complex cognitive judgement than the perception of control. Chance, as implied by Einstein in his famous phrase, 'God does not play dice with the Universe', is not really a category with which we can causally explain anything. As long as we accept a deterministic view of the world, an attribution to chance amounts merely to an admission that the finer determinants of an outcome were beyond our detailed understanding and were, therefore, unpredictable. Thus, if a die is rolled and a particular number appears and we ask the question, why that number as opposed to any other?, explanations at a variety of levels are possible. At one level it is quite accurate to say that the person who rolled the die caused the outcome since had he or she rolled it differently other outcomes would have resulted. Nevertheless, the attribution of chance in this case is valid because the person could not possibly have had any idea of which outcomes would result from particular actions. However, in everyday life people may not fully discount for this lack of foreknowledge, and in particular they may find the benefits of hindsight too alluring to make such compensations. In a series of experiments Fischhoff (1975) has found that people tend to believe that an outcome was more predictable and inevitable when they have the benefit of hindsight and clearly, therefore, knowledge of outcomes must make it relatively difficult to ascribe events to chance.

Many of the findings discussed by Wortman and Langer concerning the beliefs that people have about random events can be explained by this sort of process. The finding, for instance, that greater control is felt when the subject is physically responsible for the outcome can be explained since such responsibility is a necessary condition for the above process to produce a 'non-chance' attribution. Similarly, variables such as knowledge beforehand of what outcomes one is trying to produce, as well as a high degree of involvement and familiarity with the task, can be expected to make it especially difficult for subjects to discount for their lack of foreknowledge. Many of the self-blame phenomena can also be explained in this cognitive, information-processing manner. To give an example, if a person is attacked after taking a particular route home, then self-blame may arise simply because, viewed with the benefit of hindsight, the decision to take that particular route may seem foolish and risky, however objectively reasonable it may have been at the time. Again, this process involves a failure to use chance as an attributional category because of the difficulty in discounting for lack of foreknowledge that the benefit of hindsight invariably gives rise to. However, the argument that people may find it cognitively difficult to ascribe events to chance should not be taken too far. Hewstone et al. (1982) have shown, for instance, that people do use chance as an attributional category in situations where group self-esteem is involved. Thus it may well be that the biases discussed by Wortman have some sort of motivational base and do not arise purely because of an inability that people have in making attributions to chance. Nevertheless, the case for a motivational basis should not be regarded as conclusively proven.

EXPLANATIONS AT THE INTERPERSONAL LEVEL

This section is concerned with the ways in which a need for control may influence the explanations and judgements that people make about the behaviour of others. One of the areas in which the influence of control motivation on attributions has been suggested most often is in the explanations that people give for accidents and misfortunes to which others fall victim. Walster's (1966) theory proposes that people frequently blame victims for their fate because they do not want to accept that such things can happen to them by chance and out of the blue. There seems to be some anecdotal evidence on this issue. Ryan (1971), for instance, found that many victims felt that others had blamed them inordinately for their fate. Symonds (1974), after talking to several hundred victims of rape, muggings, kidnappings and assaults, came to the same conclusion.

The experimental evidence for these defensive attributions is however much less clear. Walster (1966) in her early work reports a study consistent with the theory in which the perpetrator/victim of an accident was blamed more if the consequences of the accident were severe than if they were mild. Subsequent work has, however, failed to find such a trend with any consistency, and Burger (1981) concludes, after a meta-analytic study of 22 experiments concerned with this issue, that there is only a weak trend in the expected direction. The situation has been somewhat complicated by Shaver's (1970) refinement, in which he argues that, if the subject identifies too closely with the perpetrator/victim, he or she may attribute less blame in anticipation of being personally involved in a similar incident in the future. Thus he argues that in some cases severity of outcome may be inversely related to the ascription of blame. This addition, while possibly being correct, has the effect of making defensive attribution theory difficult to test through manipulations of severity since it is hard to determine objectively just how much a person identifies with the perpetrator/victim. One study that attempted to test Shaver's theory by manipulating severity and similarity was conducted by Fincham and Hewstone (1982), and this found little evidence to support Shaver's position. In all, it would be fair to say that the results in this area are equivocal. As Fincham and Jaspars (1980) have pointed out, this may be due to the fact that studies vary in the definition of responsibility, the relevance of the stories for subjects, as well as the degree of objective similarity between subject and perpetrator/victim. An added complication seems to be that studies vary in whether the perpetrator of an accident is the only victim or if others are also involved. In the latter cases, if severity is positively related to blame, it may reflect a retributive motive rather than anything to do with feelings of threatened control on the part of the subject.

In short, the evidence on severity and responsibility does not provide conclusive support for the influence of control motivation on attributions. The work reported earlier, which found that victims feel in general that they are over-blamed for their fate, provides better support, but even here questions abound concerning the interpretation of this phenomenon. As has been noted by several authors, such findings can be easily explained in terms of Lerner's 'just world' theory (Lerner, 1970), which suggests that we have to derogate victims or blame them for their fate in order to preserve a view of the world as just. It should be emphasized that a controllable world and a just world are not necessarily the same thing. Of course, derogation of victims can also be explained by reference to the same cognitive process that was offered for the self-blame findings in the previous section.

The effect of control motivation on interpersonal perception has tended to be seen almost exclusively in terms of the phenomenon of victim derogation. However, it is possible that there is an influence on the way we explain other people's everyday behaviour even when misfortunes or accidents are not involved. In an experiment directly related to this issue, D. T. Miller et al. (1978) made subjects listen to two people playing a 'prisoner's dilemma' type of strategic game. After viewing, some of the subjects were led to believe that they would have to play a similar game with one of the participants, and it was found that this group tended to make more dispositional attributions for that player's behaviour as well as to believe that they knew the player's personality better. Miller explains this finding by suggesting that confidence in the dispositional qualities of the player made subjects feel more confident about their own anticipated game. This interpretation seems to be supported by the results of a follow-up experiment in which the authors devised a need for control scale and found that the effect described above was more pronounced among those who scored highly on that scale. This last finding also seems to suggest that the results cannot be completely explained simply by reference to Jones and Davis' (1965) theory that people make more dispositional inferences when the target person's behaviour is 'hedonically relevant'. Smith and Brehm (1981) have essentially replicated the Miller et al. study and, furthermore, found that type A coronary-prone individuals are more likely to infer dispositions when put in such a situation. Again, this supports the interpretation of the phenomena in terms of control (D. T. Miller et al., 1978), in that type A's are generally thought to have a high need for controlling their environment. Berscheid et al. (1976) have also reported data that show the increased tendency for people to infer dispositional traits when anticipating interaction. Finally, Swann et al. (1981) have added further weight to the control interpretation of all the above studies by finding that prior experience of control deprivation enhances people's tendency to search for diagnostic personality information in subsequent interaction with others.

The generalizability of all the above findings to ordinary social life may be quite high, since many social interactions resemble a game of strategy in which success is crucially dependent upon accurate knowledge of one's partners. Against this background it would not be surprising if people exaggerated the extent to which they could infer a person's true character on the basis of predictor information purely in order to give them greater confidence and certainty in social interaction. Certainly, the literature seems to suggest that people have exaggerated notions concerning the stability of behaviour across situations (Mischel, 1968) and that they tend towards 'non-conservative' prediction of one variable from knowledge of another (see, for instance, Ross, 1977; Tversky and Kahneman, 1974). Tversky and Kahneman have shown that people over-rely on representativeness (predictor) information at the cost of background statistical information. It is possible that, while such tendencies inevitably result in a fall in accuracy, they are psychologically satisfying because, potentially at least, greater social certainty is likely to result from an exaggeration of the diagnosticity of representativeness information.

However, it should be emphasized that strong dispositional inferences about a person are likely to increase one's sense of control only if it is important to *predict* that person's behaviour in the future. If, however, one's objective is to *change* the behaviour, then *situational* attributions may be more appropriate. To test this an experiment was carried out by Bains (1982a) in which white female subjects were shown a video of two white people having a discussion on 'West Indians in Britain' in which both participants expressed some racist views. There were three conditions. One group was told after viewing that they would be asked later to predict the woman's attitudes on a number of political issues. Another group was told that they would have to meet the woman and attempt to change her attitudes in a less racist direction, and the third group did not anticipate having to do anything. Analysis of the results broadly confirms the predictions, in that subjects who anticipated having to change the woman's views believed that her attitudes were less strongly held, compared with the beliefs of subjects in the other two groups. On the other hand, the 'prediction' group made much stronger dispositional judgements than either the 'attitude change' or 'control' groups. The functional nature of these shifts in attributions is obvious, and the results suggest that control motivation may not always lead to strong dispositional-type inferences.

Although the above experiment is highly artificial, it is possible to suggest that there may be many instances in everyday life when needing to change a person's behaviour may reduce the likelihood of strong dispositional attributions. A study that seems to support this type of reasoning has found that social workers make situational attributions for alcoholism, whereas doctors make dispositional and particularly biological attributions (Robinson, 1978). One interpretation of this finding is that each profession seems to favour attributions to the level at which they themselves can be most successful in effecting a change.

In all, there seems to be quite good evidence that control motiviation may influence interpersonal attributions. Future research should move away from the, at present, rather one-sided concern with the phenomenon of victim derogation and look to the influence on interpersonal perception in general. In doing this, however, the distinction between needing to predict or needing to change the target person's behaviour should be kept in mind.

EXPLANATIONS AT THE SOCIAL LEVEL

This section is concerned with the way in which control motivation may influence explanations for societal events as well as the way in which certain intergroup phenomena may be understood by reference to control. The concern will be with three social irrationalities: stereotyping, superstition and scapegoating. The first of these will not be discussed in any detail since it has been amply dealt with elsewhere. Briefly, however, stereotyping may be broadly defined as the ascription of qualities to groups without adequate recognition of individual differences within groups and with an exaggeration of differences between groups. The most convincing psychological accounts of stereotyping specify that it arises inevitably from our attempt to categorize and simplify the world, which in turn is determined to a large extent by a need for prediction and control (Allport, 1954; D. Hamilton, 1979; Tajfel, 1969). Thus, one of the effects, and indeed purposes, of stereotyping is the greater sense of predictability and control that occurs in believing that, simply by looking at someone or by knowing his or her group membership, it is possible accurately to infer a wide number of underlying traits and to predict his or her behaviour in a variety of situations. In this sense stereotyping may be seen as a specific manifestation at the intergroup level of the 'quick inference' type strategy that Miller's subjects were reported to have used when their control needs were elevated. Thus, a strong belief in stereotypes may provide an illusory confidence in one's ability to know how to act with people, how to get what one wants from them and, perhaps most of all, since many stereotypes emphasize the negative and threatening aspects of various groups, how to avoid being harmed by them. Adorno et al. (1950) explicitly recognize the importance of the last of these when they suggest that the authoritarian's stereotypes are essentially 'devices for mastering this world by being completely able to pigeonhole its negative aspects' (p. 623).

Particularly powerful evidence for the influence of control motivation on explanations at the social/societal level is to be found in the popularity of susperstitious beliefs. It is possible to interpret the existence, both in Third World countries today and historically speaking in the West also, of such beliefs about causation as arising in large part from the need to avoid feelings of passivity in the face of natural and social calamities. Thus Thomas writes:

> The control offered by magical rites is necessarily illusory, for charms cannot make crops grow or wounds heal. But though magic itself is vain, it has valuable side-effects. It lessens anxiety and relieves pent-up frustration and makes the practitioner feel that he is doing something positive toward the solution of his problems. By its agency he is converted from a helpless bystander into an active agent. [Thomas, 1971, p. 647]

Witchcraft as a theory of causality lends itself particularly well to this interpretation. Witches were blamed in medieval Europe for a variety of events ranging from the calamitous to the mundane. Central to the whole notion of witchcraft was the belief that finding the witch responsible would alleviate the problem. Psychological explanations for the popularity of such theories and other superstitions typically emphasize their explanatory function. Thus, Tajfel (1981) argues that the attraction of witchcraft-type theories was due mainly to the fact that they explained the inexplicable. However, what seems to have been ignored in these interpretations is that almost all magical and superstitious beliefs attribute negative events to controllable causes. They almost all suggest easy actions in order, first, to prevent an unwanted situation from occuring; if it has already taken place, they provide remedies that may be used to restore the world to its original state. Belief in these causal theories brings relief in that a variety of threatening events are at least potentially rendered controllable. Thomas seems to recognize this distinction when he suggests that the reason for the especially high popularity of witchcraft-type theories was due to the fact that 'they held out the possibility of redress. They did not merely offer the intellectual satisfaction of identifying the cause of the mishap' (1971, p. 545).

Theories that attempt to explain the decline of superstitious beliefs are consistent with the view that one of their main functions was the enhancement of control. Thus Wilson and Wilson (1945) comment that 'magic is dominant when control of the environment is weakest' (p. 95) and suggest that societies' increasing ability to control the environment is responsible for the decline of such beliefs. Thomas is more guarded about the exact correspondence between lack of environmental control and superstitious beliefs. He argues that in many cases the decline of superstitious theories about a particular problem preceded its conquest by technological and scientific means. Nevertheless, his suggestion that an important reason for this was often the sense of general confidence in the ability of the human spirit to overcome all hurdles, prompted by the rise of Protestantism and by localized scientific advances of more symbolic than practical significance, is consistent with the general notion of control. Here decline is attributed to the rise of alternative 'ideologies' of feeling in control – a belief in the efficacy and power of humans.

Naturally, a control explanation for all forms of superstitious beliefs would be simplistic. Some superstitious theories, for instance, attribute events to factors that could be regarded as fundamentally uncontrollable, such as the stars or even God, and it is difficult to see how belief in these enhances one's sense of control. One possibility is that they enhance the predictability of the world. Thus, a belief that plagues or droughts are preceded by the appearance of a comet or by a certain configuration of planets, while having no implications for control, may be psychologically satisfying in that a certain element of predictability is introduced. However, it is clear that even the extension of control to include predictability does not provide a complete explanation for all forms of superstitious beliefs. Many may simply exist in order to complement a particular cosmological theory adhered to by a society, and thus have no psychological function as such. Nevertheless, the control function of many superstitious beliefs cannot be disputed, and the fact that such theories have been held by societies for thousands of years is testimony to the powerful way in which motives can influence the perception of causal relationships in the world.

It should not be assumed that today people are perfectly rational in the explanations that they give for social events. Under certain conditions, the twentieth century too can throw up explanations as bizarre and as out of touch with reality as anything ever seen in the Dark Ages. It only requires the right situation – one of attributional ambiguity, and which people also find very threatening. Such a situation possibly occurred with the calamitous economic collapse of Weimar Germany in 1929. The Republic was suddenly and without warning 'stricken by forces which its leaders did not understand and which they felt were beyond men's control. How was it possible that suddenly there could be so much suffering in the midst of so much plenty?' (Shirer, 1972, p. 172). The Nazi party, which leapt overnight from regional obscurity to national prominence as a result of this collapse, gave an explanation for it that was very different from that offered by other parties: 'Instead of rational analysis they offered a series of scapegoats: the November Traitors, Marxists, Freemasons, Jesuits even, but most of all the Jews who were depicted as the root cause of all Germany's problems' (Carr, 1969, p. 345).

Traditionally, psychological explanations for the attractiveness of Nazi ideology in general and of the Jewish theory in particular have emphasized either its scapegoating function or its role in providing a simple and economic explanation for a variety of sudden inexplicable events. Certainly it is true that groups tend to protect self-esteem by appropriate attributional strategies (Hewstone and Jaspars, 1982a; Tajfel, 1981; D. M. Taylor and Jaggi, 1974), and the Jewish theory might have been attractive because it provided for a shift of responsibility for the crisis to an outgroup. It is also true, as Billig (1978) points out that, reducing as it did the twin 'evils' of capitalism and communism to the activities of the same ethnic group, the theory provided a simple but potent explanation for almost all the world's problems and conflicts. However, while both these accounts go some way towards explaining the attractiveness of the Jewish theory, they perhaps neglect the fact that an important part of its appeal to many Germans, in 1929 and subsequently, lay in the fact that it gave them hope by attributing the crisis to causes that were easily controllable – the activities of small groups of people. As Herzstein (1980), in his review of Nazi ideology, writes 'Nazism was in many ways one of the most optimistic of ideologies . . . optimistic because the physical destruction of a people could salvage the world for an ideal Germany of goodness and virtue' (p. 26). This hope was not merely implicit in the attribution of the crisis to the Jews. Other facets of Nazi ideology also contributed. Thus, the 1914 war was lost not because Germany was too weak to fight a war on both fronts and had been overwhelmed by superior forces, but because the 'November Traitors' had stabbed the country in the back. Without such people Germany could in the future, ran the claim, win back the territories that had been lost. Central to Nazism was also the belief in the power of the human will and mythical notions concerning the abilities of the Aryan super-race – there was nothing that could not be conquered by resolution and determination. All this was coupled with a seemingly paradoxical belief in superstition and the occult.

All in all, one can go a long way towards understanding the structure of Nazi ideology, as well as its appeal, by seeing it as a 'package of control' offered to a people rendered passive and helpless by the turn of world events. This is not to say that other factors were not also implicated in its attractiveness. Nor is it to say that the psychological appeal of Nazi ideology was the only or even most important component of the success of National Socialism in Germany. But any social psychological analysis of the phenomena cannot disregard the role of control. On a more general level, it can be suggested that an important function of the attribution of calamitous social and economic events to a small minority group, whether it is witches, Jews, the 'November Traitors' or blacks, is to preserve a view of the world as controllable. All that becomes necessary in order to save the situation is to deal with the group responsible. In fact, this might be why the group selected for such attributions is often highly visible and very small in size – the smaller it is, the easier it is to deal with.

INDIVIDUAL DIFFERENCES

An interesting question is whether there are any consistent individual differences in the tendency to engage in the kinds of control biases discussed above. Clearly, one would expect people who have a high need for exerting control over the environment to show greater evidence of such biases than others. In addition, if self-blame for failure, derogation of victims, quick interpersonal inference, superstition, stereotyping and scapegoating are all hypothesized, at least in part, as serving the same underlying psychological function, then one might expect measures of each of these at the individual level to intercorrelate with each other.

These predictions were tested by Bains (1982b) by devising a need for control scale and measures of all the above biases with the exception of scapegoating, which it was felt would be difficult to measure because of social desirability factors. In general, the results were encouraging for the broad theory that has been outlined above. Not only did measures of most of the biases intercorrelate within persons, but they also showed, with the exception of superstition, significant correlations with the need for control measure. Factor analysis of the intercorrelation matrix for all the biases revealed two distinct but intercorrelated factors. Self-blame and derogation of victims loaded highly on one dimension, indicating a factor that may be termed a belief in 'persons as origins'; that is to say, a belief that people in general are responsible for what happens to them. The second factor was composed of the scales measuring superstition, 'quick interpersonal inference' and stereotyping, and may be termed a 'belief in the world as predictable'. These results suggest two distinct but intercorrelated strategies that people with a high need for control might use in order to enhance the controllability of their world. They might increase their belief in the extent to which people control what happens to them and/or enhance, by various strategies, the predictability of their world. All in all, the data present good support for the notion that control motivation influences the way people interpret the world. However, a cautionary note should be added. Some of the biases may intercorrelate for reasons that have nothing to do with control. In particular, superstition and stereotyping might intercorrelate at the personal level because of a third variable such as education or even social desirability. Further work may be needed to partial out the effects of the hidden variables. Nevertheless, it seems unlikely that the whole pattern of results can be explained by such factors.

The idea that there may be consistent individual differences in the need to cast the world in a controllable light may be used to understand certain personality constructs in psychology. In particular, it can help explain certain features of the 'Authoritarian Personality' (Adorno et al., 1950). One of the most prominent themes in this work is the extent to which the individuals studied have a 'drive for power, strength, success and self-determination' (p. 474). This orientation is exhibited in all arenas of life, expressing itself in the career domain with a concern for status and power and in the inter-personal area with an 'exploitative–manipulative type of power orientation' (p. 400) towards people. As the authors observe, 'It appears that he (the Authoritarian) wants to get power, to have it and not to lose it' (p. 237).

Given these inclinations, an examination of the modes of explanation typically utilized by Authoritarians might be of interest. In particular, is there any evidence that such individuals bias their perceptions of the world in order to render it more controllable? One observation that is of interest in this context is that Authoritarians seem to have a highly internal locus of control. 'The tendency to believe that will-power and cheerfulness can solve all problems seems of special importance' (Adorno et al., 1950, p. 425). Authoritarians are also much more prone to make dispositional judgements of people. They strongly believe in personality traits and place much emphasis on dispositional determinants of behaviour; a fact that is interesting in the light of Miller's argument that this serves to render interpersonal relations as more predictable and controllable. A tendency closely related to this is the Authoritarian's readiness to endorse stereotypical views about the intrinsic and unchangeable characteristics of various minority groups.

Authoritarians are also very quick to blame ethnic groups and in particular Jews for various social and economic problems. This again is interesting in the context of the suggestion made earlier that such attributions serve to enhance one's feelings of mastery in the face of complex and often insoluble problems. Again, Adorno et al., recognize this function: 'Charging the Jews with all existing evils seems to penetrate the darkness of reality like a searchlight and to allow for quick and all compromising orientation – it is the great panacea providing at once intellectual equilibrium, counter-cathexis and a cannalisation of wishes for a change' (1950, p. 619).

Other Authoritarian tendencies – the disdain for weaker sections of society, political and economic conservatism, dislike of welfare programmes and strong endorsement of ideas such as 'people get pretty much what they deserve' (Adorno et al., 1950, p. 155) – can also be interpreted as arising from their need to view the world as controllable. For very much the same reasons as subjects seem to blame people for the misfortunes that they suffer, the Authoritarian has a strong need to believe that a person's position in society reflects his or her worth, and that anyone who suffers does so because of his or her own mistakes and shortcomings. To believe otherwise would be to allow the possibility that one may also suffer through no fault of one's own – it would threaten the perceived controllability of one's world.

The finding by Adorno et al. that Authoritarians are much more superstitious than other people also fits in with the view expressed earlier on the functions of such beliefs. In addition, it is consistent with the finding of historians that many of the leading Nazi politicians were highly superstitious characters.

One final aspect of the Authoritarian personality that may be interpreted in control terms is the intolerance of ambiguity and uncertainty. If knowledge is power, then by definition, ambiguity and uncertainty must be the opposite of power. Always to know the cause of events in the world and always to be certain of one's conclusions is probably one of the best ways of preserving one's sense of mastery. In the final analysis, the accuracy of this 'knowledge' is immaterial. As Goebbels, who must rank as one of the most Authoritarian characters of all time, once said, 'For people it is not what they believe that is important; it is only important that they believe.'

Adorno et al. were mainly concerned, in *The Authoritarian Personality*, to show that a variety of traits, beliefs and modes of explanation came together in the same personality type. They did not primarily address themselves to the underlying reason for such a coherence, and, to the extent that they did, they relied on psycho-analytic theory. The suggestion being made here is that, at least in part, the beliefs and modes of explanation that Authoritarians present can be understood as a coherent whole if they are seen to arise from high need to cast the world in a controllable light. However, it should be emphasized that such an interpretation cannot explain all aspects of the Authoritarian syndrome. For instance, one characteristic of such types is a willingness to take orders and bow down to authority, and it is difficult to see how this can be linked to a high need for control. Similarly, Authoritarians are alleged to have extra-punitive tendencies in the face of personal failure, and this does not coincide at all with the statement earlier that self-blame is often a useful strategy for preserving control in such situations. Thus, while there may be a substantial overlap beween the high-need-for-control person, who is especially prone to the biases discussed above, and the Authoritarian, there are also certain differences. It is possible that many of these differences may be explained by suggesting that the Authoritarian, apart from having a high need for control, also has an especially low or vulnerable self-esteem. This vulnerability may make self-serving biases dominate over control biases in the face of failure and result in the observed extra-punitive tendencies. It may also mean that Authoritarians, despite certain inclinations against being dominated by others, submit to those who are deemed to be superior and more powerful than themselves, in a way that those with a more robust sense of self-esteem would not. Finally, the extreme prejudice of such people and their general downgrading of outgroups can be seen as an attempt at the group level to sustain self-esteem by self-serving tendencies.

Clearly, one implication of this approach to the Authoritarian personality is that the F scale is really bi-factorial. In this context it is interesting to note a study conducted by O'Neil and Levinson (1954). The authors gave several social attitude scales, including a shortened version of the F scale, to a number of subjects and factor-analysed the results. Contrary to expectations, they found that the F scale factors were split roughly in half on two orthogonal factors. The first of these the authors labelled 'masculine strength facade', a factor that emphasized personal invulnerability, toughness and high self-control; clearly, this corresponds well to all the attributes that one might expect from a high-need-for-control person. The second and unrelated factor on which half the F scale items loaded was labelled by the authors as 'authoritarian submission'. The implication of this study is that we may need two psychological principles to explain the full Authoritarian personality, and as such it supports the interpretation offered in this paper of the syndrome in terms of need for control and fragile self-esteem.

It would be inappropriate to end this section without a word on how the much-used internal–external (I–E) locus of control distinction maps on to some of the personality structures discussed above. Theoretically, the Rotter (1966) I–E scale measures perceptions of causality in the world, and in principle this is quite distinct from *need* for control. However, it is possible to suggest, and this is the central point of this section, that a high need for control might motivate a perception of the world as controllable. On the same grounds, one might also predict a relationship between internality and certain components of Authoritarianism.

The suggestion that both Authoritarianism and internality may in fact be seen as cognitive/explanatory orientations to the world prompted by a high need for control, and that therefore there is a substantial overlap between the two constructs, raises an interesting issue. Since the publication of the Rotter scale in 1966, there has been an avalanche of work on the I–E personality distinction. Almost without exception, this work has contained an implicit positive evaluation of the 'internal' and a tendency to portray the 'external' as someone with disordered and maladaptive cognitions. If the substantial similarities between internality and Authoritarianism are accepted, then one is forced to the sad conclusion that the Authoritarian of the 1950s has surfaced in the 1970s under new labels and values. This unquestioning positive approach to the high 'internal' is, however, beginning to be eroded. Thus McGarry and Newbury (1981) have challenged the view that externality equals irrationality in finding that strong and active belief in superstitions is actually correlated with internality. This finding, while perhaps being counter-intuitive, is entirely in accord with the general position being advanced in this paper, and indeed can really be explained only by suggesting that both superstition and an internal locus of control may reflect a defensive attempt to enhance the controllability of one's world.

CONCLUSIONS

In ending this discussion on the role of control as an organizing principle for the understanding of explanations given in a variety of contexts, a few points need to be clarified. First, it is not being assumed that control represents the only motivational influence on explanations. Self-esteem-protecting motives have already been mentioned, and clearly they may in some cases, as for instance in the case of failure, operate in a different attributional direction to control motivation. A second point concerns an impression that may have been created that, by and large, 'control biases' reflect an attempt at the individual level to preserve a particular view of the world. It is possible, however, that in the main such biases are not arrived at through individual experience, but on the contrary are culturally shared ways of explaining the world into which an individual is socialized (see Moscovici and Hewstone, chapter 6, above). Within-cultural variance in the incidence of such biases may well be dwarfed by variance between cultures (see Bond chapter 8 below). It is certainly true that different cultures have very different ways of enhancing the controllability of their world. In many Third World countries this is achieved by a belief in superstitious theories of causality, whereas in the West this has been superseded by the 'religion of persons as origins'. There is a case to be made for suggesting that the fundamental attribution error has replaced superstition as the new ideology of control. It is also important to remember that, while different cultures may adopt different strategies for enhancing control, like individuals they may vary in the extent to which they value control – just as with certain individuals we may find all forms of 'control biases' represented more in some cultures than in others.

In any case, whatever the cross-cultural incidence of such biases, it seems that, in modern Western society at least, a worthwhile account of many explanations given by people for personal, interpersonal and societal events can be achieved by recognizing the importance of control. While it is true that, for some of the biases, less motivationally tinged explanations are possible, an account in terms of control has the advantage of being more parsimonious and is therefore preferable. Nevertheless, further empirical proof is required to sort out the various interpretations. It is hoped that such work will contribute to the reinstatement of motivational concepts and thinking to social psychology – a development that is long overdue.

8 A Proposal for Cross-Cultural Studies of Attribution

Michael H. Bond

入 境 隨 俗

Before entering a country, learn about its customs.
Books of Rites, 206BC – AD 25

INTRODUCTION

In the autumn of 1972 I sat with a respectful Japanese audience listening to Harold Kelley deliver a lecture on his current thinking about attribution theory. A strained silence followed the presentation as Dr Kelley awaited reactions and comments from the floor. With the embarrassment becoming palpable, the President of the Japanese Society for Social Psychology leaned across to me and pleaded that I 'ask something interesting'. The mandatory question was posed, Dr Kelley responded, and the lecture was quickly brought to a close. Form, at least, had been served.

I had initially attributed the silence of the audience members to their reluctance about addressing the speaker in English. I now believe this construction was incorrect. Many of the audience spoke fluent English, and translators were available should difficulties have arisen. The formality of the occasion and Dr Kelley's revered position were undoubtedly important factors, of course. It has also occurred to me recently, however, that the unresponsiveness of the Japanese audience may have reflected something more disturbing. Is the question of how lay persons explain the causes of interpersonal events simply irrelevant to Japanese thinking? Or is the answer so obvious that the question seems unworthy of the asking? Or are the constructs used by Japanese persons to explain behaviour unrelatable to those used by Western attribution theorists?

Today, it is easier to advance these intriguing possibilities for the Japanese silence than it would have been in the autumn of 1972. The early 1970s witnessed an avalanche of professional self-examination during which many of our guiding principles and methodologies were challenged (Elms, 1975; Gergen, 1973; Israel and Tajfel, 1972; W. J. McGuire, 1973). Instead of observing and analysing the interplay of universal truths, it was widely suggested that we were merely viewing a unique historical drama, typically played out on the rarified and idiosyncratic stage of a social psychology laboratory (Gergen, 1978; Ring, 1967). On the heels of this general challenge came a salvo from another flank, arguing that the very assumptions underlying mainstream social psychology were shot through with the ideological and normative biases of American social philosophy (Hogan and Emler, 1978; Pepitone, 1976; Sampson, 1977). Gradually the *Zeitgeist* had developed to stimulate the conjecture that the American, Dr Kelley, had simply been talking past, beside, or around his Japanese audience. One culture's issue and approach were simply not another's. What kind of support might there be for such speculation?

THE INFLUENCE OF CULTURE

The ideological argument

In a recent paper Sampson (1981) has argued that cognitivism has become a dominant focus in psychology because it reflects and supports an ideological order. This normative order is individualistic, giving a primacy to the isolated knower and emphasizing the subjective determinants of behaviour. Psychology conducted within this framework tends to yield reified constructs framed at the individual level and abstracted from the historical–social context in which the individuals are embedded. Sampson further argues that such a construction of reality serves what Habermas (1971) called the 'technical interests of knowledge'. In Sampson's words, 'Knowledge constituted within the purview of the technical interest is founded on social practices involving work, in particular the achievement of a technical mastery and control over nature and people' (Sampson, 1981, p. 739).

The study of how lay persons explain the causes of social behaviour is obviously related to this general analysis. For the concern of attribution researchers is in large part with examining the conditions under which the cause of an individual's behaviour is believed to lie 'within' the individual, i.e., to reflect his or her personality. When the locus of causality is determined to be individual, the panoply of control mechanisms can then be engaged to effect changes favourable to these technical interests. In this way the contemporary fascination with attribution can be construed as a reflection of a wider social and historical process organized to achieve domination over nature. If this argument has merit, then it would follow that, in cultural settings organized to satisfy different interests, the question of what causes social behaviour and the locating of that cause in the individual would enjoy less currency.

Some anthropological input

The concept of the separate person is central to all theories of attribution. Under specified circumstances the individual will be assigned the role of agent whose intentions, motives and dispositions have caused the behaviour under consideration. Such analyses obviously presuppose a conception of the person as a distinct entity that can be set apart from other persons and his or her natural environment.

Geertz (1975), however, maintains that this fundamental epistemological assumption is 'a rather peculiar idea within the context of the world's cultures' (p. 48). This startling assertion is based on a considerable wealth of observation by one of the most experienced of anthropologists. If it is true, there would seem to be little likelihood in many cultures of developing a lay conception of the contribution made by discrete individuals in generating their own behaviour. Naturally occurring explanations for interpersonal behaviour may still exist, but the individualistic input of personalities would be irrelevant (see also Hsu, 1971).

Even where there is a conception of persons as agents of intended behaviour, there may be little need to develop a lay person's conception of the role played by unique and individual personalities in producing the observed behaviours. Take yet another quotation from the same article by Geertz:

> There is in Bali a persistent and systematic attempt to stylize all aspects of personal expression to the point where anything idiosyncratic, anything characteristic of the individual merely because he is who he is physically, psychologically, or biographically, is muted in favor of his assigned place in the continuing and, so it is thought, never-changing pageant that is Balinese life. It is dramatis personae, not actors, that endure; indeed, it is dramatis personae, not actors, that in the proper sense really exist. [Geertz, 1975, p. 50]

In such a culture individual behaviour could generally be explained by reference to the roles played by the various actors (see Selby, 1975). There would be little variation outside these channels. One is reminded here of Boldt's (1978) construct of structural tightness. In societies characterized as structurally tight, role expectations are imposed with little room for flexible interpretation in their enactment. Status instantiation is 'less open to negotiation, improvisation and innovation' (Boldt, 1978, p. 157). Many cultural groups, like the Balinese, are structurally tight. What need would they have had to develop a naive theory of personality? The attributional functions of providing explanations and enabling predictions (Forsyth, 1980) could be easily fulfilled without reference to individual personalities.

Such is not the case in cultures with a political and social philosophy of individualism (Hofstede, 1980). In such societies, role-based constraints are weakened by the value placed on freedom of expression and the flexibility of role enactment built into the social structure. Predicting others' behaviour becomes more problematic, increasing the likelihood that lay persons will formulate theories to explain such variable behaviour. Not surprisingly, these theories have featured the personality of the actor as a fundamental component.

The contribution of cross-cultural psychology

The obvious response to the ideological and anthropological challenges would be to export our attribution models to see how robust and useful they are in different cultural milieux. Should they prove marketable, we have grounds for claiming that we are discussing universal social and cognitive processes uncompromised by the socio-historical context of their origin. If not, we can begin isolating the culturally varying factors that must be introduced to make our theories generalize beyond the context of their origin.

Perhaps some examples would help illustrate these two processes. One of the best-known demonstrations of the first outcome concerns the judgement of emotions communicated by different facial expressions. In his 1872 classic, *The Expression of the Emotions in Man and Animals*, Darwin asserted that various facial configurations were derived from movements once functional in emotion-arousing situations. So, for example, raising the lips and flaring the nostrils in anger are part of the biting response used in defence or attack. Given their evolutionary heritage, such forms of emotional display must be innate and therefore recognizable across cultures.

This hypothesis has been carefully examined by Ekman and his co-workers (Ekman et al., 1969). They selected photographs of Americans whose facial expressions of eight basic emotions had been identified with a high degree of reliability by other Americans. These photographs were then shown to a group of indigenous natives in New Guinea and Borneo who had no previous contact with Westerners, in person or through the media. The facial expressions of happiness, anger, disgust and interest were identified as such with extremely high levels of agreement across cultures. Shame, sorrow, fear and surprise produced lower levels of agreement across cultures, but much higher than would have resulted merely from chance. Given their previous work in yet other cultures, Ekman et al. believed their evidence supported Darwin's contention that the facial expression of emotion was innately determined. If not, how could the same facial configurations be identified across so much cultural diversity as communicating the same emotion? It is the search for this sort of invariant relationship that animates much cross-cultural research (Foschi, 1980; Jahoda, 1979; Segall, 1979, chapter 2; Triandis, 1975).

Of course, not all such research programmes discover the trans-cultural relationships initially expected. The early American work on psychological differentation (Witkin et al., 1962) unearthed a small, but consistent sex difference such that females showed less differentiation than males. Given the Gestalt theory underpinning this work, it was speculated that this sex difference had some genetic basis and would therefore be reproduced in other cultures. Replications, however, soon established that the sex difference was an inpredictable will-o'-the-wisp – its size varied from culture to culture, disappearing altogether in certain societies.

In their review of the literature, Witkin and Berry (1975) integrated the disparate results by suggesting that the size of the sex difference was a function of pressures towards conformity operating in a given society. This conclusion not only brought order out of apparent chaos; it also strengthened the theory of psychological differentiation by linking socialization evidence about conformity within societies to similar evidence across societies. In this case, then, the cross-cultural extensions served to advance the theory they were designed to test and also pointed to an important dimension of cultural variation (see Berry, 1979).

So, cross-cultural extensions of mainstream psychology will either confirm the generalizability of our findings or point towards theoretical improvements. Given that we will benefit either way, why is so little work being done?

The lack of research in a cross-cultural framework

As Triandis (1976) has pointed out, the issues dominating Western consciousness often pale in other cultures; the priorities elsewhere are different. Also, there seems to be a lamentable narrowness of vision, an indifference to the cultural question on the part of most psychologists. Schwartz (1981), for example, contends that: 'To many psychologists culture has always seemed a vague concept with which they cannot come to grips. . . . Culture is an obstacle in their quest for universal human nature, to be filtered out where encountered or ignored as "content" where what is wanted is process or structure' (p. 8).

Another telling reason is that revealing cross-cultural work requires collaboration of individuals from the cultures involved. Such coordination itself is often frustrating and time-consuming. In addition, as Faucheux (1976) correctly points out, this collaboration must be structured by the parties concerned in such a way that each culture's perspective is capable of being represented. Cultural imperialism and the rigid teacher–student model must be avoided at all costs. A more egalitarian, respectful approach is required. For many of us this is a most exacting requirement. Finally, the research methodologies required to advance our understanding are demanding, particularly with a topic like attribution. Let us substantiate this last claim by looking at some of the questions that seem worth asking in our initial forays across culture.

FUNDAMENTAL ISSUES IN CROSS-CULTURAL EXPLORATIONS OF ATTRIBUTION

There are many possible questions that could be raised to help focus our extension of attribution research into the cross-cultural domain. The first two selected arise from the concerns voiced by social philosophers and anthropologists. If they can be adequately addressed, then we may move on to consider additional problems posed to sharpen our inquiries.

How frequently do people engage in attributional activity?

A facetious riposte to this question would be, 'Endlessly. Just look at the number of journal articles on the topic!' Despite this apparent affirmation, a number of North American psychologists are beginning to question whether people are quite so thought-filled about their day-to-day activity as a trip through the psychological literature would suggest (e.g., Langer et al., 1978). Regarding attributional activity, Manis (1977) has likewise questioned the extent to which most people are spontaneously concerned about the causes of the social behaviour they experience. This meta-issue has arisen because attribution theorists have been much more concerned with testing theories about attribution than with testing the ecological validity of attribution. This oversight is partially understandable, since we as psychologists are intensely interested in the causes of behaviour and interact with undergraduates who share this interest. The consequence, however, is that we have not addressed the question of whether persons engage in such attributional reflections spontaneously in the course of their activities outside an experimental setting. If attribution has any significance beyond psychological journals, it is in persons' lives as lived that it must be observed to occur.

To do so, we need less obtrusive techniques that do not themselves create or channel the attributional behaviour. A step in this direction has recently been undertaken (e.g. Harvey et al., 1980). In this paradigm, people are exposed to videotaped episodes where actors engage in various surprising, unusual or negatively valenced behaviour. Later, the research subjects are given an opportunity to write down their recollection of thoughts and feelings they experienced while observing these episodes. These written reactions are then scored for attribution judgements.

Harvey et al. maintain, convincingly I believe, that demand characteristics are held to a minimum in this procedure. Subjects are given an open-ended opportunity to respond in any way and at any length they choose. Their responses can then be assessed for the proportion of attributional analysis and its nature.

Such an approach is of obvious value within any given culture where psychologists are exploring the contextual determinants of attribution. Additionally, however, it must be used in trying to answer Pepitone's (1981) recent question, 'Do all people everywhere make causal attributions [about interpersonal events]?' To many psychologists the asking of this question will seem hopelessly naive. However, the process of trying to understand interpersonal behaviour may itself be an undertaking whose interest, importance and salience is determined by fundamental dimensions of cultural variation.

For example, many psychologists have argued that persons engage in attribution because of a need to explain and control the world around them (e.g., Bains, chapter 7 above; Forsyth, 1980; Heider, 1944, 1958; D. T. Miller et al., 1978). In this regard, it is suggestive to note that orientation towards nature along the dimension of control–adaptiveness–subjugation is a fundamental aspect of intercultural variation (Triandis, 1981). This value perspective was originally proposed by Kluckhohn and Strodtbeck (1961), and concerns whether a society organizes itself towards mastering nature, towards a harmonious relationship, or towards a submissiveness to its demands. How would members of cultures varying in their location along this dimension differ in their unstructured responses to a selection of representative interpersonal events? I would expect that persons from cultures whose orientation encourages domination over nature would engage in much more attributional activity. Many dimensions of cultural variation such as uncertainty avoidance and power distance (Hofstede, 1980) would appear to be similarly related to attributional undertakings.

Note that the question at issue is not whether different cultural groups *can* engage in attribution. According to Dixon (1977), the semantic class of human propensity (i.e., trait-type vocabulary) exists in all known languages. Presumably these judgements are reached through some form of attribution. Furthermore, research shows that members of various cultures can make reliable and functionally meaningful attributions *when asked* (e.g., in Nigeria – Boski, 1982; in Hong Kong – Bond and Goodman, 1980); in India – Singh et al., 1979; in Japan – Shaw and Iwawaki, 1972). The question at issue is rather *how frequently* such activity is undertaken. To answer this we must ask, as did Harvey et al. (1980), in a way that allows us to see the process elicited in as unfettering and non-directive a manner possible. Otherwise, we may simply confirm yet again the wisdom of the Chinese adage, 'The suspicious mind creates its own shadows' (Lieh Tzu).

What causal categories are used?

The self-serving bias is a phenomenon reflecting the tendency of persons to attribute desirable compared with undesirable outcomes more to internal characteristics; undesirable compared with desirable outcomes are attributed more to external factors (Zuckerman, 1979). Recently, Chandler et al. (1981) reported a study that explored the self-serving bias in five cultures. To do so, they administered the Multidimensional-Multiattributional Causality Scale (MMCS, Lefcourt et al., 1979) to university students in India, Japan, South Africa, Yugoslavia and the United States. This scale consists of 48 items, half tapping the achievement domain, half the affiliation domain. Within each domain there are six items for attributions to the explanatory categories of ability, effort, task and luck, three items each for success and three each for failure. Among their findings is the fact that, across cultures, attributions to ability for achievement successes were higher than were attributions to (lack of) ability for failure. Furthermore, this self-serving bias interacted with culture such that the size of the bias was three times for Indian subjects what it was for Japanese subjects.

Now these are provocative results which on the surface suggest that this motivational pattern for attributions may constitute a universal process with cultural variations influencing its size. It is equally plausible that the comparisons are invalid for many reasons, one of which could be the differing relevance or complete irrelevance of the ability, effort, task and luck categories for causal explanations in the four cultures importing the scale. If, for example, luck is not a salient category for achievement attributions in India, what sense are we to make of the fact that Indians showed no attributional differences to this causal category as a function of outcomes resulting in success or failure?

These four causal categories were developed by Weiner et al. (1971). As *a priori* structures they have been used in a variety of North American studies, showing considerable construct validity. The obvious problem is that such structuring may limit the amount and content of the causal explanations elicited from the respondents (F. R. Smith, 1977). In response to this concern a number of American studies have recently been published using a free-response format (Elig and Frieze, 1979; Frieze, 1976; Orvis et al., 1976; Mann, 1980; F. R. Smith, 1977). These have generally confirmed the various theoretical constructs advanced by Weiner et al. and others as constituting the fundamental attributional categories.

One problem in interpreting the Chandler et al. (1981) results is that we have no such reassurance that the categories provided are the categories actually used in the remaining four cultures. In all fairness to the authors, they acknowledge this problem with their results. They would clearly subscribe to the view that, in the initial stages of cross-cultural research, a free-response format is essential. Despite the added labour of content analysis they impose, open-ended probes give a maximum opportunity for each cultural group to indicate which categories it spontaneously uses in the causal and non-causal explanation of interpersonal events. By allowing the data to suggest their own categories, we avoid the problem of imposing one culture's theoretical constructs upon the respondents of another culture. They can then cast their own shadows, rather than selecting from the imported shadows projected by foreign psychologists.

Cross-cultural research that elicits such unstructured responses may indicate the generality of the categories, in which case we can proceed with our comparisons. They may, however, deliver an unexpected bonus by indicating constructs used with markedly different frequency in the cultures contrasted. For example, Shweder and Bourne (1982) were interested in pursuing the implications of Geertz's (1975) assertion that the notion of the individual isolated from his or her social relationships is an unusual concept among the world's cultures. They argued that, when persons from most cultures describe others, they will rely more on contextual qualifiers to trait labels than will Americans. Instead of asserting that 'Jack is aggressive', they might state that 'Jack is aggressive with younger persons.' Put in other terms, the people of most cultures are interactionists rather than trait theorists. To test this hypothesis, Shweder and Bourne (1982) analysed the free descriptions of other persons made by Oriyan (India) and American (United States) respondents. The data supported the validity of their analysis, with the Oriyans using more contextual qualifiers and behavioural descriptions than persons from the United States.

What these results suggest is that attribution categories like Kelley's (1967) person, stimulus and circumstance are probably too discrete and restrictive when used separately in many cultures. They probably will not overlap with the categories used as causal explanations by persons from these other cultures. Could this possibility help explain the Japanese silence that greeted Kelley's presentation? Could it help explain the relative lack of attribution research done in cultures like Japan and India where there are many social psychologists but little attribution data? The cultural bias of individualism animating North American social psychology in general (Hogan and Emler, 1978; Pepitone, 1976; Sampson, 1977) and attributional analyses in particular (Sampson, 1981) may have made much of it unexportable.

If this is so, and we are in no position yet to be certain, it raises the provocative question of how behaviour is explained by lay persons in these other cultures. The models presently available from the world's great traditions such as the Chinese, Indian and Japanese (see Pedersen, 1977) do not seem helpful, at least in their present depictions. If we begin to ask unrestricting questions, however, some fascinating results may well emerge. With the benefit of our present perspective, we may begin to develop alternative models of the attribution process (e.g., V. L. Hamilton, 1980).

The case should not be overstated, however. A number of pilot comparisons by students in my cross-cultural courses at the Chinese University of Hong Kong indicate that many of the North American-based theories are culturally robust and usable. In one study, for example, analyses were conducted of explanations for academic success and failure provided by United States and Hong Kong students to a free-response questionnaire. The categories elicited were remarkably similar, with the four main categories of Weiner et al. (1971) featuring prominently for both groups.

In another such study students of these two cultural groups were asked to explain four different interpersonal events with positive and negative outcomes, again using open-ended response formats. The answers were carefully assessed by both American and Chinese class members. They decided that an elaboration of Mann's (1980) coding procedure, itself based on Kelley's (1967) model, was satisfactory in categorizing the responses. There were no differences in the frequency with which person, stimulus or circumstance categories were used by the two cultural groups. Finer analyses within these three main categories, however, revealed suggestive differences. The circumstance category was divided into physical (e.g., accidents) and social (e.g., duties) subgroups. The Chinese respondents were found to use a higher proportion of social-to-physical responses than were those from the United States. Likewise, the situation category was divided into subgroups of relationship with the other and needs of the other. Chinese respondents used a higher proportion of relationship compared with need explanations than did their counterparts from the United States.

These results have been produced in ways that create confidence in the generalizability of the model and its categories. Careful attention to the unstructured answers additionally suggests finer categorical analyses, which permit cross-cultural differences in frequency to be detected. These differences may, and in this case do, point towards important cultural factors influencing the outcome of attributional analyses.

For the next question, I have borrowed the subtitle from an important but generally overlooked article on cognitive dissonance (Tedeschi et al., 1971). In that paper they argued that the literature supporting Festinger's (1957) theory of cognitive dissonance could be reconceptualized. Previously it had been generally assumed that our various dependent measures were tapping fundamental cognitive processes. Tedeschi et al. argued that these measures served an interpersonal function. Specifically, they offered subjects the opportunity to demonstrate to the experimenter that they subscribed to the American norm of consistency. By avoiding 'dissonance' the subjects were engaging in an act of self-presentation calculated to construct an acceptable public self in the eyes of the experimenter (Baumeister, 1982).

An analogous argument has been made for attribution responses in experimental settings (Bradley, 1978; Weary, 1979). It is based on the position that attributions frequently serve an interpersonal function (Forsyth, 1980), and that most attributional data are collected from subjects in ways that make their responses identifiable to the experimenter. Consequently, the subjects' responses can be regarded as tactical self-presentations towards a higher-status audience – the experimenter.

This interpersonal aspect of attributional behaviour is important in its own right and fully worthy of study. If, however, we are interested in making statements about the cognitive processes underlying observed attributions, it is prudent to eliminate the public nature of attribution. This goal can be achieved by affording subjects the opportunity to make their attributions anonymously *vis-à-vis* the experimenter or any other audience. Anonymous and public attributions may, of course, be similarly related to our independent variables, but available studies suggest that different patterns often occur, both for attributions about others (Gould et al., 1977) and for attributions about the self (House, 1980; Weary et al., 1983).

The goal of our cross-cultural comparison will dictate whether we collect subjects' responses publicly or anonymously *vis-à-vis* the experimenter. Interpersonal norms across cultures are addressed by attributions taken in the presence of an audience. So, for example, it appears as if Indians (Fry and Ghosh, 1980) and Hong Kong Chinese (Wan and Bond, 1982) show a reversal of the self-serving bias on the dimension of luck when attributions are made with high subject identifiability in the eyes of the experimenter. Americans, on the other hand, show a self-serving pattern of public attributions to luck on similar tasks (Snyder et al., 1976; Stephan et al., 1976). We believe that self-effacing attributions to luck are used by Orientals to attenuate their immodest attribution on the dimensions of effort and ability. The need to appear modest is, of course, an interpersonal concern and is best tapped by collecting responses in a highly public way.

On the other hand, underlying cognitive activity across cultures is illuminated when subjects perceive that their attributions are being made anonymously. So, as mentioned previously, respondents to the anonymous Chandler et al. (1981) survey in five cultures all showed a self-serving bias on the dimension of ability, a finding also found for Hong Kong Chinese on a recent extension of the study to this population. These results suggest that such a bias is a universal aspect of private functioning. It may well be a component of perceived self-efficacy (Bandura, 1982), at least among clinically normal persons. This contention could be advanced, however, only if the responses had been collected with some guarantee of anonymity. Otherwise, they could be construed as reflecting needs for acceptable public self-construction (Baumeister, 1982), rather than as aspects of personal cognition.

Given the preceding argument, it is hoped that cross-cultural researchers will collect their data in ways maximally suited to answering the questions they are posing.

How does 'culture' exercise its impact?

Culture may be regarded as an elaborately confounded variable. The ways in which a typical member of one culture may differ from a typical member of another are legion. Consequently it is not very helpful simply to find a difference in attribution between members of various cultures. The question will always arise, 'Which difference between members of the two cultures has led to the observed difference in attribution?'

Take, for example, Shaw and Iwawaki's (1972) study, which examined attributions of responsibility (AR) by Japanese and Americans using Shaw's AR questionnaire. They found, among other things, that Japanese were more responsive to outcome intensity than the Americans. They explained this result in terms of different value orientations and child-rearing practices between the two cultures. This hypothesis is perfectly reasonable, of course. But in the absence of any data on the relationship between attribution of responsibility and values or child-rearing practices, the hypothesis is purely speculative. We are left much where we began, without any sound insight into the factor responsible for the observed cultural effect. Had such data been available as a part of the study, we would be in a position to expand our knowledge about the pan-cultural determinants of responsibility attribution.

What we need are studies that examine the impact of variations in both culture *and* these other variables. Detweiler's (1978) research is a model of this approach. He was concerned with discovering whether culture had any effects on patterns of personality judgement over and above the effects on these judgements produced by the personality variable of category width. To disentangle their respective impacts, he first assessed his Trukese and American subjects on their tendency to group perceptual objects into large or small categories (broad versus narrow categorizers). He later administered his stimulus materials which served as a basis for making personality judgements. Through careful statistical analysis, he was able to establish that culture affected category width, which in turn affected the attribution of personality characteristics. Culture had no effect beyond its impact on category width.

He could, of course, have found that category width was not the critical variable accounting for the difference. He would then have had a sound reason for exploring other possible mediators. Alternatively, he could have found that culture still had an impact over and above its effects on category width. Just such a conclusion has been reached by Ickes (1981) in assessing the impact of sex (culture?) and self-esteem on internal versus external styles of attribution. With this latter type of outcome, the effects of the personality variable on attribution have been generalized across cultures, as in Detweiler's study; but also, one is alerted to search for other personality variables which are further mediating the impact of culture on attribution. And so the search could continue but on an ever more solid empirical foundation.

Many personality variables are prime candidates for inclusion in such studies. Perhaps the most obvious is the locus-of-control variable, which has been widely explored across cultures (Hui, 1982) and has also shown an impact on attribution in American research (Krovetz, 1974; Lefcourt et al., 1975). Regardless of which personality variable is chosen, the thrust of this proposal seems clear: we must move beyond simple comparisons between cultures and focus on ferreting out the personality variables common to both cultures and which are mediating the cultural differences. Such a procedure enables us to establish personality–attribution linkages that hold across cultural variation. These sorts of linkage are essential building blocks for a universal (pan-cultural) theory of social behaviour (Triandis, 1978).

CONCLUDING REMARKS

We have every reason to be excited with the exploration of how people from different cultural traditions understand their social world. In this search, however, we must be careful to refrain from creating their world in the image of our own. To avoid this pitfall we need to adopt a less structured and less obtrusive approach. Such an approach is ideally suited for addressing the first two issues raised: how frequently people engage in attributional activity, and the categories that are used. In answering these questions in this way, we can be more confident that we are reflecting another culture's reality rather than describing the shadows we have ourselves cast.

Once on firmer ground we can begin asking more pointed questions. Two have recently emerged from the literature as being of basic importance; public spectacle versus private ratiocination, and the way in which culture exercises its impact. The first focuses our attention on what realm of activity is being illuminated by the subjects' responses; the second, on how the process operates.

To borrow from a commentary on McDougall's classic, *Social Psychology*, the bags are packed but the journey has not yet begun. It is hoped that this chapter has suggested some useful directions for this journey to take.

ACKNOWLEDGEMENTS
I wish to thank Miles Hewstone, David Schneider and two anonymous reviewers of an earlier version for their thoughtful contributions towards sharpening my thinking on this topic. Its shortcomings cannot, unfortunately, be attributed to them, despite their originating from different cultures than mine.

PART III
Applications of Attribution Theory

9   From Attributions to Behaviour

J. Richard Eiser

It is an indispensable part of any research activity that one should limit one's attention to certain kinds of questions and certain kinds of approaches. The success of research is measured, in the first instance, by how well specific questions have been answered. But once such preliminary success is achieved, the need arises to set such answers in a broader context, and to show that they are of potential interest and importance for researchers who have been concentrating on other topics and even for a more general audience who have no involvement in research at all. To consider the applications of attribution theory is to evaluate the success of that theory in terms of these latter kinds of criteria. It is here that the literature on attribution processes displays both a sharp division and a curious imbalance. This is perhaps best illustrated in the review by Kelley and Michela (1980). They provide a 'general model of the attribution field', as shown in figure 1. As may be seen, a distinction is drawn between 'attribution theories', which are concerned primarily with the relationship between attributions and their antecedents, and 'attributional theories', which are concerned with the consequences of attributions.

This figure has a number of interesting details. First, one can see that no attempt is made to specify how information, beliefs and motivation interact to influence how people make attributions. As a 'general model' it is silent on how information-processing factors, such as are described in Kelley's own (1967) ANOVA model, interact with motivational or functional biases. This silence is something that a number of other chapters in this book are attempting to break. There are many areas where such functional biases may be important. Attributions for successful and unsuccessful performance (Weiner, 1974) have mainly been studied in the context of educational achievement, but a variety of other kinds of performance should be amenable to similar analyses – for example, among many others, athletic, occupational, rehabilitative and more general personal coping (cf. Brewin, 1981). In this volume, the chapters by Fincham (chapter 11) and King (chapter 10) examine the relevance of such concepts to problems in clinical and health psychology. Questions of personal health, whether mental or physical, are obviously important for individuals in terms of their consequences, in a way that many of the more abstract experimental tasks used in the literature arguably are not.

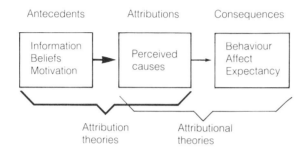

FIGURE 1 *General model of the attribution field*
Reproduced, with permission, from the Annual Review of Psychology, *vol. 31,*
1980, by Annual Reviews Inc.

Second, if one looks at the box entitled 'Attributions', the only entry is 'perceived causes'. This identification of attributions with perceptions of causality derives historically from Heider's (e.g. 1944) work on phenomenal causality and causal unit formation (cf. Eiser, 1983), but may de-emphasize the social and interpersonal aspects of attributions as *accounts* (Semin and Manstead, 1983) and as assignments of blame or responsibility (Fincham, chapter 11 below).

Third, the thickness of the bracket and arrow that join the 'Antecedents' and 'Attributions' boxes, compared with those joining the 'Attributions' and 'Consequences' boxes, is no accident. On the contrary, it reflects both the preponderance of the research literature and Kelley and Michela's own implicit view of the 'proper' scope of attribution theory. The suffix in their term 'attributional' signals an accusation of illegitimacy as visibly as a bend sinister in medieval heraldry. Finally, the 'Consequences' box contains behaviour, affect and expectancy without specification of their interactions and interdependence, but with the clear insistence that these are all dependent on how causes are attributed to events.

Kelley and Michela (1980) are right in claiming that the traditional formulations of attribution theory have little to say about the consequences of attributions. This, however, is perhaps the single most telling criticism of the traditional formulations. Much of the work on attribution processes has been interested in social perception as an end in itself. In other words, the issue is that of how events that have happened are construed, interpreted and explained. The emphasis has been epistemological, rather than behavioural. Of course, none of the workers in this tradition would go so far as to *deny* that attributions had behavioural consequences. If challenged, they would surely reply that social behaviour *must* be shaped by the way one perceives and interprets one's social world. However, the fact remains that this tradition has had little to say about *how* attributions lead to behaviour. Heider may have regarded his theories as attempts to model what Lewin (1951) would have called the 'life-space' of the perceiver, but the dynamic or motivational aspects of Lewin's approach – the concept of movement within that life-space – are left behind. More particularly, although it is a truism to say that social behaviour is influenced by social perception, it cannot simply be assumed that the main part of this influence is dependent on perception of causality.

In describing traditional attribution research as epistemological rather than behavioural, I do not wish to imply an evaluation. If researchers want to study processes of social perception 'for their own sake', that is a perfectly respectable thing to do. The only danger is that such a standpoint might lead to a model of people's social perceptual processes – of their 'lay epistemology' (cf. Kruglanski et al. chapter 5 above) – which itself is less behavioural than people are themselves. Put differently, although some researchers may not be very interested in behavioural consequences, ordinary people may be, *and this may be reflected in the kinds of attribution processes in which they engage.*

WHEN DO PEOPLE MAKE ATTRIBUTIONS?

One of the most widely cited experiments in the attribution literature is that by McArthur (1972). This involved male university students reading a series of short, highly stylized descriptions of behaviour in which consensus, distinctiveness and consistency information (cf. Kelley, 1967) were significantly varied. Subjects were told: 'Your task is to decide, on the basis of the information given, what *probably caused* the event to occur' (p. 174; italics added). Response categories allowed for attributions to the person, the stimulus, the particular circumstances or some combination of these three. The results, though open to alternative interpretations (cf. Jaspars, chapter 2 above), were seen as broadly supporting Kelley's (1967) ANOVA model of causal attribution.

But despite the fact that such experiments seem to 'work' (and there have been many in a similar mould), they arguably fail to make the case that these same processes are operating in everyday real-life encounters. The fundamental question, and it still remains, is not whether people *can* make causal attributions, but how they come to define or encode events as ones for which causal attributions need to be made. This definitional or encoding process, which is bound to involve related processes of learning, memory and attention – and no doubt motivational and emotional processes as well – is simply not looked at by this kind of experiment. Furthermore, one cannot conclude that people *typically* offer causal explanations for events on the basis of experiments where subjects are explicitly instructed to think in causal terms. When attempts are made to give subjects greater freedom in how to express their interpretation of events – and also when descriptions of real-life events are used – subjects' responses may bear little resemblance to the standard categories of causal explanation used as dependent measures in more constrained experiments (Antaki, 1982). Ordinary language interpretation, in other words, may often have little obvious to do with causal explanation.

Wong and Weiner (1981) were concerned not with people's interpretations of events, but with the kind of questions that people tend to ask, specifically in imagined contexts of expected or unexpected success or failure. Their overall conclusion, on the basis of five separate experiments, was that people do engage in 'spontaneous attributional search', but that this tendency is stronger in contexts of failure than of success, and when the outcome is unexpected rather than expected. In other words, their suggestion is that attributional processes primarily come into play if a person feels there is something that needs to be explained.

Even in this study, however, one can question the full extent to which subjects were attempting to ascribe causes. The main feature of this study was a 'self-probe methodology', in which subjects were asked to write down what questions, if any, they would be likely to ask themselves. In the first experiment, 'Attribution questions' were defined as '"why" questions concerned with the possible causes of the outcome' (Wong and Weiner, 1981, p. 652). It is not stated whether all "why" questions were assumed to be causal, or whether any non-causal "why" questions were found. In experiments 2 and 3 instructions (given after the first 'self-probe' task) informed subjects: 'In seeking an explanation for success or failure, people often ask themselves questions regarding possible *causes*' (p. 655; italics added). The five attributional dimensions of locus, control, intention, stability and generality were explained to the subjects, who then coded their own questions which they had previously written down. According to subjects' own use of these dimensions, questions about locus and control had 'higher priority', i.e. occurred earlier. Reasonable confirmation of this effect was found in experiment 4, using different instructions and responses. Experiment 5 provided subjects with the opportunity to seek information 'to help them determine the cause(s)' (p. 659) of their performance in a recent examination. Information relevant to questions of locus and control was sought most often.

The point about these details is that, for all their claims concerning the 'spontaneity' of their subjects' attributional search, Wong and Weiner still might be thought to have led their subjects towards a causal explanatory response set through the particular instructions they used. In fairness to Wong and Weiner, however, it should be pointed out that their concept of 'causal explanation' is a rather generic one, and that, in common with many attribution theorists, they make little attempt to distinguish, for instance, locus of causality from locus of responsibility.

Despite these reservations, the central conclusion, that attributional search is primarily a response to negative or unexpected events, remains noteworthy. There are, after all, many situational factors other than experimental instructions that can lead people to ask 'why' questions. These themselves can provide a focus for applied social psychological research – for example, how do clinicians attribute causes, jurists attribute intentionality or insurance inspectors attribute responsibility? There is also the very important set of questions that relate to how people make attributions concerning problematic aspects of their own behaviour.

The implication, though, is that there are many events in our lives that do not engage the kinds of reflective and analytical processes proposed by attribution theorists. In fact, some researchers, notably Langer (e.g. 1978) would go even further, and claim that social interaction is typically 'mindless', in the sense of relying on only rather gross and overlearnt routines for the processing of information that involves the minimum of conscious attention. The challenge posed by trying to 'apply' attribution theory is, to a great extent, one of specifying appropriate contexts for its application. It is not particularly illuminating to say that attribution theory *can* be applied to different kinds of problems. Still less would it be helpful to behave as though attributions are the only social cognitive processes for which claims of applicability can be made. Rather, one needs to specify when, and if, and how people engage in the kinds of inference processes hypothesized by attribution theorists. Chapters 10 and 11 by King and Fincham meet this challenge by providing evidence of contexts in which people do make attributions, while neither claims that people are making attributions all the time.

EXPECTANCY AND PREDICTION

Turning to the consequences of attributions, a great deal of work has focused on the concept of *expectancy*, particularly within the context of experiences of success or failure. Broadly speaking, research has shown that such experiences can, depending on the circumstances, lead to expectancies for future success or failure, and that these expectancies can be self-fulfilling.

The best-known attempt to formulate the relationships between attributions and expectancy has been put forward by Weiner. According to Weiner (1974), the perceived causes of success or failure may be categorized in terms of the three dimensions of internality, stability and intentionality. Thus, for example, ability (or the lack of it) would be categorized as 'stable–internal' and luck as 'unstable–external'. In contrast to workers in the locus of control tradition (Rotter, 1966), Weiner denies that the internal–external dimension *per se* influences expectancy for future achievement. Instead, he argues, it is the stable–unstable dimension that is crucial. If success is attributed to a stable cause, or failure to an unstable one, expectancy for future success is higher than if success is attributed to an unstable cause or failure to a stable one. The concept of intentionality is treated less systematically by Weiner, although, for instance, he uses it to distinguish effort (intentional) from ability (unintentional), or teacher bias (intentional) from task difficulty (unintentional).

One specific instance of support for Weiner's position comes from a study of smokers attempting to give up cigarettes (Eiser, 1982). As may be imagined, many smokers who try to give up have tried and failed to do so in the past, and consequently often have rather pessimistic views of their chances of success. In this study, measures were obtained of smokers' intentions to give up, their expectancies of success, and their attributions for why 'so many' smokers who try to stop fail to do so. These attributions were coded so as to provide two indices, one relating to internality, the other to stability. Whereas the stability index contributed strongly to expectancy, the internality index did not. Expectancy in turn contributed strongly to intention, and intention to behaviour (actually making an attempt to give up by the time of a follow-up).

Weiner's views on the influence of attributions on emotions is more complex. His earlier view (e.g. Weiner, 1976) was that internal attributions led to pride in the case of success and shame in the case of failure, these reactions being absent in the case of external attributions. His more recent position is considerably more complex. Weiner, Russell and Lerman (1978, 1979) noted that success and failure produced broad differences in affective reactions regardless of attributions. However, particular kinds of affective reactions – e.g. feelings of competence, satisfaction, contentment, gratitude or relief in the case of success or incompetence, fear, guilt, anger or stupidity in the case of failure – depended critically on the kinds of attributions made. These differences could not be compressed into a simple internal–external dichotomy. How such differences in affective reaction might lead to different kinds of behavioural effects is not considered in the Weiner et al. (1979) paper. This is clearly a topic for future research. Affective reactions should clearly give us some insight into the reinforcement value of particular kinds of success or failure, and without this it is difficult to see how one can really talk of a theory of achievement *motivation*.

The concept of expectancy, however, is also important for another reason. It provides an important bridge to other research in social cognition concerned with probabilistic reasoning and judgement under conditions of uncertainty. Interestingly, although Heider argued that a most important function of attributions is to render the subjective environment more predictable, he did not really talk about prediction in probabilistic terms. A number of researchers (e.g. Fischhoff, 1976; Kahneman and Tversky, 1973; Nisbett and Ross, 1980), on the other hand, have set out to explain how people's probabilistic judgements depart from prescriptive models of statistical reasoning. In explaining these departures, an influential concept is that of 'cognitive heuristics'. Broadly speaking, a cognitive heuristic is a device that allows a decision to be made, as it were by a rule of thumb, without full attention being paid to all available evidence. This makes for economical, but sometimes errorful, processing of information.

This research includes some suggestive findings relevent to the relationship between prediction and causal attribution. Ajzen (1977) finds evidence for what he terms a 'causality heuristic', reflected in subjects' predictions being influenced more by information that is causally relevant than by information that is equally informative statistically, but does not fit into a causal schema.

Tversky and Kahneman (1980) draw a similar conclusion, and point to what they call the dominance of 'causal inference' over 'diagnostic inferences'. By a 'causal inference' they refer to an inference of the form 'if X, then Y' where X is seen as the cause of Y. A 'diagnostic inference' of the form 'if X, then Y' is where Y is the cause of X. If X is what is observed, and Y is what is inferred, this means that 'causal inference', in the Tversky and Kahneman sense, refers to *predicting* the effects of given event, whereas 'diagnostic inference' refers to *explaining* why the event occurred – in short, to making attributions. Tversky and Kahneman provide persuasive data to suggest that, when faced with information that can allow either predictive ('causal') or attributional ('diagnostic') inferences, we tend to go for prediction rather than attribution.

ATTRIBUTIONS, LEARNING AND BEHAVIOUR

The distinction between causal (predictive) and diagnostic (attributional) inferences to which Tversky and Kahneman (1980) draw attention may also be viewed more generally as one relating to the temporal sequence of the events about which inferences are made. The diagnostician, the person seeking explanations or assigning responsibility for what has happened, must attempt to go back in time to reconstruct past circumstances. For the predictive decision-maker, however, there is compatibility between the direction of the inference and the temporal sequence of events.

If we are considering real events, and not just abstract problems, this temporal sequence has a simple but fundamental significance. Events provide *feedback* regarding the accuracy of the decision-maker's inferences. If we cast this in the form of the Kelley and Michela (1980) model (figure 1), it is not just that attributions can have behavioural consequences: rather, it is that behaviour itself provides actors with information that may confirm or disconfirm their attributions. In short, behaviour can produce cognitive changes that are as much antecedents as consequences of attributions. The distinction between 'information, beliefs and motivation' on the one hand and 'behaviour, affect and expectancy' on the other becomes harder and harder to draw. Behaviour is a source of information, expectancy is a sub-class of belief, affect is closely intertwined with motivation.

In short, the division that Kelley and Michela (1980) propose between attribution research and attributional research has become less and less helpful and less and less defensible. The attempt to consider social cognition in isolation from behaviour has run its course. By itself, this approach can take us no further. What is required is an integration of theories of social cognition and theories of behaviour. We need to know how cognitive change can lead to behavoural change, and vice versa. A theory of social cognition and decision-making must also ultimately imply a theory of learning.

It is interesting to note the kinds of changes that have in fact taken place in learning theory while the attention of attribution researchers has been directed elsewhere. Traditional theories of learning and conditioning rested on a distinction between Pavlovian or classical conditioning and associative learning on the one hand, and operant conditioning and instrumental learning on the other. Although, of course, the observation of either form of learning requires the occurrence of some form of behavioural change, Pavlovian conditioning is concerned not with the acquisition of *new* responses, but rather with the acquisition of new associations between stimuli. In other words, theories of Pavlovian conditioning relate to how subjects learn about the properties of stimuli. Theories of operant conditioning, on the other hand, relate to how subjects learn about the properties (mainly the consequences) of responses. One way of expressing this division is to refer to it as the distinction between stimulus learning and response learning.

So what do modern theories of stimulus learning and response learning look like? The most striking feature is the prominence of essentially *cognitive* concepts in a field that once sought to avoid terms that had the remotest mentalistic associations. Stimulus learning may be defined, according to this view, as the acquisition of expectancies concerning stimuli, whereas response learning may be defined as the acquisition of expectancies concerning responses (Tarpy, 1982). Probably the most influential work in the development of this approach is that of Rescorla (e.g. 1967), who showed that the strength of the conditioned stimulus – unconditioned stimulus (CS–US) association in Pavlovian conditioning depends on the *predictability* with which the US follows the CS.

The use of cognitive terminology in modern learning theory, however, is not the only or even the most remarkable sign of convergence, or at least of parallelism, between the two research fields. Just as in much research on social cognition there has been a separation between the study of cognitive structures in themselves and the study of behavioural decision-making, so there has often been an attempt to draw the line between stimulus learning and response learning quite sharply. The most recent position, however, is that stimulus and response learning are governed by essentially common principles (Tarpy, 1982), so that there is no fundamental difference between predicting whether one stimulus will follow another, or whether a particular outcome will follow a response. Moreover, the two sorts of learning can combine with one another. A class of experiments termed 'stimulus-response interaction' studies incorporate both Pavlovian and instrumental conditioning procedures (Rescorla and Solomon, 1967). These show broadly that conditioned emotional states (the results of Pavlovian conditioning) can either augment or reduce the level of instrumental responding to stimuli with which such emotional states are associated. There is room for speculation here concerning how emotions and response outcome expectancies might combine in influencing human behaviour in contexts such as achievement motivation (Weiner, et al., 1979) or depression and learned helplessness (Seligman, 1975).

This is not the place, however, to explore the question of how far effects observed in animal learning have parallels in social cognition, or vice versa. Suffice it to say that, at a meta-theoretical level, both social cognition and learning research are at the point where it may be more fruitful to consider how cognitive change and behavioural change interrelate than to consider how they differ from one another.

Perhaps it is no bad thing if we all try to invent the wheel now and again. Learning theorists appear to have 'rediscovered' the concept of predictive inference, and are prepared to consider how animals may think in order to understand how they may behave. Cognitive social psychologists have taken it for granted that people have the capacity to make inferences, but have tended to overlook the functional significance of that capacity for adaptive behaviour. It is for such reasons that a more broadly attributional approach, which looks specifically at the interactions between social cognition and behaviour, is essential to the development of the field. Other chapters in this volume, and particularly the following two concerned specifically with applications, should be regarded in this light.

CONCLUSIONS

Attribution theory has emphasized many of the seemingly more sophisticated, analytical and reflective aspects of our cognitive capacities. This emphasis has often resulted in a relative neglect of the consequences of attributions, and also a tendency to consider attributions in isolation from other cognitive and behavioural processes.

This is regrettable for a number of reasons. First, it sets limits to the practical utility of attribution theory in applied contexts. Second, it sets limits to the conceptual power of the theory itself, by building a model of inferential processing around what may be relatively uncommon types of inference in the context of everyday interaction and information-processing. Third, consideration of affective and emotional states is generally unsatisfactory. Either these are conceived of as sources of bias or, as in Weiner's work, they are treated merely as consequences rather than as an integral part of the attribution process. Fourth, there is no thorough consideration of the temporal context of attributions, and of the way that environment and behaviour provide feedback to the perceiver. Finally, and more generally, the orthodox formulations of attribution theory set limits to the possibility of any conceptual cross-fertilization between different areas of psychology.

10 Attribution Theory and the Health Belief Model

Jennifer King

> When the patient has a prejudice, the doctor must either keep it in countenance or lose his patient. . . . If he gets ahead of the superstitions of his patient he is a ruined man.
>
> George Bernard Shaw, *The Doctor's Dilemma*

INTRODUCTION

Attribution theory and research have been concerned largely with the ways in which people interpret the causes of certain events or behaviours, and it is suggested that these causal attributions play an important role in determining reactions to these events. Despite this fundamental idea, there has been a surprising neglect of the relationship between attributions and behaviour – more specifically, of the functions of certain types of causal attribution for behaviour.

One area in which this relationship is becoming increasingly significant is behaviour related to health and illness, particularly in the realms of coping with serious illness and in preventive actions. This chapter will discuss the existing evidence in this area, in order to illustrate the potential significance of the attribution–behaviour relationship within this particular context of health behaviour. In order to demonstrate this relationship more systematically, however, it needs to be examined within the context of the theories of attribution. The models of Kelley and Weiner have never been applied, as such, to attributions of illness. Thus, a major purpose of the chapter will be to examine these potential applications and to present some preliminary evidence for them.

Most research on health-related behaviour has relied upon a social–psychological approach, known as the Health Belief Model (Becker et al., 1977; Rosenstock, 1966). This is derived from theories of decision-making under uncertainty, and in particular from the value-expectancy approach of Atkinson and Feather (1966). The model includes several specific health beliefs which, it is suggested, govern an individual's decision to undertake certain health-related actions.

Its relevance to the area of attribution theory lies in the issue of the determinants of the health beliefs themselves. It will be proposed that the way in which a person explains or interprets the cause of a particular illness will influence certain beliefs about the illness, which in turn will affect behaviour. Thus, it is suggested that causal attributions play a major role in this model of health behaviour. The major purpose of this chapter is to discuss and illustrate this theoretical synthesis between attribution theory and the Health Belief Model. This integration is seen to have advantages for each theoretical approach. An attributional input to the Health Belief Model is expected to give this model greater predictive power. Conversely, applying attribution theory to the area of health behaviour provides an ideal opportunity both for studying the attribution–behaviour link and for emphasizing the applications of the theory. In particular, the *functions* of attributions for health behaviour can be demonstrated using this approach.

The chapter will begin by discussing the Health Belief Model in greater detail, to illustrate the major aspect of the area of health beliefs and behaviour. The second section will discuss the need for an attributional input. This will be supported by a review of existing evidence in the field of attributions of illness. The third part of the chapter will consider the potential application of the theories of Kelley and Weiner to the prediction of health behaviour, and will discuss how these might be integrated with the Health Belief Model. Some preliminary evidence for this synthesis will then be presented. Finally, the chapter will consider the implications of this approach for both theories, and for medical practice.

THE HEALTH BELIEF MODEL (HBM)

The model postulates that an individual's decision to undertake health-related actions is governed by specific health beliefs: namely, the patient's perceived vulnerability to, and the perceived severity of, a particular illness, and his or her perception of efficacy, costs and benefits involved in the recommended health action. Additional influences may be demographic, social or cultural, and various 'triggers' such as a letter from the doctor or illness in the family (see figure 1). These beliefs, both singly and in combination, have been found to predict a wide variety of preventive behaviours such as attendance at screenings for cancer, tuberculosis and immunizations, and actions to prevent coronary heart disease and unplanned pregnancies (see Becker, 1979, and Rosenstock, 1974, for reviews.) In addition, the HBM has been applied to many types of compliance with both short-and long-term treatments and therapies (Kasl, 1974). In short, the model has been applied to the behaviour of asymptomatic individuals

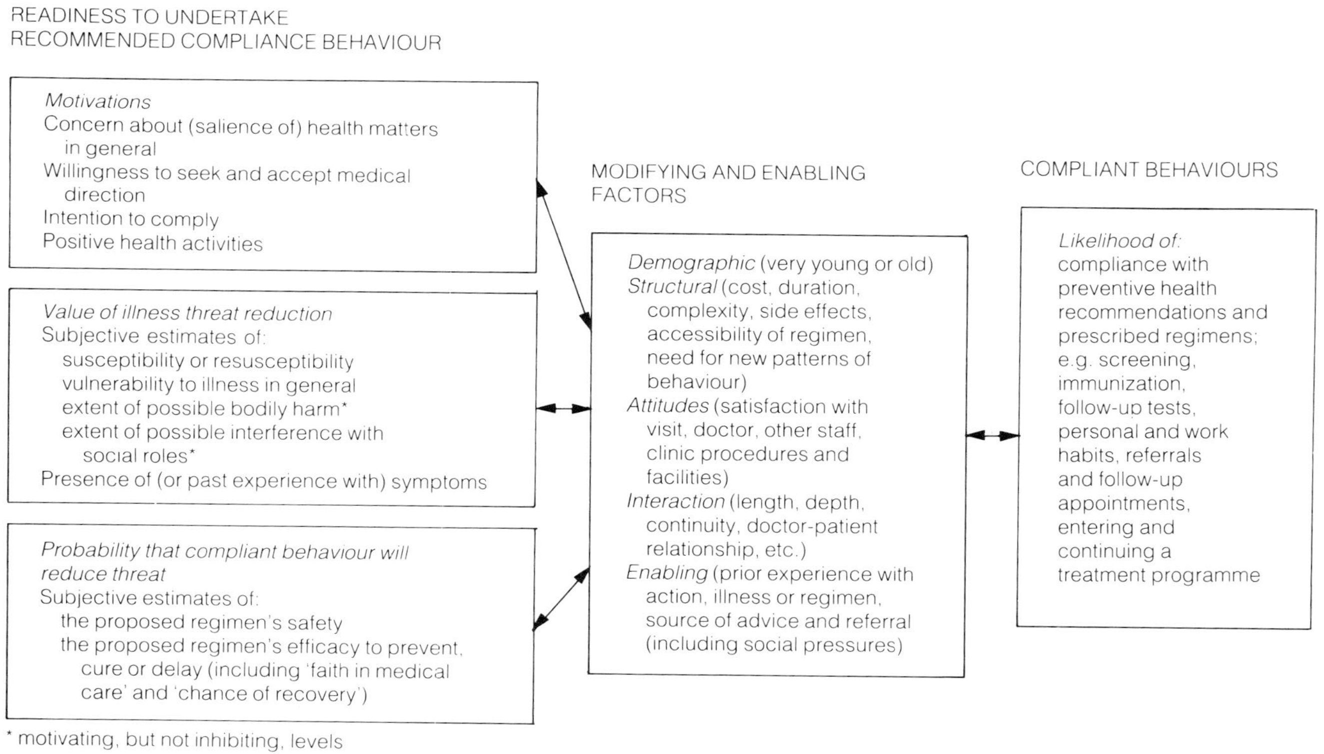

READINESS TO UNDERTAKE
RECOMMENDED COMPLIANCE BEHAVIOUR

Motivations
Concern about (salience of) health matters
   in general
Willingness to seek and accept medical
   direction
Intention to comply
Positive health activities

Value of illness threat reduction
Subjective estimates of:
   susceptibility or resusceptibility
   vulnerability to illness in general
   extent of possible bodily harm*
   extent of possible interference with
      social roles*
Presence of (or past experience with) symptoms

*Probability that compliant behaviour will
reduce threat*
Subjective estimates of:
   the proposed regimen's safety
   the proposed regimen's efficacy to prevent,
   cure or delay (including 'faith in medical
   care' and 'chance of recovery')

* motivating, but not inhibiting, levels

MODIFYING AND ENABLING
FACTORS

Demographic (very young or old)
Structural (cost, duration,
   complexity, side effects,
   accessibility of regimen,
   need for new patterns of
   behaviour)
Attitudes (satisfaction with
   visit, doctor, other staff,
   clinic procedures and
   facilities)
Interaction (length, depth,
   continuity, doctor-patient
   relationship, etc.)
Enabling (prior experience with
   action, illness or regimen,
   source of advice and referral
   (including social pressures)

COMPLIANT BEHAVIOURS

Likelihood of:
   compliance with
   preventive health
   recommendations and
   prescribed regimens;
   e.g. screening,
   immunization,
   follow-up tests,
   personal and work
   habits, referrals
   and follow-up
   appointments,
   entering and
   continuing a
   treatment programme

FIGURE 1 The Health Belief Model: hypothesized model for explaining and predicting health-related behaviour (after Becker et al., 1977)
The arrows indicate the relationships between the blocks of variables, but do not imply influences between one variable and another (e.g. motivations cannot influence demographic factors)

(health behaviour), to the behaviour of people with symptoms (illness behaviour) and to the behaviour of patients already under treatment (sick role behaviour).

The model has succeeded where many previous attempts have failed (Sackett and Haynes, 1976) to explain the widely documented problem of non-compliance (Ley, 1977), by providing a patient-centred approach to health decisions. Its great merit is its emphasis on the cognitive and evaluative response of the individual, rather than relying on socio-demographic characteristics or vague allusions to global attitudes. Nevertheless, this model should not be relied upon exclusively as the only approach to health beliefs and behaviour. The predictive and explanatory power of the model could be much improved by an understanding of the determinants of the beliefs themselves. There is very little evidence from the HBM on how beliefs about risk, for example, are actually acquired or formulated. It is possible that the notion of risk may be determined, in part, by different types of causal explanations about the illness itself. This hypothesis is explored below. In short, the HBM may be describing only one (albeit major) part of the decision-making process underlying health behaviour. Other psychological processes may also contribute, as evidence from other areas of research strongly suggests. The following sections will discuss evidence tending to support the proposal that the HBM would benefit from an attributional extension.

THE FUNCTIONS OF EXPLANATIONS OF ILLNESS

Locus of control

This concept, formulated by Rotter (1966), is an attempt to characterize individuals in terms of the extent to which they feel they can control the outcomes of their behaviour. An 'external locus of control' would imply a fatalistic approach, or the belief that events are controlled by external influences. An 'internal locus of control' corresponds to the belief that events can be influenced by personal behaviour.

This concept has been applied extensively, and with considerable success, to the area of health (Strickland, 1978). Wallston and Wallston (1978), 1981) developed a Health Locus of Control scale which found, for example, that 'externals' were less likely to take a variety of preventive measures than 'internals'. Other evidence (Auerbach et al., 1976) suggests that enhancing patients' feelings of personal control improves their ability to cope with pain after surgery. In addition, the concept of control has been incorporated in several HBM studies. Kirscht and Rosenstock (1977) found, for example, that adherence to anti-hypertensive treatment was greater in patients with a stronger sense of personal control and less dependence on the doctor.

Although locus of control does not on its own predict compliance, it seems to be significant in conjunction with other health beliefs. It is, nevertheless, a somewhat static and global characteristic, representing a generalized form of explanation by the individual. Both theoretically and practically, it would be more interesting to investigate more specific explanations related to illness, in order to predict when certain explanations are made, and how they affect behaviour. The evidence reviewed below suggests that a more appropriate theoretical approach lies in attribution theory.

Attribution, prevention and coping

The developing literature on attributions of illness suggests that the way in which a patient perceives or interprets an illness has a profound effect on the ability to cope with the illness, and on the tendency to take preventive measures. Initially, however, there is a need to distinguish between locus of control and locus of causality – a distinction that is confounded in the traditional scale of expectancies ('I–E') used by Rotter. An individual may believe that an illness is controlled by personal behaviour, but at the same time that the illness is also caused by something external, such as a virus. Conversely, a person with an external locus of control may nevertheless perceive the cause of an illness as internal, such as a heart attack, but may still believe him/herself powerless to prevent a further attack.

Research on causal attributions of illness has been characterized by the operation of perceptual biases which typically arise under conditions of uncertainty or anxiety – as in the case of serious illness. These kinds of attributions are clearly an attempt to gain some control over an inexplicable and distressing event, and in this sense they should not (as is often the case) be thought of as attributional 'errors' but rather as a kind of heuristic with a particular function – that is, coping and control (see Bains, chapter 7 above). The best documented of this type of attribution is 'self-blame', found in cancer victims (Abrams and Finesinger, 1953; Taylor and Levin, 1976), in spinal cord-injured patients (Silver and Wortman, 1980) and in parents of children with severe illness (Chodoff et al., 1964; Gardner, 1969).

There are two conflicting views concerning the functions of self-blame. Some investigators argue that self-blame may be adaptive (cf. Bulman and Wortman, 1977), since successful rehabilitation involved active efforts by the patient. Gardner suggests that this ubiquitous guilt reaction is an attempt to gain control over a calamity, since personal control is strongly implied in the idea, 'It's my fault'. In addition, Chodoff et al. suggest that self-blame represents a search for meaning since it serves the defensive purpose of denying the intolerable conclusion that no one is responsible, and that therefore nothing can be done about an impersonal or meaningless event. This is also consistent with the 'just world hypothesis' (Lerner, 1970; Walster, 1966), which postulates the need to believe that people 'get what they deserve and deserve what they get'.

Other studies suggest that there are situations in which self-blame can be maladaptive (Silver and Wortman, 1980). This was found in the case of parents whose children died from 'cot deaths' or Sudden Infant Death Syndrome (e.g. Stitt, 1971). Since there was no action that the parents could take to alter or improve the situation, their self-blame tended to result in depression and delayed recovery. Similar consequences of self-blame have been suggested in cancer victims, who delay in reporting their symptoms to the doctor as a result (in part) of their feelings of guilt (e.g. Blackwell, 1963). Finally, the tendency to self-blame has also been associated with the 'Type A coronary-prone personality' (e.g. Glass, 1977), characterized in particular by a strong need for control. This results both in self-blame and the denial of coronary symptoms, which can of course have dire consequences.

The relationship between guilt, self-blame and personal responsibility is still not fully understood, although all of them clearly represent internal attributions. Many types of external attributions can also have maladaptive consequences. Clear examples of this can be seen in the use of drugs (Morris and Kanouse, 1979). The decision to medicate may stem initially from the difficulty in distinguishing symptoms of a medical condition from the impact of temporary environmental factors; for example, attributing a stomach ache to overeating rather than influenza, or chest pains to indigestion rather than a heart attack. Such a decision validates the medical nature of the condition. Moreover, from a self-perception or attributional standpoint, taking a drug introduces a new cognition about one's own behaviour, a fact that can later modify inferences about the severity of one's symptoms ('My headache was so bad I had to take three aspirins'). Self-perception theory would suggest that people gauge the severity of the headache in part by the number of aspirins taken (Bem, 1972).

The choice of a drug, rather than a disease, attribution as the cause for a therapy's failure can have important consequences, especially in the case of diseases for which society regards the individual as responsible. People who suffer from obesity or impotence, for example, may suffer extreme self-doubt if drugs that are presumed to be effective are actually inadequate to treat their condition. Morris and Kanouse review this area in depth, and conclude that making erroneous attributions can have serious consequences for drug-taking, such as discontinuing the drug before it has served its purpose, or taking unnecessary medication. They suggest that a fuller understanding of these types of attributional processes would be invaluable for health professionals in enabling patients to use drugs more wisely and effectively. This could be achieved by helping patients to make correct causal assignments to drug, disease and other environmental factors, and thus gain greater control over their health.

The relevance of these attributional processes for certain types of therapy has been recognized increasingly (see Fincham, chapter 11 below). These therapies acknowledge the importance of modifying patients' explanations as well as treating their physical condition. This principle is also extremely important to health education and preventive medicine. The literature discussed above has paid relatively little attention to the significance of attributions to preventive behaviour. The research described later in the chapter addresses this issue and, in the final section, considers the implications of patients' attributions for health education.

Actor–observer differences in health and illness

Another type of attributional phenomenon is known as the 'actor–observer' or the 'divergent perspectives' hypothesis (Jones and Nisbett, 1971; see Farr and Anderson, chapter 3 above). This suggests that an actor's behaviour is attributed by the actor to characteristics of the situation, but is attributed by an observer to the disposition of the actor. Eiser and colleagues have neatly applied this to explanations of smoking (Eiser et al., 1978). Their data suggested that smokers (actors) made more situational attributions for their smoking, such as the pleasure derived from the cigarette, whereas non-smokers (observers) made more dispositional attributions for the smoking habit. Similarly, Rodin (1978) points to the relevance of these 'divergent perspectives' in the context of doctor–patient communication. The doctor attributes the patient's failure to follow the prescribed treatment to 'laziness' in the patient, whereas the patient explains this non-compliance in terms of external causes such as the nauseous side-effects of the drug.

The actor–observer difference hypothesis was not confirmed, however, when applied to attributions of alcoholism (McHugh et al., 1979). The prediction that non-alcoholics (observers) would make more dispositional attributions for alcoholism than alcoholics (actors) was not supported. In summary, McHugh found that alcoholics appeared to accept a large amount of personal responsibility for their drinking problem, indicating the same phenomenon of self-blame that was found in cancer patients. This conforms to findings of other studies of uncontrollable life-events which suggest that people exaggerate their ability to control such outcomes and that even innocent victims have been shown to suffer great guilt (Wortman, 1976).

There is now considerable evidence to suggest that specific causal explanations have a powerful impact on various aspects of behaviour related to both health and illness, as well as on different types of therapy, and on the doctor–patient relationship. In particular, such research draws attention to the functional role of attribution processes in coping with and treating illness, and in attempts to gain some control over it. This might suggest, therefore, that causal attributions also have a functional relationship with health beliefs (such as those described in the Health Belief Model), as well as with actual behaviour. The relationship of causal explanations to the Health Belief Model has never been explicitly examined in this context, although several investigators have acknowledged the potential significance of such explanations (Kasl, 1974; Lindsay-Reid and Osborn, 1980). Kasl suggests that an important omission from the HBM, especially in its application to the sick role, is its failure to take into account the patient's 'social representation' (see Moscovici and Hewstone, chapter 6 above) of the illness, a concept that receives detailed attention in an investigation by Herzlich (1973). This study has, however, been criticized by Farr (1977), who suggests that replies to the questions concerning the causes of illness resulted from an attributional artefact known as the 'fundamental attribution error' (cf. Ross, 1977), namely that favourable outcomes (i.e. health) tend to be attributed to the self, and unfavourable outcomes (i.e. illness) to the environment.

Apart from the now-apparent functional role of attributions in relation to illness, there are some sound theoretical reasons for incorporating causal attribution processes systematically within the HBM framework. These reasons relate to both the HBM and attribution theory. With regard to the HBM, the most outstanding question that remains concerns the determinants of the elements of the model – in particular, of perceived risk or vulnerability. A discussion of how attribution theory might contribute to this issue follows below. With regard to attribution theory itself, such a synthesis with the HBM could potentially achieve at least three things. First, it would enable investigation of the much-neglected relationship between attributions and behaviour. Second, it might enable some application of the theories of attribution to a practical field such as the study of health behaviour. Third, this application would, in turn, emphasize and enable empirical testing of the functional significance of illness attributions for decisions related to health.

The way in which this synthesis of attribution theory and the HBM might be achieved is, first, to consider in some detail the basic principles of attribution theory and their potential correspondence with the area of health behaviour. Previous approaches to explanations of health and illness have been based mainly upon particular attributional phenomena, rather than upon the more fundamental *models* of attribution. The two attribution approaches to be considered and applied to this context are those of Kelley (1967), which deals with the 'determinants' of explanations, and Weiner (1979), whose model categorizes different types of explanations. Using this distinction, some relationships between these two models can be drawn. At the same time, each can be related to the HBM.

Kelley's model of attribution

Kelley suggested that three types of information combine in certain ways to form attributions in terms of the person, the stimulus or the circumstances. 'Consensus' information concerns the degree to which other people behave similarly in the same situation. 'Consistency' information concerns the degree to which an individual has behaved similarly in similar situations in the past. 'Distinctiveness' information concerns the degree to which an individual responds similarly to other kinds of situations. Specific combinations of these variables determine whether an attribution is made to the person, the stimulus or the circumstance (or any combination of these three). Certain correspondences might be postulated with regard to illness, such that consensus represents the 'commonness' of an illness, consistency represents the frequency of occurrence of an illness (chronic, temporary or recurrent) and distinctiveness represents the number of possible causes of an illness (one distinctive cause or several causes).

It seems likely that particular causal explanations of an illness may govern, or at least be related to, certain health beliefs concerning that illness, in particular to perceived vulnerability. Research by Tversky and Kahneman (e.g., 1974) suggests that, in estimating the probability that an event will occur, people largely ignore base-rate or consensus information, in favour of simplified 'heuristics' or biases (cf. Nisbett and Borgida, 1975; Slovic et al., 1979). In addition, concrete information has been found to affect estimates of risk, and predictions, more strongly than abstract statistical information (Nisbett et al., 1976). De Carufel et al. (1981) applied these findings to the study of attitudes to breast self-examination (a measure for detecting breast cancer), and found each type of information to be at least equal in importance. Similarly, in a study of smoking during pregnancy, King and Eiser (1981) found that mothers' decisions to reduce or continue smoking were strongly affected by concrete examples of their own children (or their friends') rather than statistical information (e.g. 'I smoked all through my other pregnancies and my babies were all right').

Related to this are the arguments of Lalljee (1981) and Hewstone and Jaspars (1983a), who point out that consensus information in everyday attributions rarely refers to all, or even most, other people in general, but rather to specific sub-samples of the population. The issue of consensus, prediction and attribution is reviewed in detail by Kassin (1979). The present approach, however, suggests that consensus information, in relation to the commonness of an illness, is only one part of the information governing the prediction or perceived risk that an illness will occur. It is proposed that the concept of 'risk' may be differentiated into three aspects, whereby the probability that an illness may occur is estimated according to how common it is (consensus); how often it has occurred in the past (consistency), and whether it has one or several causes (distinctiveness).

Weiner's model of attribution

The set of attributional principles proposed by Weiner and colleagues was originally developed in the context of achievement motivation (Weiner et al., 1972). Explanations of success and failure were found to be based on four factors: ability, effort, task difficulty and luck. These factors vary along three dimensions: stability, internality and control. Thus, according to Weiner, ability is a stable, internal and uncontrollable factor; effort is unstable, internal and controllable; whereas task difficulty is external, stable and uncontrollable; and luck is external, unstable and uncontrollable. Certain correspondences with attributions of health and illness might be postulated. 'Ability', being internal and stable, might be equated with genetic or metabolic factors. 'Effort' might correspond with personal health behaviour. 'Task difficulty' is equivalent to difficulties and stress from a job or from home, for example. 'Luck' represents a fatalistic attribution of illness, or possibly a religious attribution (external and unstable).

There are other possible ways in which attribution might influence health beliefs: for example, the overall perception of threat (the combination of susceptibility and severity) may be affected by explanations in terms of Weiner's categories. Thus, for example, the perceived threat of an illness may be greater if that illness were attributed to an unstable, external and uncontrollable cause such as an accident, a virus or even 'bad luck'. These attributions might thereby indirectly affect behaviour, via the health beliefs, or in some cases might have a direct influence on behaviour. A commonly heard statement from patients is 'If I knew what caused it I'd be able to do something about it.'

The relationship between Kelley's and Weiner's theories of attribution

It has so far been suggested that explanations of illness may be based on two types of attributions, as outlined in separate theoretical statements. It may be said that Weiner's categories of explanations are affected by Kelley's three types of information – however, these two types of attributions are not independent of one another. When trying to understand attributions of illness, therefore, the model would be more comprehensive if these two 'strands' of attribution theory could be interwoven. Kelley suggests that it is the different combinations or patterns of consensus, consistency and distinctiveness information that lead to a person, stimulus or circumstance attribution. The results from a study by Frieze and Weiner (1971) implied that the same information that determines Kelley's system of attributions also affects Weiner's categories of explanation. Thus, person attributions were functionally equivalent to an ability explanation, stimulus attributions to task difficulty, person–situation attributions to effort, and circumstance attributions to luck. The proposed connection between Kelley and Weiner can be represented in terms of illness attributions, as in figure 2.

Kelley (Information)	Kelley (Attributions)	Weiner (Attributions)	'Natural' explanations of illness
CS D CY →	Stimulus (S)	= Task difficulty (external, stable uncontrollable)	= Stress from family, job
$\overline{CS}$ $\overline{D}$ CY →	Person (P)	= Ability (internal, stable, uncontrollable)	= Personality, heredity, metabolism
CS $\overline{D}$ $\overline{CY}$ →	Circumstance (C)	= Luck (external, unstable. uncontrollable)	= Chance, luck
$\overline{CS}$ D $\overline{CY}$ →	S × P	= Effort (internal, unstable, controllable)	= Moods, habits, states

$\overline{CS}$, $\overline{CY}$, $\overline{D}$ denote low consensus, consistency, distinctiveness

FIGURE 2 Summary of relationships between attributional models and 'natural' explanations of illness

Developing an 'Attribution–Health Belief Model'

These models of Kelley and Weiner can be related to health beliefs and behaviour in the following way, on the basis of the discussion so far. *Information* from Kelley's model is expected to influence both *explanations* and *health beliefs*. These variables in turn, it is suggested, combine to predict behaviour. These relationships can be formulated in terms of a model, shown in figure 3.

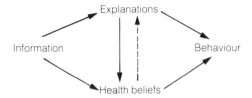

FIGURE 3 Model indicating proposed relationships between attributions, health beliefs and behaviour

The empirical studies below attempt to examine the following relationships from the model:

(1)   information (consensus, etc.) and health beliefs;
(2)   explanations and health beliefs;
(3)   explanations, health beliefs and behaviour.

RECENT EMPIRICAL STUDIES

Explanations of heart disease – their effects on health beliefs and compliance

This study examines issues (2) and (3) above. Eighty-three heart patients suffering various forms of heart disease were given questionnaires examining their individual health beliefs about their condition (using HBM variables). These included perceived risk of recurring heart trouble, perceived severity of (degree of concern over) their condition, satisfaction with treatment, and difficulties in keeping to the advice from the doctor. In addition, patients were asked to give their own causal explanations of their condition, referred to as 'natural' explanations (as distinct from theoretical categories). These included 'stress', 'poor diet', 'heredity' and 'bad luck'. The aim of the study was to examine the effect of both health beliefs and explanations on reported compliance with medical advice. The model in figure 3 would predict that compliance should be a function of a combination of health beliefs and explanations, and that the health beliefs themselves would be influenced (at least in part) by causal explanations.

The most striking findings concerned the patients' causal explanations, both at a descriptive level and in terms of their effect on various health beliefs. Most commonly cited causes of heart disease were those related to stress, worry and tension or to rheumatic fever in childhood. Other medically accepted causes of heart disease such as smoking, overeating and lack of exercise were cited considerably less frequently. This finding clearly lends itself to an interpretation in terms of 'defensive attribution' (Walster, 1966) or, perhaps more specifically, a tendency to attribute the condition to an external and uncontrollable factor such as smoking. This has the effect of absolving the patients of personal responsibility for the illness, representing a form of 'self-serving bias' (Miller and Ross, 1975).

Most significant was the effect that certain causal explanations had on health beliefs – in particular, on perceptions of risk. When these explanations were entered into a multiple regression analysis, and regressed on perceived risk, four explanations accounted for most of the variance. Thus, patients who believed their heart trouble was more likely to occur attributed their condition to 'stress from family illness', 'congenital factors', 'a sudden change of lifestyle' and 'bad luck'. The remaining variables, all from the HBM itself, had no significant effect on the degree of perceived risk. This suggests, in summary, that patients' estimates of their susceptibility to further heart trouble are governed not by beliefs about the severity of the condition, or even about the treatment received, but primarily by the interpretation of the *cause* of the illness.

Other health beliefs were also influenced by causal explanations – although generally in combination with other HBM variables. Perceived severity was particularly well predicted by such a combination, which accounted for 53 per cent of the variance in this belief. Thus, patients were more likely to perceive their heart condition as serious if they found greater difficulties in following their treatment, and if they attributed their illness to 'overweight', 'a sudden change of lifestyle', 'tension', 'smoking' and the 'will of God'. Similar explanations were also found to be associated with satisfaction with treatment.

This type of investigation demonstrates the value of using patients' 'natural explanations' in relation to health beliefs and behaviour, rather than imposing a rigid theoretical classification (such as Weiner's) upon the explanations offered. The significant focus of interest is the way the patients themselves interpret their illness – therefore, using these natural categories would seem to be more appropriate, as patients may not actually perceive the causes in Weiner's terms. This is not to deny, however, that Weiner's system can be used to classify their explanations of illness. But whether or not these categories accurately reflect the patients' interpretations is another issue and deserves investigation, especially in cases where explanations are ambiguous and could be regarded as either internal or external, such as stress or smoking.

Explanations of high blood pressure: predicting attendance at screening

This study (King, 1982) examined the health beliefs and causal attributions that predispose patients to attend a screening for high blood pressure (HBP), in response to a request from their doctor. In order to show that attributions may *predict* health behaviour, a prospective design was used, such that data were obtained before patients had actually attended the screening.

Questionnaires included three main categories derived from the proposed model in figure 3:

(1)   *information* – measures of consensus (commonness), consistency (chronicity) and distinctiveness (causal generality) of HBP;

(2)   *explanations* – 'natural' explanations of HBP and theoretical dimensions of locus, stability and control;

(3)   *health beliefs* – from the Health Belief Model.

A discriminant analysis revealed seven characteristics that clearly distinguished between attenders and non-attenders. These were (in order of importance):

intention to be screened;
lack of control over health;
situational attribution of HBP;
barriers to screening;
controllability of cause of HBP;
benefits of screening;
efficacy of screening (in reducing susceptibility to HBP);
consensus (commonness of HBP).

Attenders expressed stronger beliefs in all these factors. The discrimination was highly significant, and 83 per cent of cases could be correctly predicted to be either attenders or non-attenders, simply on the basis of their health beliefs and explanations. Most of the variance in attendance was accounted for by intention. This would be predicted by attitude theory (Fishbein and Ajzen, 1972). When intention was excluded from the analysis, however, these variables were shown to have a direct effect on behaviour. An additional discriminating factor to emerge was perceived risk. This suggests that people do not always act in line with what they say they will do, and will evidently attend the screening only if they possess certain specific beliefs and explanations – in particular, perceived risk of HBP, lack of control over health, attribution of HBP to a situational cause, commonness of HBP, and benefits of the screening.

Particularly significant is the role of attributional variables in the prediction of attendance – these clearly emerged in both analyses. In order to illustrate even more strongly their contribution to behaviour, a third discriminant analysis identified attenders and non-attenders from their 'natural' explanations for HBP. These included, simply, 15 causes (such as 'stress' and 'smoking'), generated by patients themselves. Six of these explanations were able to discriminate clearly between the two groups. Attenders were more likely to attribute HBP to 'stress' and 'worry', while non-attenders tended to cite 'too much exercise', 'lack of vitamins' and 'bad luck' – suggesting a more fatalistic view. These explanations were able correctly to predict a total of 73 per cent of cases.

In summary, these findings clearly demonstrate that attributions directly affect health behaviour; the prospective design shows that they are not simply *post hoc* justifications, but actual *predictors* of attendance at screening. The study further emphasizes the value of using patients' 'natural explanations' as well as the theoretical dimensions of attribution.

CONCLUSIONS AND IMPLICATIONS

The central focus of this chapter has been the relationship between attributions and health behaviour. It was suggested that such behaviour was influenced not only by health beliefs, as the traditional Health Belief Model would suggest, but also by causal explanations of a particular illness. In addition, it was suggested that these explanations affect health beliefs themselves. These proposals were formulated in terms of a model and tested in two empirical studies. Each of these has provided substantial support for the contribution of causal attributions to two types of health behaviour: compliance and preventive actions. The influence of explanations was mainly on health beliefs, thus indirectly contributing to behaviour. In the second study, attributions were shown, in several forms, to have a direct and predictive influence on behaviour. The application of attribution theory to the context of health has thus provided an ideal opportunity to examine the neglected attribution–behaviour relationship.

Previous research reviewed above suggested that attributions were functional in coping with serious illness. The evidence in this chapter has shown that attributions are functional also in preventive health behaviour. This earlier literature, moreover, did not systematically apply the original attributional models to the study of health behaviour. This chapter has demonstrated the plausibility of applying these models to this area, emphasizing the value of practical applications of attribution theory. Conversely, this attributional input has improved the predictive scope of the Health Belief Model and allowed some departure from this rather unitary approach to health behaviour.

Implications for medical practice

Attribution research has sometimes been criticized for failing to study attributions in their natural or social context (e.g. Semin, 1980). This criticism is patently unfounded, as demonstrated in this chapter. In view of the increasing evidence for the role of attributions in the clinical context, several implications arise for medical practice and health education. Evidently patients' explanations are often highly significant to the way they cope with an illness, to their decision to comply with medical advice or to take certain preventive health measures. These explanations could be an extremely valuable diagnostic and therapeutic tool for a medical practitioner. They may be sensitive indicators of the way a patient is interpreting and coping with an illness and of what he/she intends to do about the problem. Thus, explanations have an important function not only for the patient, but also for the doctor. Difficulty may arise in actually eliciting attributions from a patient. This problem might be resolved by asking patients what they think they 'have', before asking what they think *caused* the illness. As Stoeckle and Barsky (1980) point out, 'An illness attribution refers both to the cognitive processes by which an individual arrives at an explanatory belief and also to the explanation itself' (p. 224). The therapeutic process could therefore be greatly enhanced by such an approach. Stimson and Webb (1975) suggested that the consultation should be a 'negotiation' between doctor and patient, whereby the views of each are shared and a diagnosis is reached that is acceptable to both parties. Taking account of the patient's illness attributions would be an important step in achieving this negotiation.

Health educators, too, could benefit from understanding why certain populations attend (or fail to attend) a preventive screening. In their efforts to persuade people to take such measures, they evidently need to impress upon them not only their personal vulnerability to the illness, and the benefits of the screening, but also the *causes* of the illness. The evidence in this chapter suggests that certain explanations predispose people to attend while others do not. If attendance is to be encouraged, certain explanations may need to be altered – particularly attributions to 'bad luck'.

Summary

The application of attribution theory to health behaviour is evidently an area for further research, both from a theoretical and practical viewpoint. Research is pointing increasingly to the functions of illness attributions for a range of coping, compliance and preventive behaviours. Future research should be directed towards the contribution of attributions to other health behaviours such as smoking, weight reduction or adherence to long-term therapies. The potential of an attributional approach to the areas of health behaviour is clearly summarized by Stoeckle and Barsky (1980): 'Attributions are . . . an important vantage point from which to study doctor–patient communication and interaction, patient adherence to medical regimens, and the implicit, covert cognitive processes occurring in physicians when they explain illness to patients' (p. 236).

ACKNOWLEDGEMENTS

I would like to thank Jos Jaspars for supervising the studies described in this chapter; Miles Hewstone for his constructive editorial comments; Professor Peter Sleight and colleagues at the John Radcliffe Hospital, Oxford and Dr Peter Tate and staff at the Marcham Road Health Centre, Abingdon, for their cooperation with this research. This chapter is based on a doctoral research programme which was funded by the Health Education Council, UK.

11 Clinical Applications of Attribution Theory: Problems and Prospects

Frank D. Fincham

INTRODUCTION

Since the inception of experimental social psychology there have been attempts to apply social psychological principles in clinical psychology (Strong, 1978). Recently, the interchange between the two fields became more apparent as attribution theory began to dominate the social psychological literature (see Kelley and Michela, 1980). This is due in part to the mandate of attribution theory to study common-sense or 'naive' psychology (Heider, 1958), the malfunction of which represents the clinician's domain. It is also partly attributable to the concurrent rise of behavioural therapies, which firmly established an empirical tradition and a greater openness to general psychological principles in clinical psychology. Consequently, during the late 1960s and early 1970s a flurry of papers appeared bearing such promising titles as 'Toward an attribution therapy' (Ross et al., 1969) or 'Attribution processes in the development and treatment of emotional disorders' (Valins and Nisbett, 1971).

The marriage between attribution theory and clinical psychology appears to have been celebrated. This chapter addresses the question of its consummation. In the first section attribution research claiming to be relevant to clinical problems is critically evaluated. The lacunae in this literature serve as a springboard for the extensions proposed in the next section. These focus on problems in close relationships such as marriage. Finally, some fundamental issues in the application of attribution concepts are discussed.

ATTRIBUTION RESEARCH CLAIMING CLINICAL RELEVANCE

A great deal of the attribution research that is considered to be clinically relevant derives from Schachter's (1964) argument that emotion is the product of physiological arousal and the cognition of its source. The basis for this viewpoint is a classic study in which subjects injected with epinephrine exhibited emotional behaviour consistent with the situational cues available for labelling their state of arousal (Schachter and Singer, 1962). Schachter consequently states his theory in terms of cognitive labelling but it is routinely inferred that subjects causally attributed their arousal to a relevant source which then led them to apply a cognitive label to themselves. The internal–external distinction is basic to his theory and has been a defining characteristic of the resultant attribution research. Indeed, it can be used to organize the literature. Roughly, there have been two foci: attempts to change attributions for current maladaptive behaviour from internal to external ones, and attempts to alter external attributions for adaptive behaviour change to internal attributions.

In turning to this literature, no attempt will be made to provide an exhaustive review[1] (see Abramson, 1983; Forsterling, 1980; Frieze et al., 1979; Kopel and Arkowitz, 1975; Strong, 1978; Weiner, 1979; Zillman, 1978). Rather, the nature of research conducted thus far is considered by examining the conceptual foundations of prototypic studies. The critical appraisal that is offered highlights the shortcomings of this research and provides a much needed balance to the claims made for the role of attribution theory in clinical work. It is my firm belief that recognizing the limitations of attribution theory in the clinic will serve ultimately to strengthen its role. The intention therefore is to dwell on weakness not as an end in itself but rather as a means to emphasize the *legitimate* contribution of attribution theory to clinical psychology.

Attributions and current behaviour

A critical, clinically relevant development occurred when Schachter's framework was used to examine the reduction of naturally occurring emotional arousal. Nisbett and Schachter (1966), in a study that became the prototype of later experiments, showed that, when subjects attributed their natural fear of an anticipated electric shock to a neutral stimulus (a pill), they perceived shocks to be less painful and also increased their pain thresholds. However, the effect was found only for subjects in a low-fear condition and not for high fear. This basic mis-attribution or re-attribution phenomenon has been found in several laboratory studies (e.g., Brodt and Zimbardo, 1981; Calvert-Boyanowsky and Leventhal, 1975; Dienstbier, 1972; Rodin, 1975; Ross et al., 1969).

The potential clinical application of this research was soon noted. For example, it was suggested that acrophobia (a fear of heights) might be treated by telling clients that their symptoms are 'a common physiological consequence of the optical effects of viewing converging vertical lines' (Ross et al., 1969, p. 288). The research that followed on naturally occurring behaviours can be traced to an influential, early study. Storms and Nisbett (1970) provided insomniacs with a placebo pill which was described as either a sedative or an arousing drug. Those in the latter group reported a reduction in the time they needed to fall asleep whereas the former group experienced an increase in time taken to fall asleep. The explanation offered for these results is simple and consistent with the mis-attribution work outlined above. It was suggested that arousal pill subjects attributed the normal symptoms associated with insomnia to the drug and hence were able to fall asleep faster. In contrast, the sedative pill subjects continued to experience their pre-sleep arousal in spite of the pill, which might lead them to believe that their condition was more critical than they had previously thought (see King, chapter 10 above). However, it is seldom noted that, despite the above behavioural differences in falling asleep, subjects did not differ in the degree to which they subjectively experienced insomnia on experimental nights. Subsequent failures to replicate this effect for insomnia (Bootzin et al., 1976; Kellogg and Baron, 1975) and public speaking anxiety (Singerman et al., 1976) compound the interpretation of the above data. Despite further analysis of the process involved (Storms et al., 1979) and a successful replication of the original finding (Lowery et al., 1979), the status of these data is questionable, as the use of a self-report measure that requires subjects to be conscious of when they become unconscious remains an enigma.

Critique

A curious feature of the above research is its continued interpretation in terms of mis-attribution despite the absence of attempts to assess the causal attributions of subjects. Where manipulation checks have been included they have generally shown that the manipulation failed (e.g., Calvert-Boyanowsky and Leventhal, 1975; Singerman et al., 1976). Indeed, even in Nisbett and Schachter's (1966) original study, post-experimental questionnaire data showed only a 50 per cent success rate in manipulating causal attributions. A possible alternative interpretation for the phenomenon is that knowledge of ensuing arousal given to subjects in the mis-attribution condition allows them to predict their experiences (see S. M. Miller, 1981; Rodin, 1975) and hence behave differently. This more parsimonious explanation is consistent with Heider's view that causal analysis is undertaken precisely to increase predictability and control (see Bains, chapter 7 above). Clearly, the fundamental assumptions made in mis-attribution research require examination.

The fact that basic assumptions in this area have not been questioned attests to the compelling intuitive appeal of simple attributional hypotheses in the application of attribution theory to clinical problems. Their uncritical acceptance has resulted in inadequate conceptual analysis, as it is apparent that no real attempt has been made to consider the mis-attribution phenomenon in terms of classic attribution theory (e.g., Heider, 1958; Kelley, 1967, 1972). The current review therefore evaluates the implications of attribution theory for clinical problems in terms of these basic writings.

Consider the laboratory mis-attribution paradigm. The subject is aroused and an attempt is made to have him/her attribute the cause of the arousal to a neutral source. The arousal occurs in an unusual situation (e.g., threat of shock), which precludes the application of previously acquired covariation information. A single instance of arousal takes place and hence causal schemata are presumably operative. Causal schemata are assumed patterns of data in Kelley's (1967) covariation (ANOVA) model of causal attribution and are used when complete covariation data are missing. Hence under natural conditions mis-attribution is likely to occur only in novel situations or where the source of the arousal is ambiguous (e.g., a drug unknown to the person). Recalling the operating principles of causal schemata (see Hewstone, chapter 1 above) indicates further limitations of mis-attribution research. The mis-attribution effect relies on the operation of the discounting principle, and thus a *plausible* neutral source needs to be offered as a cause of the arousal. Previous research becomes intelligible when interpreted in terms of the above caveats. For example, as the effect of the discounting is to lead to causal ambiguity, one would expect attribution to the neutral stimulus to occur at the level of chance. This is consistent with the data obtained when manipulation checks are used (e.g. Nisbett and Schachter, 1966). In a similar vein, the fact that no mis-attribution effect was found for subjects in the high-fear condition of Nisbett and Schachter's (1966) experiment makes considerable sense. These subjects knew how they felt based on past experience with fear, and most likely rejected anticipated shock as a plausible cause of their feeling.

Clinically, the above argument is critical. In therapy one deals with more intense emotional behaviour, and the above finding regarding degree of emotionality appears to be robust (see Marshal and Zimbardo, 1979; Schachter and Singer, 1979). Such data are hardly surprising when viewed in attributional terms. Persons with real fears or phobias usually have historical information available to them. Hence single instances of contradictory information are most likely discredited. Attempts to change attributions in therapy should therefore take into account the 'consistency' information available to the client. Indeed, all three dimensions in the ANOVA model need to be addressed, as it is the pattern of data on these dimensions that determines the client's causal attribution. It is the failure to do this in conjunction with an insensitivity to the severity of the problem behaviours studied that probably accounts for the inconsistent results obtained to date.

Given the role of deception in much of the research, its inconsistent findings and the exclusive reliance on self-diagnosed, college student subjects, one may legitimately ask whether it has any clinical implications. The above analysis suggests the conditions under which it does: namely, the presence of novel symptoms for which there is a plausible non-arousing cause. Infrequent events (no consistency information), which do not fit into a more parsimonious conditioning paradigm, are particularly relevant. For example, difficulties in adapting to a new culture, new job and so on may give rise to damaging self-attributions when the external sources of the difficulties are underplayed. Similarly, having the client reattribute the symptom to another cause may be appropriate when a symptom occurs that the client finds embarrassing (lack of consensus information) and therefore does not socially validate (e.g., an erectile failure/inorgasmia; emotional lability experienced as inability to cope with aphasia). Therapy groups where the client gains normative information regarding the symptom are valuable for this reason (e.g., that persons with healthy sex lives can experience occasional erectile failure/inorgasmia; that emotional lability is commonly experienced by aphasics). However, the therapist as expert and representative of society can fulfil the same role, especially when the behaviour is bizarre to the client (see Valins and Nisbett, 1971; Johnson et al., 1977 for case studies).

Three further caveats need to be remembered in applying the research considered thus far. First, reattribution should not be considered when the symptom results from a skill deficit which in turn generates the data used to make the causal attributions. Instead, the deficit should be remediated. Second, the new source of the symptom should be plausible and its plausibility should not be based on deception. Third, the new attribution should not be contingent on the continued presence of the alternative cause. This deals with the maintenance of behaviour change, which is now addressed.

Causal attribution and behaviour change

Kopel and Arkowitz (1975, p. 207) have argued that the major clinical implication of attribution research involves inducing cognitions that 'will facilitate the maintenance and generalization of behaviour change'.

Maintenance and generalization are fundamental issues in behaviour therapy (cf. Stokes and Baer, 1977), yet surprisingly few studies examine the role of cognitions in these processes. None the less, it is widely believed that self-attributed changes are more durable than those attributed to external variables. Two studies are routinely cited to support the claim, and they have even been used to justify therapeutic strategies (S. Brehm, 1976).

Davison and Valins (1969) measured subjects' tolerance of shock and then gave them a drug compound (placebo) that would decrease skin sensitivity and thereby increase shock tolerance. A second series of shocks was then administered but the intensity of the shock was actually halved. Hence subjects observed themselves apparently tolerating more shocks. Following this trial, half the subjects were told they had received a placebo, thus implying that they, and not the drug, were responsible for the change. During a third trial conducted under the guise of a different experiment, these subjects tolerated more shocks than those who thought that their previous behaviour had been drug-induced. The major problem with this study is that the authors produced 'maintenance' by affecting subjects' beliefs and not their actual prior behaviour. Moreover, the clinical significance of the experiment is open to question.

In a more clinically oriented study, Davison et al. (1973) treated self-referred insomniacs using a combination of drug and relaxation techniques. After one week half the subjects were told that they had received a minimum dosage of the drug (self-attribution) and the remainder were informed that they had received an optimal dosage (drug attribution). As predicted, the time taken to fall asleep was higher in the latter group following the intervention. Criticisms of this study include the fact that the maintenance phase was only four days long and that attributions were never directly measured (see Grimm, 1980, for a further critique).

Recently, Colletti and Kopel (1979, p. 616) claim to have done 'the first applied research study' that shows an association between self-attribution and long-term behaviour change. They found a significant correlation ($r = 0.38$) between reduced cigarette smoking one year after a treatment programme and the degree to which subjects felt the reduction was due to changed attitudes. Unfortunately, their data do not speak to the primacy of attributions versus behaviour change, as they did not attempt any causal statistical analysis.

The above critique is not intended to deny the importance of this line of inquiry. On the contrary, an attributional conception of therapy emphasizes its importance – a persistent symptom occurs in the absence of therapy and then disappears with therapy. Applying the covariation principle to this minimal information suggests that the symptom should again be present following the termination of therapy. Hence, from an attributional perspective the very fact of successful therapeutic intervention mitigates against maintenance of behaviour change, and this issue therefore demands attention.

Recent developments

Thus far the focus has been on more traditional attempts to make attribution theory clinically relevant. It was motivated in part by the absence of a critical and integrative evaluation of this frequently cited work and in part by the desire to give the reader some historical perspective regarding the application of attribution theory to clinical psychology. However, the potential contribution of attributionally oriented research lies not only in a more thorough and systematic continuation of these beginnings but also in several new, exciting developments.

Recently attempts have been made to apply attribution theory to such problems as loneliness (Peplau et al., 1979), addiction (Eiser, 1982), severe physical incapacitation (Bulman and Wortman, 1977), the exacerbation of emotional behaviour (Storms and McCaul, 1976), self-esteem (Ickes and Layden, 1978) and community mental health (Strickland and Janoff-Bulman, 1980; Sue and Nolan, 1980). Space limitations preclude examination of these newer developments, and their omission is partly justified by the fact that they have not yet led to a systematic body of empirical research. However, the attributional reformulation of the learned helplessness model of depression (Abramson et al., 1978) is one recent development that has already had a marked impact on the field. Consideration of this growing literature is also beyond the scope of the present chapter (see Abramson and Martin, 1981; Beach et al., 1982), but this new application none the less needs to be addressed briefly.

The learned helplessness model posits that the symptoms of depression result from a lack of perceived contingency between one's actions and outcomes related to those actions. That is, events are experienced as uncontrollable. According to the attributional reformulation of learned helplessness, it is really the attributions made along specific causal dimensions that mediate the symptoms of depression. The internal–external dimension relates to self-esteem deficits in depression; the global–specific dimension to the generality of the symptoms; and the stable–unstable dimension affects their chronicity (see Wortman and Dintzer, 1978, for a critique of the model). Even though no attempt has been made to link these dimensions to Kelley's (1967) criteria of consensus, distinctiveness and consistency, they are very similar if not identical. The reformulation therefore reflects classic attribution notions more closely than other clinically applied work to date. Consequently, it speaks to ·several of the criticisms raised in relation to previous research, but at the same time it suffers the same deficiencies as the covariation model.

The reformulation, like the ANOVA cube, tends to be interpreted in terms of main effects and thus violates Kelley's original notions (see Jaspars, chapter 2 above). However, some attention has been paid to how attributions along the dimensions of the model covary in depression (Metalsky and Abramson, 1980; Seligman et al., 1979). This elaboration of the notion of attributional style (see Ickes and Layden, 1978) is note-worthy. First, the possibility that people make particular kinds of causal inferences across situations and time implies that they tend to use consis-tently certain kinds of similar information. This highlights the importance of prior causal beliefs that individuals bring to the task of making causal inferences. In the clinical context this is especially important, as empha-sized in the preceding review. The potentially useful interchange between basic and applied research in this area is apparent. Second, causal beliefs may arise from many sources, but one of the most important is prior experience. Hence a possible link between covariation and schema models of attribution may be forged. The client with his/her causal theory regard-ing the symptom forces the clinician to address this link.

Thus far, only implications derived from existing clinical applications of attribution theory have been considered. The lacunae in clinical attribution research also carry implications for future study. Most studies to date have dealt almost exclusively with individual or intrapersonal problems. The interpersonal field, where the problem entails two or more people, com-prises an important extension in the application of attribution theory to clinical problems.

EXTENDING APPLICATIONS OF ATTRIBUTION THEORY TO INTERPERSONAL PROBLEMS

The study of attribution at the interpersonal level has been an integral part of attribution research. One might therefore expect to find a rich source of information which is potentially useful in understanding the role of causal attributions in interpersonal problems. Unfortunately, most attribution research has involved persons who are unfamiliar with each other, and its utility is therefore limited to client problems which involve difficulties relating to persons with whom the client is minimally acquainted (e.g., social anxiety, shyness, etc.). When an understanding of intimate relationships is sought, this source of data is not particularly useful. Recently, however, a spate of studies (e.g., Doherty, 1982; Harvey, Ickes and Kidd, 1978; Madden and Janoff-Bulman, 1981; Newman and Langer, 1981; Orvis et al., 1976; Passer et al., 1978; Sillars, 1981; Thompson and Kelley, 1981) and theortical statements (e.g., Kelley, 1979; Newman, 1981a, 1981b; Newman and Langer 1983) have examined attributions in close relationships. Marital and family therapists have been quick to note its implications for their clinical work (e.g., Arias, 1982; Baucom, 1981; Doherty, 1981a, 1981b; Hotaling, 1980).

Unfortunately, not enough attention has been given in the above writings to the nature of close relationships and the consequent implications for understanding causal attributions among intimates. Several researchers have simply extrapolated ideas that have proved useful at the intrapersonal level to interpersonal problems. For example, Baucom (1981) has included explicit instruction on the ANOVA model in behavioural therapy with couples. In view of the lack of attention given to the nature of intimate relationships, several of their salient features are examined. The marital relationship is used to illustrate the ensuing arguments.

A striking feature of marital interaction is its reciprocal nature. A given behaviour by partner A is simultaneously a stimulus (in so far as it is followed by a behaviour by partner B) and a response (in so far as it follows an action by B) in an uninterrupted chain of interchanges. Each behaviour carries implications for the relationship, and hence it is important to determine the causes of the other person's behaviour (Orvis et al., 1976; Newman and Langer, 1983). This poses a dilemma. Where does one begin the causal analysis? Orvis et al. (1976) were confronted with this problem when they found that subjects sometimes related a causal sequence in reporting events for which they and their partners had different explanations. They chose to code only the most immediate cause and hence, like most social psychologists, neglected the issue of causal chains in examining phenomenal causality (see Fincham and Jaspars, 1980; Fincham and Shultz, 1981).

Clearly, there is no objectively correct solution to the above problem, as any attempt to impose a linear cause–effect structure on intimate interactions is arbitrary. This does not imply that such structures are alien to partners' perceptions of their relationships, nor does it suggest that rules for imposing such structures do not exist. On the contrary, communication theorists have long recognized that the segmentation or 'punctuation' of interaction organizes behaviour and is therefore vital to it (Watzlawick et al., 1967). They argue that relationship problems can arise from 'faulty punctuation', where each partner justifies his/her behaviour as a response to the other's prior behaviour (e.g., wife nags . . . husband withdraws . . . wife nags . . . husband withdraws, etc.). The extent to which causal connections are traced can thus be critical, and may differentiate distressed from non-distressed relationships. Consider the case of

Mr Z, who tells his wife at the breakfast table that he will be late home from work because of a prior assignment which has to be prepared for tomorrow's deadline. Mrs Z may either console her husband and sympathize with him regarding work pressures, or she may berate him for not having worked harder in the preceeding days and believe that his 'inaction' denotes his lack of care for her or the relationship. The happily married Mrs Z will most likely choose the former action, whereas the maritally distressed Mrs Z is likely to choose the latter.

The above example illustrates how causal attributions can often play a functional role in the relationship. This is possible because in real life, as opposed to the typical laboratory situation, there are usually a number of plausible causes for an event even after a rigorous covariance analysis. Hence it is not surprising that partners in a relationship can offer equally plausible yet widely disparate explanations for sources of conflict between them (Orvis et al., 1976). Recognition of the functional role of causal attributions means that in the clinical context one is faced with the task of replacing a set of causal perceptions that are instrumental in maintaining the problem with an alternative set that will be functional for the individual/couple in overcoming their problem. One is engaged not in helping the client to seek veridical causes but rather in altering the perceived plausibility of alternative causes.

The functional nature of causal attributions is recognized, albeit implicitly, by therapists of differing orientations. Systems theorists (e.g. Minuchin, 1974; Watzlawick et al., 1974) argue that a couple's/family's problem is shaped by the contextual frame within which it is perceived. The technique of 'reframing', while not couched in attribution terms, in effect constitutes a form of re-attribution that enhances a sense of mastery over the problem. Behavioural marital therapists (e.g., Jacobson and Margolin, 1979) are now also including relabelling (re-attribution) of behaviour in their therapeutic armamentarium. The use of the above strategies is predicated on the assumption that causal chains are important in relationship dysfunction and that their segmentation does not provide veridical attributions.

Recent data provide support for the above argument. In his investigation of conflict between roomates, Sillars (1981) found that punctuation differences or different segmentations of causal chains were common, especially among dissatisfied roommates. Lower satisfaction was also associated with blame directed towards the other person and stable causal attributions for the conflict. Both these factors suppressed conflict resolution strategies that promoted mutually satisfying outcomes. However, the direction of the causality is not clear. Orvis et al. (1976) examined attributional conflict in young couples and found that subjects tend to give explanations of their partner's behaviour, which leads to conflict, in terms of the personal properties (characteristics or attitudes) of their partner. On the other hand, the explanations given by the partner whose behaviour is under consideration took the form of excuses or justifications. Similar results emerged when Passer et al. (1978) examined the meaning given to causes of negative interpersonal behaviour. The 'attitude toward the partner' was an important dimension for both actor and partner. The 'intentional–unintentional' dimension also emerged in the actor condition and corresponded to the distinction between justifying and excusing conditions found by Orvis et al. (1976). A similar parallel in results occurred in the partner condition as 'states versus actor's traits' comprised the second dimension.

Two major implications of these results are noteworthy in the present context. First, the fact that attitude towards the partner was a dimension for both actor and partner conditions suggests that distressed and non-distressed spouses should differ in the causal attributions they make for both their own and their spouse's behaviour. Second, to the extent that the provision of justifications or excuses (accounts) prevents conflict by 'verbally bridging the gap between action and expectation' (Lyman and Scott, 1970, p. 112), this process is likely to have broken down in distressed relationships.

Fincham and O'Leary (1983) investigated the first of the above implications, which is strongly emphasized in theoretical writings (Epstein, 1982; Jacobson and Margolin, 1979). Couples seeking marital therapy were compared with a non-distressed control group in terms of the dimensions underlying their perceived causes of spouse behaviour (spouse–external to spouse, global–specific, stable–unstable, controllable–uncontrollable). The results showed that distressed spouses considered the causes of negative spouse behaviour to be more global than non-distressed spouses while the inverse pattern obtained for positive behaviour. The other difference found involved perceived controllability – distressed spouses considered the causes of positive behaviour to be more uncontrollable than non-distressed spouses. Only partial evidence was therefore obtained to suggest that distressed and non-distressed couples differ in the causal inferences they make for spouse behaviour.

One obvious implication of this finding is that causal dimensions different from those traditionally used in individually oriented research may be important in studying intimates. Research is currently being conducted to examine this hypothesis. In addition, Newman (1981a, 1981b) has emphasized an interpersonal attribution category to supplement the dispositional and situational categories that have dominated research. Interpersonal attributions focus on 'one's perception of "self in regard to other" and "other in regard to self" ' (Newman, 1981a, p. 63). However, this still leaves an incomplete picture. For example, attributions that identify the relationship as cause and point to the interaction or transactional process need to be examined. Even though Orvis et al. (1976) found little evidence for such attributions, their importance is emphasized by the fact that they play an integral part in therapy and have been identified as a necessary component of behaviour change (Jacobson and Margolin, 1979).

The second issue raised, concerning the preventative role of causal attributions in intimate conflict, has not been investigated in distressed and non-distressed couples. The view of causal attributions as accounts that bridge the gap between expectation and action suggests various points of possible relationship malfunction. First, the problem may lie at the level of partner expectation arising from unrealistic or irrational beliefs. In fact, Geiss and O'Leary (1981) found that marital and family therapists report unrealistic expectations as the second most frequent cause of marital distress, and they are, moreover, negatively associated with improvement in therapy (Epstein and Eidelson, 1981). Rational restructuring (Ellis and Greiger, 1977) concerning partner beliefs is an appropriate intervention in this case. Second, the degree of divergence in the causal perceptions of actor and partner may be so large that any attempt to provide an account becomes futile and may result in conflict (Sillars, 1981). Such differences can arise from a variety of sources (e.g., punctuation differences, behaviour incompatible with the account, etc.), and therefore several strategies may be appropriate as interventions (e.g., role play of each other's positions, explicitly examining the *transactional* process, behaviour change, etc.). Third, relationship goals may be at variance with current accounts (for example, partner may want to separate while actor's account, if accepted, would imply continuation of the relationship). Fourth, the individual and/or the relationship may be entering a different developmental stage which requires a change in the level of explanation (e.g., reduced interpersonal involvement or crises may require more elaborate accounts). Other possibilities exist, and clearly research is needed to examine differences between satisfactory and distressed relationships.

When causal attributions among intimates are considered from the viewpoint of accounts as portrayed above, it becomes obvious that one is dealing not simply with perceived causality but also with expectations which infuse the causal perceptions with their meaning and evaluative content. The expectation component has been implicitly assumed in previous writings (e.g., Orvis et al., 1976) and may explain why causal attributions are often equated with perceived blame. Given a set of expectations regarding reasonable behaviour (often shared by reader and writer, client and therapist), a partner-directed causal attribution can amount to a charge that requires rebuttal. From this analysis it is apparent that research on responsibility attribution is more relevant to relationship dysfunction than the study of perceived causality as traditionally conceived in the attribution literature. The quintessence of responsibility is answerability or accountability. Hence, responsibilities exist only in relation to concomitant duties and need not even involve causal connections. The energy expended coaching distressed spouses in the ANOVA principles of causality (Baucom, 1981) could then more profitably be spent teaching them rules of responsibility attribution (see Fincham and Jaspars, 1980). Even the various meanings of responsibility might prove useful in this respect. For example, the fact that one can only be held responsible when certain mental criteria are met (capacity responsibility) finds its analogue in close relationships in the situation where a partner lacks the requisite skills required to meet his/her partner's expectations (e.g., to be intimate, communicate freely).

The above analysis has important implications for both therapy and research. When couples in therapy present problems where causal attributions are central, one needs to focus not only on the attributions themselves but also on the expectations that make them so important. These may be implicit and not apparent to the couple, or they may be explicit. For some distressed couples a lack of awareness regarding partner expectations may be the root of their problems (e.g., that partner is expected to infer actor's feelings so that when this does not occur it is seen as a lack of caring; that disagreement is necessarily destructive and hence when partner does disagree it indicates his or her desire to erode the relationship; etc.) In sum, the therapist may wish to focus on expectations, attributions or both depending on the circumstances of the case.

As regards research implications, there is an obvious need to examine forms of explanations or accounts that are not given in terms of perceived causality but that none the less serve the same functional role as causal attributions (Antaki, 1981). Causal attributions, when verbalized, constitute behaviours that might profitably be examined by standard behavioural assessment techniques. For instance, a functional analysis in which the immediate stimuli preceding the verbalization of an attribution and its consequences are systematically monitored would elucidate the conditions under which causal attributions are articulated and would show how they are shaped by social interaction (see Kidd and Amabile, 1981). Such procedures have also been underutilized in cognitive therapy with couples.

The functional nature of causal attributions is most apparent when they constitute part of the relationship dialogue. Attributions as verbalized communications between partners have been discussed elsewhere (see

Newman, 1981b; Newman and Langer, 1983, Orvis et al., 1976) However, it is worth noting that many causal attributions remain unarticulated in a relationship, and that this in itself can lead to relationship problems. For example, even though there is evidence to suggest that persons act as hypothesis-testers in generating causal attributions (Snyder and Gangestad, 1981), partners in a close relationship may make causal attributions about each other and not mention or test these precisely because of their familiarity with the other person. Alternatively, this may occur because it is functional for the perceiver at the intrapersonal, evaluative level. For example, when partners make an important relationship decision or experience a strong emotion they may selectively infer positive or negative causes for the other's behaviour to justify their decision/feeling. Such a process is likely to be particularly important during relationship termination (Newman and Langer, 1983). Thus the goals of the partners in the relationship need to be carefully considered when analysing the causal inferences they make. (See Lalljee and Abelson, chapter 4 above, regarding the importance of goals in relation to explanations.)

Implicit and untested causal attributions are perhaps most deleterious when the partner's behaviour is perceived as significant in relation to self when, in fact, it may merely reflect the partner's idiosyncracies or own intrapersonal problems. Newman and Langer (1983) suggest that this 'attributional error' is as fundamental as the traditional tendency to favour dispositional attributions over situational ones. Inferring such behaviours as having communicative or interactive importance is particularly likely to occur in distressed relationships characterized by conflict and hence therapists should be sensitive to this phenomenon.

The impression given thus far suggests an active processor continually analysing and explaining his/her partner's behaviour. However, partners are likely to build a 'schema' or script (see Lalljee and Abelson, chapter 4 above) regarding their relationship and to process self and partner behaviour within this schema in the same way that individuals process incoming information in terms of their self schema (Markus, 1977). Such processing is likely to occur at an automatic, less mindful, level and can potentially involve a great deal of distortion. Perhaps the most important therapeutic implication concerns positive behavioural changes brought about in therapy. To maintain such gains, the therapist should ensure that the couple process these changes in an adaptive manner lest they assimilate them to an existent (malfunctional) schema and/or discount them. For example, a partner's change should be attributed to factors such as his/her own effort or changed feelings and not to a belief that the couple are responsive to each other only during crisis (relationship schema), the therapist's intervention or a behavioural contract (discounting). It naturally follows that every appropriate opportunity should be used to have clients process interaction in the service of building a new, positive relationship schema. The issues of partner and relationship schemata and of mindful-versus-mindless attribution are likely to be critical in understanding relationship dysfunction, and await research.

In sum, it is apparent that in close relationships causal attributions are not the logical products portrayed by some attribution theorists. On the contrary, they are part of the fabric of the relationship, altering and being altered by its course. Thus causal attributions should be viewed as functional to the relationship, and they may serve to help maintain or terminate it. At times they constitute part of the discourse of the relationship and in this respect constitute one of several forms of explanation. However, they can also remain unarticulated and can be made with differing degrees of mindfulness. In any event, their potence derives from expectations that are discrepant with behaviour, a fact that tends to have been overlooked. Consequently, the process of responsibility attribution models causal attributions in close relationships more veridically than does traditional research on perceived causality. It seems, then, that attribution theory offers a fresh perspective in studying dysfunction in intimate relationships, and that new models of the attribution process that address the issues raised in this section will enhance, even further, our understanding of such interpersonal problems.

CONCLUSION

Clearly, certain areas at the interface of attribution theory and clinical psychology (e.g., re-attribution) have been the object of research for some time. Others, such as the attributional reformulation of learned helplessness, represent recent developments whose full potential has yet to be realized. Further topics (e.g., an attributional analysis of relationship dysfunction) are beginning to receive the attention they deserve, while yet others still need to be recognized. For example, the investigation of the clinician as a professional causal attributor, in contrast to the lay (student) attributor studied in the bulk of attribution research, is potentially fruitful in terms of both clinical application and basic theory (see Furnham et al., 1983); the psychodiagnostic process is an obvious starting point for such research. Overall, then, it seems that the application of attribution theory to clinical problems holds a great deal of potential. However, it is equally apparent that the attribution–clinical interface is replete with problems, and the attempt to serve two masters can easily result in satisfying neither.

From the viewpoint of clinical practitioners, the ultimate concern is with the practical utility of an attributional approach. They may legitimately ask whether clinical efficacy has been demonstrated. The current answer must be a resounding 'no', as studies using clinical populations are rare, and outcome research that specifically evaluates the contribution of attributional interventions to therapeutic efficacy is lacking. The absence of clinical research may appear to be incongruous when it is recalled that causal attributions are held to be an integral part of cognitive therapies. For example, Beck (Beck et al., 1979) stresses reattribution techniques for clients who unrealistically attribute negative occurrences to a personal deficiency. Herein lies a kernel problem in clinical applications of attributional theory. 'Attribution therapy', like its parent attribution theory, is largely implicit, and its 'principles' are only partially articulated. Yet it retains an appeal because it is so intuitively obvious. It is hard to imagine a therapy that did not address the issue of causal connections at some level as they are germane to our language (Kanouse et al., 1981). However, this should not blind us to the issue at hand. First, it is the explicit focus on causal attributions in therapy that is in question. Second, it is the evaluation of interventions dealing with causal attributions *per se* that is required. Thus, even if the efficacy of Beck's cognitive therapy is not in doubt, the role of re-attribution in this therapy remains unexamined.

Another critical issue is that *cognitive* therapies, which seem to provide indirect support for an attribution approach, rely heavily on *behavioural* techniques (e.g., Beck et al., 1979; Ellis and Greiger, 1977). The demonstrated efficacy of behavioural therapy (see Kazdin and Wilson, 1978) prompts the sceptic to question the role of cognitive techniques in producing therapeutic change as compared with their *a posteriori* role in understanding such change (Wilson, 1982, makes a similar distinction). Attribution theorists recognize the necessity of developing 'attributional theories' to show how attributions affect behaviour (Kelley and Michela, 1980), but this issue currently remains unresolved. Rather than adopt an either/or stance, a more fruitful goal would be to discover the conditions under which attributions are more potent determinants of behaviour and vice versa. Further progress would also be aided by keeping distinct two separate issues: altering causal attributions as a means of facilitating behaviour change, and changing attributions as an end in itself. The latter is a far less controversial goal for any 'attribution therapy'.

Whatever the ultimate status of causal attributions *vis-à-vis* behaviour, it behooves one to remember that causal inferences constitute only one of the many forms of inferences clients make. Rarely will an intervention that focuses solely on causal attributions be sufficient. As indicated in this chapter, serious consideration of a client's causal inferences leads one into new territories that are beyond the boundaries of traditional attribution theory. It is in following these leads that the greatest contribution of attribution theory to clinical psychology lies. None the less, it remains an open question as to whether any 'attribution therapy' will ever be more than a therapeutic adjunct in the armamentarium of the well-rounded clinician. Its most important role may be as a precursor to intervention. When clients are helped to recognize several plausible causes for their problem they are more likely to acknowledge multiple possible solutions, which in turn is likely to facilitate change. If this proves to be the only explicit role of attribution in the therapeutic process, it is none the less a useful one.

Finally, in returning to the question of the consummation of the marriage between attribution theory and clinical psychology, one thing is apparent; the honeymoon phase is over. The time for more sound and clinically meaningful research is long overdue. However, such research presupposes careful and explicit conceptual analysis of the potential application and *limitations* of attribution theory in the clinic. The present chapter represents a step in this direction, for until it takes place the field faces the danger of falling under its own weight.

ACKNOWLEDGEMENTS
The author would like to thank Ileana Arias, Bob Emery, Susan Kemp-Fincham, Marv Goldfried, Miles Hewstone, Fred Kanfer and Steve Beach for their comments on an earlier draft of this chapter.

NOTE
1   References to many primary sources have been omitted in favour of review papers owing to an editorial request. Moreover, only research on adults is considered in the present chapter. For an attributional perspective of child behaviour problems see Fincham and Diener (1982).

PART IV
Commentary

12 On the Continued Vitality of the Attributional Approach

John H. Harvey and Ben Harris

INTRODUCTION

The task of the present chapter is to evaluate the contributions of the essays in this volume to the attribution literature. Before embarking upon this task, it may be useful to examine the historical context of the present volume.

After Heider's pioneering work on attributional processes from the early 1920s to the production of his 1958 book, there was a period during the 1960s when little work was done on attributional problems. But toward the late 1960s, with the appearance of Jones and Davis's (1965) and Kelley's (1967) influential papers, the attribution domain began to expand and become a major area for research in social psychology. This development was given considerable momentum by the fertile idea exchange that occurred at the 1969 UCLA Conference on Attribution Theory. The well-known proceedings of this conference are the 1972 book by Jones, Kanouse, Kelley, Nisbett, Valins, and Weiner. A multitude of graduate students interested in attributional processes 'cut their teeth' on this book. Many of these young scholars produced works that became influential in their own right in the attribution field during the 1970s.

As Hewstone suggests in the introduction to this volume, the 1970s can be termed the halcyon days of attribution research. The progress achieved during this period is reflected in the hundreds of journal articles on attribution (see S. S. Smith et al., 1980; Kelley and Michela, 1980), a host of edited volumes (Harvey, Ickes and Kidd, 1976, 1978, 1981; Frieze, Bar-Tal, and Carroll, 1979; Antaki, 1981), and even a pair of textbooks focusing exclusively on attributional phenomena (Shaver, 1975; Harvey and Weary, 1981).

So, indeed, the attribution field has been a productive one. But these are the 1980s. Where is the field headed during the next two decades? As some have suggested, will it become as dormant as the once-vigorous dissonance field became during the 1970s? The present volume will not answer these major questions, nor should it be so accountable. But, if it is to make a contribution, we should be able to see some signs of vitality and direction. And we do. Hewstone himself provides sufficient argument about vitality in his knowledgeable, marvelously balanced and statesman-like introduction to the volume. Future directions may be seen in parts of most of the papers in the various sections. For both vitality and direction, we agree with Moscovici and Hewstone's suggestion that it now is time to 'consider the wider aspects of attribution work'. The basic foundation work of the 1960s and 1970s must continually be re-assessed and modified in the light of new ideas and data. But we believe that the attribution field can progress significantly in coming years only to the extent that it embodies a concern with a wider array of human phenomena and problems. As for the durability of the attribution conception, no greater *raison d'être* for the field's continuation in this long and probable long-term future could be provided than that given by Kelley (1978) and Heider (1976) in separate interviews with them:

> I think the very way it [the attribution field] developed – it wasn't some bright idea that somebody had, that somebody forced on somebody's data or tried to extend by brute force. It came out of a lot of phenomena that social psychologists have looked at and tried to interpret. I just can't imagine that the phenomena that are hooked into that kind of cognition will change or be modified. They'll never go away. We'll always have to have that kind of explanation. [Kelley, 1978, p. 384]

> It [attribution] is all-pervasive and important. It [the field] can go any-where. . . . Attribution is part of our cognition of the environment. Whenever you cognize your environment you will find attribution occurr-ing. [Heider, 1976, p. 18]

THEORETICAL EXTENSIONS

The principal questions that may be asked about the chapters described as involving theoretical extensions are: What are the extensions, and are they likely to stimulate research and further theoretical work in the attribution field? One of our impressions of recent edited volumes on attribution is that there have been few theoretical contributions that could even begin to have the stimulant value displayed by earlier analyses such as Jones and Nisbett's (1971) provocative statement of the divergent perspectives hypo-thesis. If true, this state of affairs is not surprising. New broad hypotheses usually come first in the development of a theory. Subsequently, work is done that qualifies those hypotheses. Often, the qualifying work is not as exciting as was the original work.

In his chapter Jaspars presents and provides empirical evidence regarding a relatively complex model of causal attribution – resembling in complexity the analysis of Kruglanski et al. Part of this model involves a subjective scaling assumption which suggests that attributors sometimes may operate as if they use a subjective scale that evaluates the constituent informational elements (such as consensus). But the data presented from a study with four-year-old children do not directly speak to such theorizing. Also, assuming some such process may be valid, many questions remain, including: How would different conditions such as success and failure at a task influence subjective scale? Does the model allow for motivational biasing? Jaspars also presents interesting, but still quite indirect, evidence that attributors may start with local, specific explanations and then continue with more general explanations as information permits. Jaspars's statement is another in a line of commentaries on Kelley's (1967) so-called ANOVA conception that involves a useful argument about how common sense causal reasoning *often* is not like scientific analysis.

Chapter 3 by Farr and Anderson, which involves an assessment of Jones and Nisbett's divergent perspectives hypothesis, comes as close as any in the book to being an exciting extension that will have an impact on mainstream attribution workers. Their statement, though, does not need to be seen as an extension of the actor–observer hypothesis, or necessarily as a counter-position to that of Jones and Nisbett. In a sense, it is a statement of a related but significantly different set of hypotheses and different accompanying theoretical logic. We believe that the authors are quite right in refocusing scholars' attention of perspectives of P both as an actor in the social scene and as an observer of the behaviour of others. Further, they make a useful contribution in suggesting that both Mead and Heider considered the self in purely relational terms and in reminding us that Ichheiser proposed what was essentially a divergent perspectives hypothesis in 1949.

The richness of the ideas that can be explored from the broader position adopted by Farr and Anderson is illustrated by their posing of the following question:

> How does one integrate the record of O's behaviour, as seen, visually, by P (i.e., the observer) with the oral 'account' which O (the 'actor' might give concerning the 'reasons' for his 'actions'? [pp. 53-4 above]

What the authors are saying in part here is that accounts, reasons and actions are phenomena in their own right and deserve particular consideration. Analysis and research during the 1970s would readily support this position, which is more refined than was apparent in Jones and Nisbett's original statement.

The foregoing question, however, also illustrates a major issue with the Farr–Anderson position. How will attribution investigators construct proper empirical operations to test such complex questions? This same difficulty has baffled researchers who have attempted to test Mead's provocative 'taking the role of the other' perspective ideas. The authors argue that research on attribution theory, so far, has singularly failed to approximate the level of mental complexity involved in the individual's inclination to interact with him- or herself. This assertion is generally true, but it applies to most of what has been done in cognitive social psychology during the last 35 years. What we need at this point is less finger-pointing and more systematic work that better shows the operation of complex mental activities.

We also are unsure of the value of Farr and Anderson's linking of the Jones and Nisbett position with behaviourism in American psychology. The logic of this linkage is difficult to follow, especially if the authors are suggesting anything more than a passing association (e.g., focus on behaviour in perception of causality).

While Farr and Anderson react against the information-processing terminology and flavour of Jones and Nisbett's conception, Lalljee and Abelson (chapter 4) present a knowledge structure approach to attribution that makes the informational tone of Jones and Nisbett's ideas seem quite modest in comparison. This approach focuses on the purpose that an action fulfils and argues that individuals (and computers) use knowledge structures to comprehend, remember and summarize text or conversation about everyday reality. We believe that Lalljee and Abelson are quite right in stressing the scriptal nature of many explanations. Also, we appreciate the authors' formulation of the concepts of constructive and contrastive attribution processes to deal with how attributors explain unscripted behaviour.

In our view, the knowledge structure approach is useful as an adjunct to traditional attributional approaches. As has been argued before about script theory, it is not clear what hypotheses follow from the main assumptions (i.e., the theory seems more descriptive than explanatory in nature). But whatever the case on the stature of the theory, scriptal ideas would be more compelling if they were tested in more involving behavioural settings than has been true in the past. Consider, for example, the inferential dilemmas encountered in close relationships: why did she leave him? Such questions often elicit a plethora of scriptal possibilities. The documentation of such important real-life patterns would do much to enhance the value of script conceptions for understanding attributional phenomena.

Kruglanski, Baldwin and Towson's chapter 5 is a theoretical extension only in the sense that it reviews Kruglanski's (1980) general theory of the knowledge acquisition process. We believe that the jury is still out on this terribly ambitious theory. The claim is that the epistemic framework outlined in the theory affords an integration of major theoretical positions such as attribution theory, cognitive consistency models and social comparison theory. This approach is highly elegant. It remains to be seen whether or not it will have significant impact on attribution work (or, more generally, on cognitive–social psychology). It does not seem probable to us, however, that concepts such as 'conclusional need' will ever have the type of widespread influence that concepts such as 'discounting' and 'correspondent inference' have had. Also, Kruglanski et al.'s position appears on the surface to be a model that assumes people to be highly logically oriented in their inferences. However, to assume that inconsistency among cognitions creates a stress to re-establish structure is not unlike the basic assumption made in cognitive consistency theories: inconsistency creates a negative motivational state that results in actions designed to reduce the negative state. This apparent similarity with drive reduction conceptions in the attitude change field is not discussed by Kruglanski et al.

An aspect of Kruglanski et al.'s argument that deserves attention is the hypothesis that certain presumed biases and errors in the attribution process may be no more than 'freezing', or temporary blockages, in the hypothesis generation process. As Kruglanski and colleagues have shown, their argument about 'freezing' is amenable to empirical tests that reveal the temporary nature of biases when hypothesis-making is 'unfrozen'.

SOCIAL EXTENSIONS

Hewstone suggests that attribution work has been rather individualistic in orientation. This suggestion is true in that most theoretical statements in the field have focused on the individual's thoughts, feelings and actions as the centrepieces for analysis and research. Such a focus is individualistic, however, only in that it does not also take into account the interactive influence of another person's thoughts, feelings and actions, or those of individuals comprising a group or even society. The focal individual in this work typically is conceived as thinking about or feeling or acting towards other(s). So the work is 'social' in nature – how 'social' may be another matter. Indeed, the question of what humans do *that is not social*, in some sense, is an imposing problem. The reclusive ('asocial'?) Emily

Dickinsons of the world reveal how intensely involved with human experience a mind may be, whether or not there is immediate and direct social interaction.

To take this reasoning one last step, it has been suggested that the study of attributional conflict in couples by Orvis et al. (1976) involved a social focus because of its emphasis on how couples use attributions as communications about what they like and dislike about one another. How is such a focus any more social than that involved, for example, in the classic attribution study by Jones et al. (1961), in which subjects made inferences about the character of a person interviewing in an appropriate or inappropriate fashion to be either an astronaut or a submariner? Both are clearly 'social psychological' investigations. The major difference we would emphasize is that Orvis et al. at least were moving towards a study of reciprocal perception and behaviour between two individuals. In contrast, Jones et al.'s focus was on a unidirectional process – perceiving and forming impressions of others. We contend that this type of distinction is more likely to be fruitful than is one in which social versus individualistic emphasis is at issue. It also is the reciprocal influence, or causal loop, type of evidence that is too sparse in the attribution literature.

Because of the futility of counterposing individually versus socially oriented attributions, we would not characterize part II of this book as social extensions of attribution theory. Rather, we see the chapters by Moscovici and Hewstone (chapter 6), Bains (chapter 7) and Bond (chapter 8) as attempts to highlight the social context or social determination of attributional processes.

Of the three chapters in part II, Moscovici and Hewstone's is the most challenging – on account of both its provocative ideas and its sheer density. In their essay, Moscovici and Hewstone first describe the processes by which knowledge in the natural sciences is transformed[1] into the common-sense knowledge of the average citizen who is said to adopt 'science as a hobby'. They then describe how similar processes are at work transforming the knowledge of the social sciences (e.g. psychology) into the average citizen's common-sense social understanding – which in turn has become the subject matter of attribution theories.

In the language of Moscovici and Hewstone, the non-scientist's knowledge is a 'social representation' of science, since it must fulfil certain psychological and social functions. For example, common-sense science must be easily communicated; and so to the average citizen entire schools of scientific thought or research are symbolized by a single scientist (e.g., Einstein, Freud, Leakey). Similarly, common-sense science serves to guide the citizen's action. Thus, everyday representations of scientific issues (i.e., the nature of mental illness) may be dominated by simple metaphors (i.e., mental illness is a disease) which suggest a direct course of action (i.e., disturbed individuals should seek medical help).

Based on this theory of social representations, it is argued that attribution theory must consider more fully the ways in which attributions correspond to transformations of the professional psychologist's causal knowledge for social needs. Thus, Moscovici and Hewstone remind the reader that the fundamental attribution error (overestimating the influence of the individual's personal attributes) can be seen as serving certain social functions in an individualistic society.

To us, this essay contains a number of worthwhile arguments. To mention just one, we agree that the term '*naive* social scientist' has an ethnocentric connotation similar to 'primitive culture', implying that anyone not sharing the assumptions of twentieth-century Western science is artless or credulous (e.g., Clodd, 1885; cited in the *Oxford English Dictionary*, 1933, vol. 7). Thus we agree with Moscovici and Hewstone's preference for 'common-sense' or 'amateur' scientist to describe the citizen whose knowledge we are studying.

At the same time as we agree on this detail, there are two major features of these authors' argument that, if we understand them correctly, we find problematic. The first is Moscovici and Hewstone's portrayal of the social relations of science; the second is their assertion that modern attribution theories have ignored the social (representational) function of the individual's interpersonal perceptions.

Although discussing the social relations of science is not the primary purpose of this volume, a majority of Moscovici and Hewstone's essay is devoted to this pursuit, and deserves comment. According to these authors, (1) the modern citizen's common sense is formal scientific knowledge transformed to everyday needs; (2) citizens generally put their confidence in 'the authority of science'; and (3) citizens today 'want to consume science' to a degree that they have 'a kind of addiction' to scientific fact and theory.

In formulations such as these, citizens' transformation of science is portrayed as a social process; but somehow their consumption of, addiction to and respect for science is treated in a non-historical manner. The development of scientific theory is also portrayed as a process removed from the influence of non-scientists, as if science existed apart from, and above, the social realm. Thus there is an identity suggested between a modern consumer of packaged scientific knowledge (i.e., as sold to corporations as a commodity by a television network) and the amateur scientist of the eighteenth or nineteenth centuries. As a corrective to this apparent ignorance of how social class and historical context can determine the scientist's work, we would urge the examination of the variety of relationships that can exist between scientific discovery and social context (e.g., C. E. Rosenberg, 1976, chapter 1).

Returning to the topic of attribution theory, Moscovici and Hewstone assert that theorists in this field have ignored the degree to which the individual's attributions are based on social scientific reasoning, transformed to fulfil social needs. As a result, they charge, attribution theory is 'often a theory of *causes without explanations*. It studies *how* explanations are made, but not *why*' (p. 121 above). To us this is an ironic assertion immediately to precede Bains's essay on the import of control motivation in attribution processes. It has been argued since the inception of attribution work that the need for control is the principal 'why' of attributions. In fact, such an argument constitutes the theme of Bains's chapter, which suggests that 'One of the most important functions of attributional inquiry is the greater control of the environment which an understanding of causal relationships enables . . .' (p. 121 above).[2]

In sum, we are more surprised by Moscovici and Hewstone's general statements about science and society than we are challenged by their analysis of the limitations of attribution theory. Considering Moscovici's record of fine work on the social determination of social psychological theories (Moscovici and Faucheux, 1972), we expected that these authors would have spent an equal amount of effort bringing the scientists down to the level of social, human being as they did on the elevating the average, formerly 'naive', citizen to that level.[3]

Following Moscovici and Hewstone, Bains discusses how control motivation may be viewed as an organizing principle in personal, interpersonal and social intergroup contexts. In our opinion, the originality of Bains's ideas for the attribution literature is greatest in his illustrations of control motivation–attribution relationships for stereotyping phenomena and activities surrounding attributions of witchcraft. What would be most useful would be archival research that better revealed these naturalistic relationships.

Even as we had difficulty with the 'why explanations' question in Moscovici and Hewstone's statement, we also could not accept Bains's beginning assumption – that attribution theory *has neglected* (no qualification such as 'often has neglected') the idea that motives can influence and distort the way we perceive events in the world. Not only did Heider emphasize this idea, but so also have many attribution analysts since the major developments in the field in the late 1960s (see Weary Bradley's (1978) review). An emphasis on this idea is implied in Wortman's (1976) discussion of control and attribution, which Bains refers to often. Without being presumptuous, we would guess that what Bains means is that the role of motivation has not been accorded major status in certain foundation attribution works.

Turning to Bond's chapter (chapter 8), we believe that he makes a reasonable argument about the need for cross-cultural studies of attributional processes. He traces and critically analyses some of the relevant work in this area. Further, he calls for work that involves a relatively unstructured and unobtrusive approach to asking people in different cultures about their attributions. In the absence of a great deal of such cross-cultural, free-response attributional research, we would suggest obtaining attributional information from sources easily sampled unobtrusively: archival accounts of human conduct.

One source of such accounts might be post-experimental interviews in non-attributional cross-cultural research – on need achievement, for example. Although such discussions of subjects' social perceptions (e.g., 'why do you think that this other subject was successful on that task?') would be contaminated by experimental variables, they might reveal different patterns of attribution across different cultures. Alternatively, one might consider the application of a Heiderian notion across cultures by comparing the implicit causal attributions found in fairy tales, legends or modern fiction from different countries (Heider, 1959; 1958 p.6).

While practicality precludes large-scale cross-cultural studies from becoming a principal line of inquiry in the field, this direction is one that is needed. As sound work is completed, we may learn about systems of understanding that differ greatly from the systems found among Western peoples. Do we as yet have any attribution principle of universal validity? The answer, as Bond suggests, is that we do not know and have only vaguely begun to consider this question.

APPLICATIONS

It is hardly novel to have a set of chapters on applications in a volume on attribution in the 1980s. The Frieze et al. (1979) volume was directed exclusively toward applications. The applications section fits well with the goal of examining the wider aspects of attribution set for the current volume.

At least in America, there is an increasingly smaller number of graduate students who are being trained to investigate mainly basic processes in social psychology, including principles of attribution. Increasingly, social psychology involves an amalgam of applied thrusts – into medical settings, industry and corporations, the judicial system, community intervention programmes, psychotherapeutic intervention and so on. It follows from these significant demographic trends that applied aspects of attribution theory will continue to be an area of growth in coming years, probably much more so than work on basic processes. As just one example, the role of attribution in depression phenomena has already yielded scores of studies and several review/theoretical works in the last five years. Thus, to go back to Hewstone's 'halcyon days' metaphor, attribution's next major period may be one of continued and even increased work on and consolidation of these applied directions.

As Hewstone admits in the Introduction, the contributors to this volume do not always agree with one another. As an example, Eiser in chapter 9 indicates that Kruglanski's conception of lay epistemology is less behavioural than people are themselves. Eiser argues that attribution approaches have devoted too little attention to attribution–behaviour relationships. We agree (see Yarkin et al., 1981). Most important, Eiser makes a quite sensible argument to the effect that attribution and behaviour are complexly related, with behaviour as likely to influence attribution (as Bem, 1972, has cogently argued) as is attribution to influence behaviour.

In their chapters on medical and on clinical psychology, King (chapter 10) and Fincham (chapter 11) suggest that our understanding of topics in these applied areas can be enriched by an attributional perspective. More importantly, they show how this enrichment depends on our ability to apply attributional theories selectively and to respect the patterning and quality of individuals' naturally occurring attributions. King's contribution to these themes is a thoughtful discussion of how an attributional orientation can inform research on health-related behaviour (e.g., compliance with therapeutic regimens).

King begins by explaining the importance in medical psychology formulations of the individual's beliefs about health and health maintenance (e.g., self-estimated risk of illness, perceived efficacy of therapy). She then goes on to propose that the causal structure surrounding these beliefs might be a source of predictive information on health-related behaviour. A valuable part of King's paper is the report of her attempts to provide empirical evidence about relationships among explanations, health beliefs and behaviour. As an illustration of her findings, she indicates that heart patients' estimates of susceptibility to further heart trouble were influenced more by their interpretations of the cause of the illness than by beliefs about the severity of the condition or the treatment received.

Unfortunately, King over-interprets some of her data, inferring a causal relationship without sufficient proof. Specifically, her first study established that the heart disease patients who most believed their diseases to be serious were most likely to attribute their illness to chronic or relatively uncontrollable factors (e.g., God's will, life changes, tension, smoking). Rather than simply stating that pessimistic self-diagnosis is associated with certain perceived causes of disease, King describes the former belief as 'influenced by causal explanations' (p. 182 above). Equally plausible, however, is a reversed causal sequence (i.e., belief in an illness's seriousness dictates certain causes) or the action of a third variable such as the general trait of pessimism.[4]

Despite this and a few other questionable interpretations, King's chapter successfully advocates a promising and overdue research programme. It is overdue because of the apparent blindness of many theorists in behavioural medicine to attribution theory (see Blanchard, 1982). To us, the resulting theoretical limitations in this field are reminiscent of the limitations of early work applying learned helplessness to humans;[5] however, the development of this latter theory suggests that it is difficult to maintain ignorance of such a major force in contemporary social psychology as attribution theory (Huesmann, 1978).

If an attribution approach indeed proves useful to health psychologists, it would be in great contrast to its utility in clinical psychology, as Fincham clearly illustrates in chapter 11. He asserts that both theoretical clarification and additional programmatic research must occur before attribution therapy is accepted as a potentially useful technique. The validity of such an assertion is most obvious in regard to the sub-field of clinical uses of mis-attribution effects. As Fincham correctly points out, research in this area is flawed by basic logical and methodological errors such as experimenters' failure to assess the causal attributions of subjects. Owing to this, and to a host of other reasons, we agree with Fincham's overall evalution of the relevance of mis-attribution work for clinical practice:

> Given the role of deception in much of the research, its inconsistent findings and the exclusive reliance on self-diagnosed, college student subjects, one may legitimately ask whether it has any clinical implications. [p. 191 above]

A second major contribution of Fincham's chapter is his discussion of the functional role of attributions in the development, maintenance and termination of close personal relationships. Specifically, we see promise in the suggestion that research on responsibility attribution may prove to be more relevant to relationship dysfunction than the study of perceived causality – since the attributions of each person in an initimate dyad often serve to blame the other and to exonerate one's self (Orvis et al., 1976).

A final contribution of Fincham is his general scepticism towards exaggerated claims for the potential of attribution therapies, and his suggestion that such approaches can, at best, serve as a therapeutic adjunct in the repertoire of the well-rounded clinician. Our own limited reading of the relevant clinical literature suggests that this criticism holds true for endeavours such as marriage counselling; for intensive psychotherapy, family therapy and certain cognitive therapies, even this mild assertion of attribution theories' usefulness may be too strong a statement.

As we see it, there are two chief difficulties encountered in any attempt to apply an attributional perspective to clinical psychology. First, as Fincham in chapter 11 and Newman (1981a,b) admit, individuals in interpersonal relationships are affected by the dynamics of the relationship, which are not reducible to a collection of the individuals' self- and other-directed attributions. Thus, the clinician's task, at minimum, must be seen as the analysis of attributions about relationships, not just about A's and O's.

A second problem faced by clinical applications of attribution theory is that even non-psychotic individuals in disturbed relationships often suffer from illogical *beliefs* (not just perceptions) maintained by illogical patterns of thinking. Moreover, the illogic of such thought in actual cases is not limited to the sort of attributional errors described in the social psychological literature.

Consider the case of an emotionally disturbed, 25–year-old man described by Watzlawick et al. (1974). The young man in question had a history of psychiatric hospitalization, was unemployed, was living in a marginal existence in a bedsitting room, and was brought into the clinic by his mother who anticipated a recurrence of her son's previous acute psychosis. The son felt that his parents treated him like a child, paying all of his bills and witholding money from him when they felt that he was acting badly. The son never openly expressed anger over this relationship; instead, he acted socially inappropriately and seemed autistic at various times during the family's initial clinical interview.

From an attributional standpoint, this case could be understood, first, as a disagreement over attributed causality, since it seems logical that the son would see his parents as the cause of tension, while the parents would see it as caused by their son. Also, this case could be understood as a disagreement over responsibility attribution, since parents and son probably would differ over the son's status as a purposeful, informed actor. Alternatively, from a family therapy perspective, what is most notable about such a case is not simply the individuals' causal perceptions or attempts at blaming, but the *patterns* of communication and the implicit *beliefs*, which constitute the family relationship and produce the individuals' attributions of self and other.

If correct, this alternative view predicts a difficult time for anyone attempting a simple reattribution therapy, since such dysfunctional beliefs and communication patterns can incorporate additional factual information without changing the participants' basic assumptions. Thus in this case, successful re-attribution of the cause of the son's irresponsible behaviour (i.e., 'it's due to his illness') would not necessarily alter the parents' belief that their son was an overly fragile object who should be treated as a child; it would also perpetuate the son's reaction.

From the perspective of structural family therapy, what must occur is not simply the re-attribution of cause but a 're-framing' of the relationship, by way of the therapist's intervention. In the case discussed by Watzlawick et al. (1974), 'in the presence of his mother it was pointed out to the son that since he felt outnumbered by his parents, he had every right to defend himself by threatening to cause a far greater expenditure by suffering another psychotic break' (p. 124). This paradoxical intervention redefined the son's behaviour as actions that he performed (in a quasi-voluntary manner) to upset and threaten his parents. As a result, both mother and son were temporarily freed from some of the constraints of their previously established beliefs and roles, resulting in significant behaviour change.[6] What is noteworthy to us is Watzlawick et al.'s assertion that 'what turned out to be changed as a result of the reframing is the *meaning* attributed to the situation . . . but not its concrete facts' (1974, p. 95; our emphasis).

Is it possible for such a change to be interpreted in terms of current attribution theories? Are the family therapist's techniques of re-labelling and re-framing forms of re-attribution (Fincham chapter 11 above, p. 196)? We have yet to see convincing evidence in support of such a proposition. Instead, we read cases in which the therapist's chief goal is (for example) 'a reconceptualization of the symptom in interpersonal terms [which] can open new pathways for change' (Minuchin, 1974, p. 155).[7] Although this might result in changed attributions (e.g., an infantilized son may be seen as more responsible), the problem in need of solution is a complex pattern of beliefs, most of which are relational (e.g., beliefs about others' beliefs).

Finally, if one looks at cognitive therapists whose primary work is not with families, but with individual clients, the applicability of attribution theory is equally problematic. In the often-cited work of Aaron Beck and Albert Ellis, for example, we think that it is incorrect to equate processes such as 'cognitive restructuring' with re-attribution. Consider a case by Ellis in which he utilizes cognitive restructuring (or 'disputing') in working with a woman whose failure to experience orgasm in sexual relations causes her much shame and guilt. Rather than convince the patient that the cause of her sexual inadequacy was not a personal quality of hers (thus promoting re-attribution), Ellis attacks the beliefs that he sees mediating between the woman's sexual problems and her negative feelings about herself (Ellis and Whiteley, 1979, p. 68).[8]

To cite another example, the prominent cognitive therapist Aaron Beck eschews an exclusive focus on the causes of events or on the responsibility attributed for them. Rather, he attacks the illogical patterns of thinking by which patients often misinterpret their enviornment ('cognitive distortions', such as arbitrary inference, selective abstraction, inexact labelling, etc.). Thus, he describes the case of a depressed woman who would see a minor amount of dust in a drawer and conclude that the entire chest of drawers was 'dirty' and that she was a failure at being a housewife. Certainly some of this woman's implicit assumptions involved faulty attribution (e.g., 'no one else has drawers this dirty' – failure to judge consensus); yet corrective attributional processes, such as looking for alternative causes for events, play only a minor role in Beck's work on cognitive distortions (Beck, 1967, p. 326).

To summarize our comments on Fincham's essay, we think that he has correctly analysed the weaknesses of experimental re-attribution therapies, and has presented interesting suggestions about the applications of an attributional perspective to counselling of couples with relatively circumscribed problems. We also agree with Fincham's call for further attention in clinical settings to attributions that involve interpersonal and transactional foci. However, it remains to be seen whether this will be possible within the parameters of current attribution theories.

CONCLUSIONS

Overall, this volume is successful in presenting some new theoretical perspectives and some social extensions and applications of attribution theory – in short, 'some wider aspects of attribution work'. We think that the diversity of ideas and emphases and the concern with real-world issues on display here are quite salutary for the attribution field. This field is hardly unified in focus. In comparison to the well-worked field of social cognition, for example, the attribution domain seems quite tattered and disarrayed. But we believe that the domain's redeeming feature is its breadth and immersion in the examination of real dilemmas and activities. In a stinging commentary, Neisser (1980) recently accused social cognition theorists of being over-specialized and of writing what appear to be bureaucratic memoranda, rather than broadly gauged scientific reports. Such an accusation would not be appropriate for the present set of papers. The papers in this volume certainly are not bureaucratic documents. At the minimum, they are true to their collective goal of emphasizing the value of studying common-sense explanations – even as Heider so compellingly dissected and presented them for a multitude of future scholars to appreciate and wonder about as he does.

NOTES

1 In more than one place, this process is referred to as the 'retooling of science'. This is an interesting metaphor, but one that seems based on a confused idea of the operation of machine shops.
2 One might then ask to what degree control or domination over the environment is a socially determined goal rather than a universal value. This seems like a fine question; we would only ask that it not be made a required topic of study for all social psychologists.
3 Of course, there is controversy over the degree to which larger social forces (e.g., social class) and certain social processes (e.g., reification) can be seen influencing the actual research of scientists. For recent discussions of such issues, relevant to psychology, see Spuhler (1982) and Lewontin et al. (1982).
4 In part to answer such questions of causal direction, King reports a second study, in which patients' causal attributions were assessed in advance of their having the chance to engage in health-related activity.
5 'Coping Behaviour: Physiological Change and Learned Helplessness', symposium held at Virginia Polytechnic Institute and State University, 8–9 October 1976.
6 To continue Watzlawick et al.'s description of the case: 'The therapist then made some concrete suggestions as to how the son should behave in order to give the impression of impending doom – these suggestions being mostly reformulations of the somewhat weird behaviour the son was engaging in anyway' (1974, p. 124). The effect of this interview was such that, later, the mother was able to express resentment (not just fear) over her son's actions, and then to challenge him to manage a monthly allowance by himself, rather than be given a daily dole. As reported by Watzlawick et al., the son responded by saving money, buying a car and thus becoming less dependent on his mother.
7 To illustrate, a therapist might define a young woman's anorexia as disobedience, and as a masterful technique for making her parents appear incompetent.
8 For example, 'I should get orgasms. If most women have orgasms, I must too. If I don't, this is unbearable and I am something awful' (Ellis and Whiteley, 1979, pp. 68–9).

References

Abbott, E.A. (1926 edn) *Flatland*. Oxford: Basil Blackwell.

Abelson R.P. (1976) Script processing in attitude formation and decision-making. In J.S. Carroll and J.W. Payne (eds), *Cognition and social behaviour*. Hillsdale, NJ: Erlbaum.

Abelson, R.P. (1981) Psychological status of the script concept. *American Psychologist*, **36**, 715–729.

Abelson, R.P., Aronson, E., McGuire, W.J., Newcomb, T.M., Rosenberg, M.J. and Tannenbaum, P.H. (eds) (1968) *Theories of cognitive consistency: A sourcebook*. Chicago: Rand McNally.

Abrams, R.D., and Finesinger, J.E. (1953) Guilt reactions in patients with cancer. *Cancer*, **6**, 474–482.

Abramson, L.Y. (ed.) (1983) *Social-personal inferences in clinical psychology*. New York: Guildford Press.

Abramson, L.Y. and Martin, D.J. (1981) Depression and the causal inference process. In J.H. Harvey, W.J. Ickes and R.F. Kidd (eds), *New directions in attribution research*, (vol 3). Hillsdale, NJ: Erlbaum.

Abramson, L.Y., Seligman, M.E.P. and Teasdale, J.D. (1978) Learned helplessness in humans: Critique and reformulation. *Journal of Abnormal Psychology*, **87**, 49–74.

Adler, A. (1949) *Understanding human nature*. New York: Perma Books

Adorno, T.W., Frenkel-Brunswick, E., Levinson, D.J. and Sanford, R.N. (1950) *The authoritarian personality*. New York: Harper.

Agar, A.H. (1981) Ethnography as an interdisciplinary campground. In J.H. Harvey (ed.), *Cognition, social behaviour and the environment*. Hillsdale, NJ: Erlbaum.

Ajzen, I. (1977) Intuitive theories of events and the effects of base-rate information on prediction. *Journal of Personality and Social Psychology*, **35**, 303–314.

Ajzen, I. and Fishbein, M. (1983) Relevance and availability in the attribution process. In J. Jaspars et al. (eds), *Attribution theory and research: Conceptual, developmental and social dimensions*. London: Academic Press.

Allport, G.W. (1954) *The nature of prejudice*. Cambridge, Mass.: Addison Wesley.

Allport, G.W. (1968) The historical background of modern social psychology. In G. Lindzey and E. Aronson (eds), *The handbook of social psychology* (vol. 1). Reading, Mass.: Addison-Wesley (2nd edn)

Allport, G.W. and Postman, L. (1947) *The psychology of rumour*. New York: Holt.

Anderson, N.H. (1965) Averaging versus adding as a stimulus-combination rule in impression formation. *Journal of Experimental Psychology*, **70**, 394–400.

Antaki, C. (ed.) (1981) *The psychology of ordinary explanations of social behaviour*. London: Academic Press.

Antaki, C. (1982) Ordinary explanation, attribution theory and verbatim accounts. Unpublished doctoral dissertation, University of Sheffield.

Apfelbaum, E. and Herzlich, C. (1970–71) La Théorie de l'attribution en psychologie sociale. *Bulletin de Psychologie*, **24**, 961–976.

Arias, I. (1982) Cognitive processes influencing marital functioning. Paper presented at the 90th Annual Convention of the American Psychological Association, Washington, DC.

Arkin, R., Appelman, A. and Burger, J. (1980) Social anxiety, self-presentation and the self-serving bias in causal attribution. *Journal of Personality and Social Psychology*, **38**, 23–35.

Atkinson, J.W. and Feather, N.T. (1966) *A theory of achievement motivation*. New York: John Wiley.

Auerbach, S.M., Kendall, P.C., Cuttler, H.F. and Levitt, N.R., (1976) Anxiety, Locus of control, type of preparatory information and adjustment to dental surgery. *Journal of Consulting and Clinical Psychology*, **44**, 809–818.

Bains, G.S., (1982a) The effects of anticipated interaction on social perception. Submitted for publication.

Bains, G.S., (1982b) A test of the effects of control motivation on social perception using an individual differences approach. Submitted for publication.

Bandura, A. (1982) Self-efficacy mechanism in human agency. *American Psychologist*, **37**, 122–147.

Bar-Tal, D. and Darom, E. (1979) Pupils' attributions of success and failure. *Child Development*, **50**, 264–267.

Baucom, D.H. (1981) Cognitive behavioral strategies in the treatment of marital discord. Paper presented at the 15th Annual Convention of the Association for the Advancement of Behaviour Therapy, Toronto.

Baumeister, R.F. (1982) A self-presentational view of social phenomena. *Psychological Bulletin*, **91**, 3–26.

Beach, S.R., Abramson, L.Y. and Levine, F.M. (1982) The attributional reformulation of learned helplessness: Therapeutic implications. In H. Glazer and J. Clarkin, *Depression: Behavioral and directive intervention strategies*. New York: Garland.

Beck, A.T. (1967) *Depression: Clinical, experimental and theoretical aspects*. Philadelphia: University of Pennsylvania Press.

Beck, A.T., Rush, A.J., Shaw, B.F. and Emery, G. (1979) *Cognitive therapy of depression*. New York: Guildford Press.

Becker, M.H. (1979) Understanding patient compliance: The contributions of attitudes and other psychosocial factors. In S.J. Cohen (ed.), *New directions in patient compliance*. Baltimore: Lexington Books.

Becker, M.H., Haefner, D.P., Kasl, S.V., Kirscht, J.P., Maiman, L.A. and Rosenstock, I.M. (1977) Selected psychosocial models and correlates of individual health-related behaviours. *Medical Care*, **15**, (Suppl), 27–46.

Bellezza, F.S. and Bower, G.H. (1982) Remembering script-based text. *Poetics*, **11**, 1–12.

Bem, D.J. (1967) Self-perception: An alternative interpretation of cognitive dissonance phenomena. *Psychological Review*, **74**, 183–200.

Bem, D.J., (1972) Self-perception theory. In L. Berkowitz (ed.), *Advances in experimental social psychology* (vol. 6). New York: Academic Press.

Berry, J.W. (1979) A cultural ecology of social behaviour. In L. Berkowitz (ed.), *Advances in experimental social psychology* (vol. 12). New York: Academic Press.

Berscheid, E., Graziano, W., Monson, T., and Dermer, M. (1976) Outcome dependency: Attention, attribution and attraction. *Journal of Personality and Social Psychology*, **34**, 978–989.

Billig, M. (1978) *Fascists: A social-psychological analysis of the National Front.* London: Academic Press.

Blackwell, B. (1963) The literature of delay in seeking medical care for chronic illnesses. *Health Education Monographs*, **16**, 3–31.

Blakar, R.M. (1973) An experimental method for inquiring into communication. *European Journal of Social Psychology*, **3**, 415–425.

Blanchard, E.B. (ed.) (1982) Special issue on behavioural medicine. *Journal of Consulting and Clinical Psychology*, **50**, (6).

Blumer, H. (1966) Sociological implications of the thought of George Herbert Mead. *American Journal of Sociology*, **71**, 535–544.

Bochner, S. (ed.) (1982) *Cultures in contact: studies in cross-cultural interaction.* Oxford: Pergamon Press.

Boldt, E.D. (1978) Structural tightness and cross-cultural research. *Journal of Cross-Cultural Psychology*, **9**, 151–166.

Bond, M.H. and Goodman, G.N. (1980) Gaze patterns and interaction contexts: Effects on personality impressions and attributions. *Psychologia*, **23**, 70–79.

Bootzin, R.R., Herman, C.P. and Nicassio, P. (1976) The power of suggestion: Another examintion of misattribution and insomnia. *Journal of Personality and Social Psychology*, **34**, 673–679.

Boski, P. (1982) Ethnicity and self vs other attributions for achievement related outcomes. Paper presented at the 6th Congress of the International Association of Cross-Cultural Psychology, Aberdeen.

Bower, G.H., Black, J.B. and Turner, T.J. (1979) Scripts in memory for text. *Cognitive Psychology*, **11**, 177–220.

Bradley, G. (1978) Self-serving biases in the attribution process: A re-examination of the fact or fiction question. *Journal of Personality and Social Psychology*, **36**, 56–71.

Brehm, J.W. (1966) *A theory of psychological reactance.* New York: Academic Press.

Brehm, S. (1976) *The application of social psychology to clinical practice.* New York: Halstead Press.

Brewin, C.R. (1981) Attributional processes and response to adversity. Unpublished doctoral dissertation, University of Sheffield.

Brodt, S.E. and Zimbardo, P.G. (1981) Modifying shyness-related social behavior through symptom misattribution. *Journal of Personality and Social Psychology*, **41**, 437–449

Bruner, J.S. (1957) On perceptual readiness. *Psychological Review*, **64**, 123–151.

Brunswik, E. (1952) The conceptual framework of psychology. In *International encyclopaedia of unified science* (vol. 1, no. 10). Chicago: University of Chicago Press.

Bulman, R.J. and Wortman, C.B. (1977) Attributions of blame and coping in the 'real world': Severe accident victims react to their lot. *Journal of Personality and Social Psychology*, **35**, 351–363.

Burger, J.M. (1981) Motivational biases in the attribution of responsibility for an accident. A meta analysis of the defensive attribution hypothesis. *Psychological Bulletin*, **90**, 496–512.

Buss, A.R. (1978) Causes and reasons in attribution theory: A conceptual critique. *Journal of Personality and Social Psychology*, **36**, 1311–1321.

Calvert-Boyanowsky, J. and Leventhal, H. (1975) The role of information in attenuating behavioral response to stress: A reinterpretation of the misattribution phenomena. *Journal of Personality and Social Psychology*, 32, 214–221.

Campbell, D.T. (1963) Social attitudes and other acquired behavioural dispositions. In S. Koch (ed.), *Psychology: A study of a science* (vol. 6). New York: McGraw-Hill.

Cancian, F.M. (1968) Varieties of functional analysis. *International Encyclopaedia of the Social Sciences* (vol. 6), 29–43.

Carnap, R. (1955) Logical foundations of the unity of science. In O. Nemeth et al. (eds), *International encyclopaedia of unified science*. Chicago: University of Chicago Press.

Carr, W. (1969) *A history of Germany, 1815–1945*. London: Weidenfeld & Nicholson.

Chaiken, S. and Baldwin, M.W. (1981) Affective–cognitive consistency and the effect of salient behavioral information on the self-perception of attitudes. *Journal of Personality and Social Psychology*, 41, 1–12.

Chandler, T.A., Shama, D.A., Wolf, F.M. and Planchard, S.K. (1981) Multi-attributional causality for achievement across five cross-national samples. *Journal of Cross-Cultural Psychology*, 12, 207–221.

Chodoff, P., Friedman, S. and Hamburg, D., (1964) Stress defences and coping behaviour: Observations in parents of children with malignant disease. *American Journal of Psychiatry*, 120, 743–749.

Clodd, E. (1885) *Myths and dreams*, London: Chatto and Windus.

Colletti, G. and Kopel, S.A. (1979) Maintaining behavior change: An investigation of three maintenance strategies and the relationship of self-attribution to the long-term reduction of cigarette smoking. *Journal of Consulting and Clinical Psychology*, 47, 614–617.

Coombs, C.H. (1964) *A theory of data*. New York: John Wiley.

Da Gloria, J. and Pagès, R. (1974–75) Problèmes et exigences d'une théorie de l'attribution. *Bulletin de Psychologie*, 28, 229–235.

Darwin, C. (1872) *The expression of the emotions in man and animals*. London: D. Appleton & Co., Reprinted in 1965 by the University of Chicago Press.

Davison, G.C., Tsujimoto, R.N. and Glaros, A.G. (1973) Attribution and the maintenance of behaviour change in falling asleep. *Journal of Abnormal Psychology*, 82, 124–133.

Davison, G.C. and Valins, S. (1969) Maintenance of self-attributed and drug-attributed behaviour change. *Journal of Personality and Social Psychology*, 11, 25–33.

Deaux, K. and Emswiller, T. (1974) Explantions of sex-linked tasks: What is skill for the male is luck for the female. *Journal of Personality and Social Psychology*, 29, 80–85.

De Carufel, A., Straszak, I. and Jabes, J. (1981) Influencing attitudes towards breast self-examination: A cognitive approach. In D.S. Leather, G.B. Hastings and J.K. Davies (ed), *Health education and the media*. Oxford: Pergamon Press.

De Charms, R. (1968) *Personal causation: The internal affective determinants of behavior*. New York: Academic Press.

Deschamps, J.-C. (1973–74) L'attribution, la catégorisation et les représentations intergroupes. *Bulletin de Psychologie*, 27, 710–721.

Deschamps, J.-C (1983) Social attribution. In Jaspars et al. (eds), *Attribution theory and research: Conceptual, developmental and social dimensions*. London: Academic Press.

Detweiler, R.A. (1978) Culture, category width, and attributions: A model-building approach to the reasons for cultural effects. *Journal of Cross-Cultural Psychology*, **9**, 259–284.

Dienstbier, R.A. (1972) The role of anxiety and arousal attribution in cheating. *Journal of Experimental Social Psychology*, **8**, 168–179.

Dixon, R.M.W. (1977) Where have all the adjectives gone? *Studies in Language*, **1**, 19–80.

Doherty, W.J. (1981a) Cognitive processes in intimate conflict: I. Extending attribution theory. *American Journal of Family Therapy*, **9**, 1–13.

Doherty, W.J. (1981b) Cognitive processes in initmate conflict: II. Efficacy and learned helplessness. *American Journal of Family Therapy*, **9**, 35–44.

Doherty, W.J. (1982) Attribution style and negative problem-solving in marriage. *Family Relations*, **31**, 23–27.

Druian, P.R. and Omessi, E. (1982) A knowledge structure theory of attribution. Unpublished manuscript, Yale University.

Duhem, P. (1962 edn) *Theories and structure of physical theory*. New York: Atheneum.

Duncan, B.L. (1976) Differential social perception and attribution of intergroup violence: Testing the lower limits of stereotyping of Blacks. *Journal of Personality and Social Psychology*, **34**, 590–598.

Duncker, K. (1945) On problem-solving. *Psychological Monographs*, **58**, (5, whole of no. 270).

Durkheim, E. (1898) Représentations individuelles et représentations collectives. *Revue de Metaphysique et de Morale*, **6**, 273–302, translated as 'Individual and collective representations', in E. Durkheim, 1974, *Sociology and philosophy*. New York: Free Press.

Duval, S. and Wicklund, R (1972) *A theory of objective self-awareness*. New York: Academic Press.

Dyer, M.G. (1982) In-depth understanding: A computer model of integrated processing for narrative comprehension. Unpublished doctoral dissertation, Yale University.

Eiser, J.R. (1980) *Cognitive social psychology*. Maidenhead: McGraw-Hill.

Eiser, J.R. (1982) Addiction as attribution: Cognitive processes in giving up smoking. In J.R. Eiser (ed.), *Social psychology and behavioural medicine*. Chichester: John Wiley.

Eiser, J.R. (1983) Attribution theory and social cognition. In J. Jaspars et al. (eds.), *Attribution theory and research: Conceptual, developmental and social dimensions*. London: Academic Press.

Eiser, J.R. Sutton S.R. and Wober, M. (1978) Smokers' and non-smokers' attributions about smoking: A case of actor-observer differences? *British Journal of Social and Clinical Psychology*, **17**, 189–90.

Ekman, R., Sorenson, E.R. and Friesen, W.V. (1969) Pancultural elements in facial displays of emotions. *Science*, **164**, 86–88.

Elig, T.W. and Frieze, I.H. (1979) Measuring causal attributions for success and failure. *Journal of Personality and Social Psychology*, **37**, 621–634.

Ellis, A. and Greiger, R. (1977) *Rational–emotive therapy: A handbook of theory and practice*. New York: Springer.

Ellis, A. and Whiteley, J.M. (eds) (1979) *Theoretical and empirical foundations of rational–emotive therapy*. Monterey, Cal.: Brooks/Cole.

Elms, A.C. (1975) The crisis of confidence in social psychology. *American Psychologist*, **30**, 967–976.

Epstein, N. (1982) Cognitive therapy with couples. *American Journal of Family Therapy*, **10**, 5–16.

Epstein, N., and Eidelson, R.J. (1981) Unrealistic beliefs of clinical couples: Their relationship to expectations, goals, and satisfaction. *American Journal of Family Therapy*, **9**, 13–22.

Evans-Pritchard, E.E. (1937) *Witchcraft, oracles and magic among the Azande*. Oxford: Oxford University Press.

Farina, A., Fisher, J.D., Getter, H. and Fisher, E.H. (1978) Some consequences of changing people's views regarding the nature of mental illness. *Journal of Abnormal Psychology*, **87**, 272–279.

Farr, R.M. (1976) Experimentation: A social psychological perspective. *British Journal of Social and Clinical Psychology*, **15**, 225–238.

Farr, R.M. (1977) Heider, Harré and Herzlich on health & illness. Some observations on the structure of 'représentations collectives'. *European Journal of Social Psychology*, **7**, 491–504.

Farr, R.M. (1978) On the social significance of artifacts in experimenting. *British Journal of Social and Clinical Psychology* **17**, 299–306.

Farr, R.M. (1980) On reading Darwin and discovering social psychology. In R. Gilmour and S. Duck (eds), *The development of social psychology*. London: Academic Press.

Farr, R.M. (1982a) Interviewing: An introduction to the social psychology of the inter-view. In F. Fransella (ed.), *Psychology for occupational therapists*. London: Macmillan.

Farr, R.M. (1982b) On going beyond the information given: attributional artifacts in the research process. In H. Heibsch, H. Brandstatter and H. Kelley (eds), *Social psychology: Revised and edited version of selected papers presented to the XXII International Congress of Psychology, Leipzig, DDR, 1980* (vol. 8). Amsterdam: North Holland.

Farr, R.M. and Moscovici, S. (1983) On the nature and role of representations in self's understanding of others and of self. In M. Cook (ed.), *Interpersonal perception*, Psychology in Progress Series. London: Methuen.

Faucheux, C. (1976) Cross-cultural research in experimental social psychology. *European Journal of Social Psychology*, **6**, 269–322.

Fauconnet, P. (1928) *La Responsabilité*. Paris: Alcan (2nd edn).

Ferguson, M. (1981) *The aquarian conspiracy: Personal and social transformation in the 1980s*. London: Routledge and Kegan Paul.

Festinger, L. (1957) *A theory of cognitive dissonance*. Evanston, Ill.: Row, Peterson.

Festinger, L. (1980) Looking backward. In L. Festinger (ed.), *Retrospections on social psychology*. New York: Oxford University Press.

Fincham, F.D. (1983) Developmental dimensions of attribution theory. In J. Jaspars et al. (eds), *Attribution theory and research: Conceptual, developmental and social dimensions*. London: Academic Press.

Fincham, F.D. and Diener, C. (1982) An attributional analysis of child behavior problems. Unpublished manuscript, University of Illinois.

Fincham, F.D. and Hewstone, M. (1982) Social categorisation and personal similarity as determinants of attribution bias: A test of defensive attribution. *British Journal of Social Psychology*, **21**, 51–56.

Fincham, F.D. and Jaspars J.M.F. (1980) Attribution of responsibility: From man the scientist to man as lawyer. In L. Berkowitz (ed.), *Advances in experimental social psychology* (vol. 13). New York: Academic Press.

Fincham, F.D. and O'Leary, K.D. (1983) Causal inferences for spouse behavior in distressed and nondistressed couples. *Journal of Social and Clinical Psychology*, forthcoming.

Fincham, F.D. and Shultz, T. (1981) Intervening causation and the mitigation of responsibility for harm-doing. *British Journal of Social Psychology*, 20, 113–120.

Fischhoff, B. (1975) Hindsight ≠ foresight: The effects of outcome knowledge on judgment under uncertainty. *Journal of Experimental Psychology: Human Perception and Performance*, 1, 288–299.

Fischhoff, B. (1976) Attribution theory and judgment under uncertainty. In J.H. Harvey et al. (eds), *New directions in attribution research* (vol. 1). Hillsdale, NJ: Erlbaum.

Fishbein, M. and Ajzen, I. (1972) Attitudes and opinions. *Annual Review of Psychology*, 23, 487–544.

Fisher, J.D. and Farina, A. (1979) Consequences of beliefs about the nature of mental disorders. *Journal of Abnormal Psychology*, 88, 320–327.

Fiske, S.T. (1981) Social cognition and affect. In J.H. Harvey (ed.), *Cognition, social behaviour and the environment*. Hillsdale, NJ: Erlbaum.

Forsterling, F. (1980) Attributional aspects of cognitive behavior modification: A theoretical approach and suggestions for techniques. *Cognitive Therapy and Research*, 4, 27–37.

Forsyth, D.R. (1980) The functions of attributions. *Social Psychology Quarterly*, 43, 184–189.

Foschi, M. (1980) Theory, experimentation, and cross-cultural comparisons in social psychology. *Canadian Journal of Sociology*, 5, 91–102.

Frank, P. (1957) *Philosophy of science*. Englewood Cliffs, NJ: Prentice-Hall.

Freedle, R. (1981) The need for a cross-cultural perspective. In J.H. Harvey (ed.). *Cognition, social behaviour and the environment*. Hillsdale, N.J.: Erlbaum.

Frenkel-Brunswick, E. (1949) Intolerance of ambiguity as emotional and perceptual personality variable. *Journal of Personality*, 18, 108–143.

Freud, S. (1893–95) *Studies on hysteria. Standard edition of the Complete psychological works of Sigmund Freud*. London: Hogarth Press.

Frieze, I. (1976) Causal attributions and information seeking to explain success and failure. *Journal of Research in Personality*, 10, 293–305.

Frieze, I., Bar-Tal, D. and Carroll, J. (eds) (1979) *Attribution theory: Applications to social problems*. San Francisco: Jossey-Bass.

Frieze, I. and Weiner, B. (1971) Cue utilization and attributional judgements for success and failure. *Journal of Personality*, 39, 592–605.

Fry, P.S. and Ghosh, R. (1980) Attributions of success and failure: Comparison of cultural differences between Asian and Caucasian children. *Journal of Cross-Cultural Psychology*, 11, 343–363.

Furnham, A. (1982a) Explanations for unemployment in Britain. *European Journal of Social Psychology*, 12, 335–352.

Furnham, A. (1982b) Why are the poor always with us? Explanations for poverty in Britain. *British Journal of Social Psychology*, 21, 311–322.

Furnham, A. (1983) Attributions for affluence. *Personality and Individual Differences*, 4, 31–40.

Furnham, A., Jaspars, J. and Fincham, F.D. (1983) Professional and naive psychology: Two approaches to the explanation of human behaviour. In J. Jaspars, F.D. Fincham and M. Hewstone (eds), *Attribution theory and research: Conceptual, developmental and social dimensions*. London: Academic Press.

Galambos, J. and Black, J.B. (1981) Why do we do what we do? *Proceedings of the Third Annual Conference of the Cognitive Science Society*. Berkeley, Cal.

Galambos, J. and Rips, L.J. (1982) Memory for routines. *Journal of Verbal Learning and Verbal Behaviour*, **21**, 260–281.

Gardner, R.A. (1969) The guilt reaction of parents of children with severe physical disease. *American Journal of Psychiatry*, **126**, 636–644.

Garfinkel, H. (1967) *Studies in ethnomethodology*. Englewood Cliffs, NJ: Prentice-Hall.

Geertz, C. (1973) *The interpretation of cultures*. New York: Basic Books.

Geertz, C. (1975) On the nature of anthropological understanding. *American Scientist*, **63**, 47–53.

Geiss, S.K. and O'Leary, K.D. (1981) Therapist ratings of frequency and severity of marital problems: Implications for research. *Journal of Marital and Family Therapy*, 515–520.

Gergen, K.J. (1973) Social psychology as history. *Journal of Personality and Social Psychology*, **26**, 309–320.

Gergen, K.J. (1978) Experimentation in social psychology: A reappraisal. *European Journal of Social Psychology*, **8**, 507–527.

Glass, D.C. (1977) *Behaviour patterns, stress and coronary disease*. Hillsdale, NJ: Erlbaum.

Goffman, E. (1969) *The presentation of self in everyday life*. London: Allen Lane.

Gould, R., Brounstein, P.J. and Sigall, H. (1977) Attributing ability to an opponent: Public aggrandizement and private denigration. *Sociometry*, **40**, 254–261.

Graesser, A.C. (1981) *Prose comprehension beyond the word*. New York: Springer-Verlag.

Greenberg, J. and Rosenfield, D. (1979) Whites' ethnocentrism and their attributions for the behaviour of blacks: A motivational bias. *Journal of Personality*, **47**, 643–657.

Greenwald, A.G. (1980) The totalitarian ego: Fabrication and revision of personal history. *American Psychologist*, **35**, 603–618.

Gregory, R.L. (1981) *Mind in science: A history of explanations in psychology and physics*. Cambridge: Cambridge University Press.

Grimm, L.G. (1980) The maintenance of self- and drug-attributed behaviour change: A critique. *Journal of Abnormal Psychology*, **89**, 282–285.

Grosz, B.J. (1978) Focusing in dialogue. In *Proceedings of theoretical issues in natural language processing: 2. An interdisciplinary workshop*. Urbana, Ill.: University of Illinois Press.

Habermas, J. (1971) *Knowledge and human interests*. Boston: Beacon Press.

Hamilton, D. (1979) A cognitive–attributional analysis of stereotyping. In L. Berkowitz (ed.), *Advances in experimental social psychology* (vol 12). New York: Academic Press.

Hamilton, V.L. (1978) Who is responsible? Toward a *social* psychology of responsibility attribution. *Social Psychology*, **41**, 316–328.

Hamilton, V.L. (1980) Intuitive psychologist or intuitive lawyer? Alternative models of the attribution process. *Journal of Personality and Social Psychology*, **39**, 767–772.

Hansen, R.D. (1980) Commonsense attribution. *Journal of Personality and Social Psychology*, **39**, 996–1009.

Hansen, R.D. and Lowe, C.A. (1976) Distinctiveness and consensus: The influence of behavioural information on actors' and observers' attributions. *Journal of Personality and Social Psychology*, **34**, 425–433.

Harré, R. and Secord, P. (1972) *The explanation of social behaviour*. Oxford: Basil Blackwell.

Harris, B. and Harvey, J.H. (1981) Attribution theory: From phenomenal causality to the intuitive scientist and beyond. In C. Antaki (ed.) *The psychology of ordinary explanations of social behaviour*. London: Academic Press.

Harvey, J.H. (1981): Do we need another gloss on 'attribution theory'? *British Journal of Social Psychology*, **20**, 301-304.

Harvey, J.H. Ickes, W.J. and Kidd, R.F. (eds) (1976) *New directions in attribution research* (vol. 1). Hillsdale, NJ: Erlbaum.

Harvey, J.H., Ickes, W.J. and Kidd, R.F. (eds) (1978) *New directions in attribution research* (vol. 2). Hillsdale, NJ: Erlbaum.

Harvey, J.H. Ickes, W.J. and Kidd, R.F. (eds) (1981) *New directions in attribution research* (vol. 3). Hillsdale, NJ: Erlbaum.

Harvey, J.H., Town, J.P. and Yarkin, K.L. (1981) How fundamental is 'The Fundamental Attribution Error'? *Journal of Personality and Social Psychology*, **40**, 346–349.

Harvey, J.H. and Weary, G. (1981) *Perspectives on attribution processes*. Dubuque, Iowa: Wm C. Brown.

Harvey, J.H., Wells, G.L. and Alvarez, M.D. (1978) Attribution in the context of close relationships. In J.H. Harvey et al. (eds), *New directions in attribution research* (vol. 2). Hillsdale, NJ: Erlbaum.

Harvey, J.H., Yarkin, K.L., Lightner, J.M. and Town, J.P. (1980) Unsolicited interpretation and recall of interpersonal events. *Journal of Personality and Social Psychology*, **38**, 551–568.

Heidbreder, E. (1973) Functionalism. In M. Henle, J. Jaynes and J.J. Sullivan (eds), *Historical conceptions of psychology*. New York: Springer.

Heider, F. (1944) Social perception and phenomenal causality. *Psychological Review*, **51**, 358–374.

Heider, F. (1958) *The psychology of interpersonal relations*. New York: John Wiley.

Heider, F. (1959) The description of the psychological environment in the work of Marcel Proust. *Psychological Issues*, **1** (3), 85–107.

Heider, F. (1973) Gestalt theory: Early history and reminiscences. In M. Henle et al. (eds), *Historical conceptions of psychology*, New York: Springer.

Heider, F. (1976) A conversation with Fritz Heider. In J.H. Harvey et al. (eds), *New directions in attribution research* (vol. 1). Hillsdale, NJ: Erlbaum.

Heider, F. and Simmel, M. (1944) An experimental study of apparent behavior. *American Journal of Psychology*, **57**, 243–249.

Henslin, J.M. (1967) 'Craps' and magic. *American Journal of Sociology*, **73**, 316–330.

Herzlich, C. (1972) La Représentation sociale. In S. Moscovici (ed.), *Introduction à la psychologie sociale*, Paris: Larousse.

Herzlich, C. (1973) *Health and illness: A social-psychologial analysis*. London: Academic Press.

Herzstein, M. (1980) *The war that Hitler won*. London: Abacus.

Hewstone, M. (1981) Social dimensions of attribution. Unpublished doctoral dissertation, University of Oxford.

Hewstone, M. (1983) The role of language in attribution processes. In J. Jaspars et al. (eds), *Attribution theory and research: Conceptual, developmental and social dimensions*. London: Academic Press.

Hewstone, M., Bond, M.H. and Wan, K.-C. (1983) Social facts and social attributions: The explanation of intergroup differences in Hong Kong. *Social Cognition*, forthcoming.

Hewstone, M. and Jaspars, J. (1982a) Intergroup relations and attribution processes. In H. Tajfel (ed.), *Social identity and intergroup relations*. Cambridge/Paris: Cambridge University Press/Maison des Sciences de l'Homme.

Hewstone, M. and Jaspars, J. (1982b) Explanations for racial discrimination: The effect of group discussion on intergroup attributions. *European Journal of Social Psychology*, **12**, 1–16.

Hewstone, M. and Jaspars, J. (1983a) A re-examination of the roles of consensus, consistency and distinctiveness: Kelley's cube revisited. *British Journal of Social Psychology*, **22**, 41–50.

Hewstone, M. and Jaspars, J. (1983b) Social dimensions of attribution. In H. Tajfel (ed.), *The social dimensions: European developments in social psychology*. Cambridge/Paris: Cambridge University Press/Maison des Sciences de l'Homme.

Hewstone, M., Jaspars, J. and Lalljee, M. (1982) Social representations, social attribution and social identity: the intergroup images of 'public' and 'comprehensive' schoolboys. *European Journal of Social Psychology*, **12**, 241–269.

Hibbert, C. (1982) *The French revolution*. Harmondsworth: Penguin.

Hofstede, G. (1980) *Culture's consequences: International differences in work-related values*. Beverly Hills: Sage.

Hogan, R.T. and Emler, N.T. (1978) The biases in contemporary social psychology. *Social Research*, **45**, 478–534.

Horai, J. (1977) Attributional conflict. *Journal of Social Issues*, **33**, 88–100.

Hotaling, G.T. (1980) Attribution processes in husband–wife violence. In M. Strauss and G. Hotaling *The social causes of husband–wife violence*. Minneapolis: University of Minnesota Press.

House, W.C. (1980) Effects of knowledge that attributions will be observed by others. *Journal of Research in Personality*, **14**, 528–545.

Hsu, F.L.K. (1971) Psychological homeostasis and jen: Conceptual tools for advancing psychological anthropology. *American Anthropologist*, **73**, 23–44.

Huesmann, L.R. (ed.) (1978) Special issue: Learned helplessness as a model of depression. *Journal of Abnormal Psychology*, **87** (1).

Hui, C.C.H. (1982) Locus of control: A review of cross-cultural research. *International Journal of Inter-cultural Relations*, **6**, 301–323.

Hutchins, E. (1980) *Culture and inference*. Cambridge, Mass.: Harvard University Press.

Ichheiser, G. (1943) Misinterpretations of personality in everyday life and the psychologist's frame of reference. *Character and Personality*, **12**, 145–160.

Ichheiser, G. (1949) Misunderstandings in human relations: A study in false social perception. *American Journal of Sociology*, **55**, 1–70.

Ickes, W. (1981) Attributional styles and the self-concept. In L.Y. Abramson (ed.), *Attributional processes and clinical psychology*. New York: Guilford Press.

Ickes, W.J. and Layden, M.A. (1978) Attribution styles. In J.H. Harvey, W.J. Ickes and R.F. Kidd (eds), *New directions in attribution research* (vol. 2). Hilldale, NJ.: Erlbaum.

Israel, J. and Tajfel, H. (eds.) (1972) *The context of social psychology: A critical assessment*. London: Academic Press.

Jacobson, N.S. and Margolin, G. (1979) *Marital therapy*. New York: Brunner/Mazel.

Jahoda, G. (1979) A cross-cultural perspective on experimental social psychology. *Personality and Social Psychology Bulletin*, **5**, 142–148.

Jaspars, J. (in press) Attitudes and social representations. In S. Moscovici and R.M. Farr (eds), *Social representations*. Cambridge/Paris: Cambridge University Press/Maison des Sciences de l'Homme.

Jaspars, J., Fincham, F.D. and Hewstone, M. (eds) (1983b) *Attribution theory and research: Conceptual, developmental and social dimensions*, London: Academic Press.

Jaspars, J., Hewstone, M. and Fincham, F.D. (1983) Attribution theory and research: The state of the art. In J. Jaspars et al. (eds), *Attribution theory and research: Conceptual, developmental and social dimensions*. London: Academic Press.

Jaspars, J., Smith, C. and Lalljee, M. (in preparation) Two wrongs do not make a right: A critical evaluation and replication of a classical attribution experiment.

Jervis, R. (1982) Perception and misperception: An upgrading of the analysis. Paper delivered at the International Society of Political Psychology. June 1972.

Jodelet, D. (1980) Les fous mentales au village. Unpublished doctoral dissertation, Ecole des Hautes Etudes En Sciences Sociales, Paris.

Johnson, W.G., Ross, J.M. and Mastria, M.A. (1977) Delusional behavior: an attribution analysis of development and modification. *Journal of Abnormal Psychology*, **86**, 421–426.

Johnson-Laird, P.N. (1980) Mental models in cognitive science. *Cognitive Science*, **4**, 71–115.

Jones, E.E. (1976) How do people perceive the causes of behaviour? *American Psychologist*, **64**, 300–305.

Jones, E.E. (1979) The rocky road from acts to dispositions. *American Psychologist*, **63**, 107–117.

Jones, E.E. and Davis, K.E. (1965) From acts to dispositions: The attribution process in social perception. In L. Berkowitz (ed.), *Advances in experimental social psychology* (vol. 2). New York: Academic Press.

Jones, E.E., Davis, K.E. and Gergen, K.J. (1961) Role playing variations and their informational value for person perception. *Journal of Abnormal and Social Psychology*, **63**, 302–310.

Jones, E.E. and De Charms, R. (1957) Changes in social perception as a function of the personal relevance of behaviour. *Sociometry*, **20**, 75–85.

Jones, E.E. and McGillis, D. (1976) Correspondent inferences and the attribution cube: A comparative reappraisal. In J.H. Harvey et al. (eds), *New directions in attribution research* (vol. 1). Hillsdale, NJ: Erlbaum.

Jones, E.E. and Nisbett, R.E. (1971) *The actor and the observer: Divergent perceptions of the causes of behavior*. Morristown, NJ: General Learning Press; reprinted in E.E. Jones et al. (eds), *Attribution: Perceiving the causes of behavior*. Morristown, NJ: General Learning Press, 1972.

Jones, E.E. and Thibaut, J.W. (1958) Interaction goals as bases of inference in interpersonal perception. In R. Tagiuri and L. Petrulo (eds), *Person perception and interpersonal behavior*. Stanford, Cal.: Stanford University Press.

Kahneman, D. and Tversky, A. (1973) On the psychology of prediction. *Psychological Review*, **80**, 237–251.

Kanouse, D.E., Gumpert, P. and Canavan-Gumpert, D. (1981) The semantics of praise. In J.H. Harvey et al. (eds), *New directions in attribution research* (vol. 3). Hillsdale, NJ: Erlbaum.

Kasl, S.V. (1974) The Health Belief Model and chronic illness behaviour. *Health Education Monographs*, **2**, 433–444.

Kassin, S.M. (1979) Consensus information, prediction and causal attribution: A review of the literature and issues. *Journal of Personality and Social Psychology*, **37**, 1966–1981.

Kassin, S.M. (1981) From laychild to 'layman': Developmental causal attribution. In S.S. Brehm, S.M. Kassin and F.X. Gibbons (eds), *Developmental social psychology*, New York: Oxford University Press.

Kazdin, A.E. and Wilson, G.T. (1978) *Evaluation of behavior therapy*. Cambridge, Mass.: Ballinger Press.

Kelley, H.H. (1967) Attribution theory in social psychology. In D. Levine (ed.), *Nebraska symposium on motivation*. Lincoln, Neb.: University of Nebraska Press.

Kelley, H.H. (1971) *Attribution in social interaction*. Morristown, NJ: General Learning Press; reprinted in E.E. Jones et al. (eds), *Attribution: Perceiving the causes of behavior*. Morristown, NJ: General Learning Press, 1972.

Kelley, H.H. (1972) Causal schemata and the attribution process. In E.E. Jones et al. (eds), *Attribution: Perceiving the causes of behavior*, Morristown, NJ: General Learning Press.

Kelley, H.H. (1973) The processes of causal attribution. *American Psychologist*, **28**, 107–128.

Kelley, H.H. (1978) A conversation with Edward E. Jones and Harold H. Kelley. In J.H. Harvey et al. (eds) *New directions in attribution research* (vol. 2). Hillsdale, NJ: Erlbaum.

Kelley, H.H. (1979) *Personal relationships: Their structure and process*. Hillsdale, NJ: Erlbaum.

Kelley, H.H. (1980) The causes of behaviour: Their perception and regulation. In L. Festinger (ed.), *Retrospections on social psychology*. New York: Oxford University Press.

Kelley, H.H. (1983) Perceived causal structures. In J. Jaspars et al. (eds), *Attribution theory and research: Conceptual, developmental and social dimensions*. London: Academic Press.

Kelley, H.H. and Michela, J.L. (1980) Attribution theory and research. *Annual Review of Psychology*, **31**, 457–503.

Kellogg, R. and Baron, S. (1975) Attribution theory, insomnia and the reverse placebo effect: A reversal of Storms and Nisbett's findings. *Journal of Personality and Social Psychology*, **32**, 231–236.

Kelly, G.A. (1955) *The psychology of personal constructs* (2 vols). New York: W.W. Norton.

Kidd, R.F. and Amabile, T.M. (1981) Causal explanations in social interaction: Some dialogues on dialogue. In J.H. Harvey, W. Ickes and R.F. Kidd (eds) *New directions in attribution research* (vol. 3). Hillsdale, NJ: Erlbaum.

King, J.B. (1982) The impact of patients' perceptions of high blood pressure on attendance at screening: An attributional extension of the Health Belief Model. *Social Science and Medicine*, **16**, 1079–1092.

King, J.B. and Eiser, J.R. (1981) A strategy for counselling pregnant smokers. *Health Education Journal*, **40**, 66–68.

Kirscht, J.P. and Rosenstock, I.M. (1977) Patient adherence to antihypertensive medical regimens. *Journal of Community Health*, **3**, 115–124.

Kluckhohn, F. and Strodtbeck, F. (1961) *Variations in value orientations*. Evanston, Ill: Row, Peterson.

Koffka, K. (1936) *Principles of gestalt psychology*, London: Routledge and Kegan Paul.

Kopel, S.A. and Arkowitz, H. (1975) The role of attribution and self perception in behaviour change. *Genetic Psychology Monographs*, **92**, 175–212.

Krovetz, M. (1974) Explaining success or failure as a function of one's locus of control. *Journal of Personality*, **42**, 175–189.

Kruglanski, A.W. (1975) The endogenous–exogenous partition in attribution theory. *Psychological Review*, **82**, 387–406.

Kruglanski, A.W. (1979) Causal explanation, teleological explanation: On radical particularism in attribution theory. *Journal of Personality and Social Psychology*, **37**, 1447–1457.

Kruglanski, A.W. (1980) Lay epistemo-logic – process and contents: Another look at attribution theory. *Psychological Review*, **87**, 70–87.

Kruglanski, A.W. and Ajzen, I. (1983) Bias and error in lay epistemology. *European Journal of Social Psychology*, **13**, 1–44.

Kruglanski, A.W., Baldwin, M.W. and Towson, S. (1983) Die Laien-Epistemologie von Kruglanski. In D. Frey and M. Irle (eds), *Sozialpsychologische Theorien Perspektiven* (vol. 2). Bern: Verlag Huber.

Kruglanski, A.W. and Freund, T. (1982) The freezing and unfreezing of lay-inferences on impressional primacy, ethnic stereotyping and numerical anchoring. Unpublished manuscript, Tel-Aviv University.

Kruglanski, A.W., Friedland, N. and Farkash, E. (1981) Lay persons' sensitivity to statistical information. Unpublished manuscript, Tel-Aviv University.

Kruglanski, A.W., Hamel, I.A., Maides, S.A. and Shwartz, J.M. (1978) Attribution theory as a special case of lay epistemology. In J.H. Harvey et al. (eds), *New directions in attribution research* (vol. 2). Hillsdale, NJ.: Erlbaum.

Kruglanski, A.W. and Jaffe, Y. (1983) Lay epistemology: A theory for cognitive therapy. In L.Y. Abramson, (ed.) *An attributional perspective in clinical psychology*. New York: Guildford Press.

Kruglanski, A.W. and Klar, I. (1982) A view from a bridge: Synthesizing the consistency and attribution paradigms from a lay-epistemic perspective. Unpublished manuscript, Tel-Aviv University.

Kruglanski, A.W. and Meschiany, A. (1981) Overcoming belief perseverance. Unpublished manuscript, Tel-Aviv University.

Kuhn, T.S. (1962) *The structure of scientific revolutions*. Chicago: University of Chicago Press.

Lalljee, M. (1981) Attribution theory and the analysis of explantions. In C. Antaki (ed.), *The psychology of ordinary explanations of social behaviour*, London: Academic Press.

Lalljee, M., Furnham, A. and Jaspars, J. (1982) Factors underlying explanations for moral behaviour. Unpublished manuscript.

Lalljee, M., Lamb, R., Furnham, A. and Jaspars, J. (in press). Explanations and information search: Induction and hypothesis–testing approaches to arriving at an explanation. *British Journal of Social Psychology*.

Lalljee, M., Watson, M. and White P. (1982) Explanations, attributions and the social context of unexpected behaviour. *European Journal of Social Psychology*, **12**, 17–29.

Lalljee, M., Watson, M. and White P. (1983) Some aspects of the explanations of young children. In J. Jaspars et al. (eds), *Attribution theory: Conceptual, developmental and social dimensions*. London: Academic Press.

Langer, E.J. (1975) The illusion of control. *Journal of Personality and Social Psychology*, **32**, 311–328.

Langer, E.J. (1978) Rethinking the role of thought in social interaction. In J.H. Harvey et al. (eds), *New directions in attribution research* (vol. 2) Hillsdale, NJ: Erlbaum.

Langer, E.J., Blank, A. and Chanowitz, B. (1978) The mindlessness of ostensibly thoughtful action: The role of 'placebic' information in interpersonal interaction. *Journal of Personality and Social Psychology*, **36**, 635–642.

Lefcourt, H.M., Hogg, E., Struthers, S. and Holmes, C. (1975) Causal attributions as a function of locus of control, initial confidence, and performance outcomes. *Journal of Personality and Social Psychology*, **32**, 391–397.

Lefcourt, H.M., Von Baeyer, C.S., Wave, E.E., and Cox, O.J. (1979) The multidimensional, multiattributional causality scale: The development of a goal-specific locus of control scale. *Canadian Journal of Behavioural Science*, **11**, 286–304.

Lehnert, W. (1978) *The process of question answering*. Hillsdale, NJ: Erlbaum.

Lerner, M.J. (1970) The desire for justice and reactions to victims. In J. Macaulay and L. Berkowitz (eds), *Altruism and helping behaviour*. New York: Academic Press.

Lévi-Strauss, C. (1962) *La Pensée sauvage*. Paris: Plon; translated as *The savage mind*, London: Weidenfeld and Nicholson, 1966.

Lévy-Bruhl, L. (1922) *La Mentalité primitive*. Paris: Alcan; translated as *Primitive mentality*, London: Allen and Unwin, 1923.

Lévy-Bruhl, L. (1925) *How natives think*. New York: Alfred A. Knopf.

Lewin, K. (1951) *Field theory in social science*. New York: Harper and Row.

Lewontin, R., Rose, S. and Kamin, L. (1982) Bourgeois ideology and the origins of biological determinism. *Race and Class*, **24**, 1–16.

Ley, P. (1977) Psychological studies of doctor-patient communication. In S. Rachman (ed.) *Contributions to medical psychology* (Vol. I). Oxford: Pergamon Press.

Lindsay-Reid, E. and Osborn R.W. (1980) Readiness for exercise adoption. *Social Science and Medicine*, **14**, 139–146.

Lloyd-Bostock, S. (1983) Attributions of cause and responsibility as social phenomena. In J. Jaspars et al. (eds), *Attribution theory and research: Conceptual, developmental and social dimensions*. London: Academic Press.

Löchel, E. (1983) Sex differences in achievement attribution. In J. Jaspars et al. (eds), *Attribution theory and research: Conceptual, developmental and social dimensions*. London: Academic Press.

Lowery, C.R., Denney, D.R. and Storms, M.D. (1979) Insomnia: A comparison of the effects of pill attributions and nonpejorative self-attributions. *Cognitive Therapy and Research*, **3**, 161–164.

Luchins, A.S. (1957) Experimental attempts to minimize the impact of first impressions. In C.E. Hovland (ed.) *The order of presentation in persuasion*. New Haven, Conn.: Yale University Press.

Lukes, S. (1973) *Individualism*. Oxford: Basil Blackwell.

Lukes, S. (1975) *Emile Durkheim: His life and work: A historical and critical study*. Harmondsworth: Penguin.

Lyman, S.M. and Scott, M.B. (1970) *A sociology of the absurd*. New York: Appleton-Century-Crofts.

Madden, M.E. and Janoff-Bulman, R. (1981) Blame, control and marital satisfaction: Wives' attributions for conflict in marriage. *Journal of Marriage and the Family*, **44**, 663–674.

Maine de Biran (1942 edn) *Oeuvres choisies de Maine de Biran.* Paris: Editions Montaigne.

Manis, M. (1977) Cognitive social psychology. *Personality and Social Psychology Bulletin*, 3, 550–566.

Mann, I.T. (1980) Free response causal attributions for interpersonal events. Paper presented at the annual convention of the American Psychological Association, Montreal.

Markus, H. (1977) Self schemas and the processing of information about the self. *Journal of Personality and Social Psychology*, 35, 63–78.

Marshal, G.D. and Zimbardo, P.G. (1979) Affective consequences of inadequately explained physiological arousal. *Journal of Personality and Social Psychology*, 37, 970–985.

McArthur, L.A. (1972) The how and what of why: Some determinants and consequences of causal attribution. *Journal of Personality and Social Psychology*, 2, 171–193.

McDermott, R.P. and Pratt, M. (1976) Attribution theory and social interaction: some ethnographic accounts. *Quarterly Newsletter of the Institute for Comparative Human Development*, 1, 3–5.

McGarry, J.J. and Newbury, B.H. (1981) Belief in paranormal phenomena and locus of control: A field study. *Journal of Personality and Social Psychology*, 41, 723–736.

McGuire, W.J. (1973) The yin and yang of progress in social psychology: Seven koan. *Journal of Personality and Social Psychology*, 26, 446–456.

McGuire, W.J. (1981) The probabilogical model of cognitive structure and attitude change. In R.E. Petty, T.M. Ostrom and T.C. Brock (eds), *Cognitive responses in persuasion.* Hillsdale, NJ: Erlbaum.

McHugh, M., Beckman, L. and Frieze, I.H. (1979) Analyzing alcoholism. In I.H. Frieze, D. Bar-Tal and J.S. Carroll (eds), *New approaches to social problems.* San Francisco: Jossey-Bass.

Mead, G.H. (1927) The objective reality of perspectives. In E.S Brightman (ed.), *Proceedings of the sixth international congress of philosophy.* New York: Longmans, Green; reprinted in G.H. Mead, *The philosophy of the present.* La Salle, Ill.: Open Court, 1932.

Mead, G.H. (1934) *Mind, self and society: from the standpoint of a social behaviourist*, edited, and with an introduction, by C.W. Morris. Chicago: University of Chicago Press.

Metalsky, G.I. and Abramson, L.Y. (1980) Attributional styles: Towards a framework for conceptualization and assessment. In P.C. Kendall and S.D. Hollon, (eds), *Cognitive-behavioral interventions: Assessment and methods.* New York: Academic Press.

Meyer, J.P. (1980) Causal attribution for success and failure: A multivariate investigation of dimensionality, formation and consequences, *Journal of Personality and Social Psychology*, 38, 704–718.

Meyer, M.E. (1921) *The psychology of the other-one: An introductory textbook.* Columbia, Missouri: Missouri Book Co.

Michotte, A.E. (1946) *La perception de la causalité.* Paris: J. Vrin; translated as *The perception of causality.* New York: Basic Books, 1963.

Milgram, S. (1974) *Obedience to authority: an experimental view.* London: Tavistock.

Miller, D.T., Norman, S.A. and Wright, E. (1978) Distortion in person perception as a consequence of the need for effective control. *Journal of Personality and Social Psychology*, **36**, 598–607.

Miller, D.T. and Ross, M. (1975) Self-serving biases in the attribution of causality: Fact or fiction? *Psychological Bulletin*, **82**, 213–225.

Miller, S.M. (1981) Predictability and human stress: Toward a clarification of evidence and theory. In L. Berkowitz (ed.), *Advances in experimental social psychology* (vol. 14). New York: Academic Press.

Minuchin, S. (1974) *Families and family therapy*. Cambridge, Mass.: Harvard University Press.

Mischel, W., (1968) *Personality and assessment*. New York: John Wiley.

Morris, L.A and Kanouse, D.E. (1979) Drug-taking for physical symptoms. In I. Frieze, D. Bar-Tal and J.S. Carroll, *New approaches to social problems*. San Francisco; Jossey-Bass.

Moscovici, S. (1961) *La Psychanalyse, son image et son public*. Paris: Presses Universitaires de France. Moscovici, S. (1976) 2nd edn of Moscovici 1961.

Moscovici, S. (1981) On social representations. In J.P. Forgas (ed.), *Social cognition: Perspectives on everyday understanding*. London: Academic Press.

Moscovici, S. (1983) The coming era of representations. In J.-P. Codol and J.-P. Leyens (eds), *Cognitive analysis of social behaviour*. The Hague: Martinus Nijhoff.

Moscovici, S. and Farr, R.M. (eds) (1983) *Social representations*. Cambridge/Paris: Cambridge University Press/Maison des Sciences de l'Homme.

Moscovici, S. and Faucheux, C. (1972) Social influence, conformity bias, and the study of active minorities. In L. Berkowitz (ed.) *Advances in experimental social psychology* (vol. 6) New York: Academic Press.

Mower White, C.J. (1977) A limitation of balance theory: The effects of identification with a member of the triad. *European Journal of Social Psychology*, **7**, 111–116.

Myers, D.G. and Lamm, H. (1976) The group polarization phenomenon. *Psychological Bulletin*, **83**, 602–627.

Neisser, U. (1966) *Cognitive psychology*. New York: Appleton-Century-Crofts.

Neisser, U. (1976) *Cognition and reality*. San Francisco: W.H. Freeman.

Neisser, U. (1980) On 'social knowing'. *Personality and Social Psychology Bulletin*, **6**, 601–605.

Nelson, K. and Gruendel, J.M. (1979) At morning it's lunchtime: A scriptal view of children's dialogues. *Discourse Processes*, **2**, 73–94.

Newman, H. (1981a) Communication within ongoing intimate relationships: An attributional perspective. *Personality and Social Psychology Bulletin*, **7**, 59–70.

Newman, H. (1981b) Interpretation and explanation: Influences on communicative exchanges within intimate relationships. *Communication Quarterly*, **8**, 123–132.

Newman, H. and Langer, E.J. (1981) Post-divorce adaptation and the attribution of responsibility. *Sex Roles*, **7**, 223–232.

Newman, H., and Langer, E.J. (1983) Investigating the development and courses of intimate relationships: A cognitive model. In L.Y. Abramson (ed.) *Social-personal inference in clinical psychology*, New York: Guilford Press.

Nielsen, G (1962) *Studies in self-confrontation: viewing a sound motion picture of self and another person in a stressful dyadic interaction*. Copenhagen: Munksgaard.

Nisbett, R.E. and Borgida, E. (1975) Attribution and the psychology of prediction. *Journal of Personality and Social Psychology*, **32**, 932–943

Nisbett, R.E., Borgida, E., Crandall, R. and Reed, H. (1976) Popular induction: Information is not necessarily informative. In J.S. Carroll and J.W. Payne (eds) *Cognition and social behaviour*. Hillsdale, NJ: Erlbaum.

Nisbett, R.E. and Caputo, G.C. (1971) Personality traits: Why other people do the things they do? Unpublished manuscript, Yale University.

Nisbett, R.E. and Ross L. (1980) *Human inference: strategies and shortcomings of social judgement*. Englewood Cliffs, NJ: Prentice-Hall.

Nisbett, R.E. and Schachter, S. (1966) Cognitive manipulation of pain. *Journal of Experimental Social Psychology*, **2**, 227–236.

O'Neil, W. and Levinson, D.J. (1954) A factorial exploration of Authoritarianism and some of its ideological concomitants. *Journal of Personality*, **22**, 449–463.

Orvis, B.R. Cunningham, J.D. and Kelley, H.H. (1975) A closer examination of causal inferences: The roles of consensus, distinctiveness and consistency information. *Journal of Personality and Social Psychology*, **32**, 605–616.

Orvis, B.R., Kelley, H.H., and Butler, D. (1976) Attributional conflict in young couples. In J.H. Harvey, W.J. Ickes and R.F. Kidd (eds), *New directions in attribution research* (vol. 1) Hillsdale, NJ: Erlbaum.

Oxford English Dictionary (1933) Oxford: Clarendon Press.

Passer, M.W., Kelley, H.H. and Michela, J.L. (1978) Multidimensional scaling of the causes for negative interpersonal behaviour. *Journal of Personality and Social Psychology*, **36**, 951–962.

Pedersen, P.B. (1977) Asian personality theory. In R. Corsini (ed). *Current personality theories*. Ithaca NY: Peacock.

Peeters, G. (1971) Causal attribution in messages as a function of inter-message semantic relations. In E. Carswell and R. Rommetveit (eds), *Social contexts of messages*. London: Academic Press.

Pepitone, A. (1976) Toward a normative and comparative biocultural social psychology. *Journal of Personality and Social Psychology*, **34**, 641–653.

Pepitone, A. (1981) Lessons from the history of social psychlogy. *American Psychologist*, **36**, 972–985.

Peplau, L.A., Russell, D. and Heim, M. (1979) An attributional analysis of loneliness. In I. Frieze, D. Bar-Tal and J. Carroll (eds), *Attribution theory: Applications to social problems*. San Francisco: Jossey-Bass.

Pettigrew, T.F. (1979) The ultimate attribution error: Extending Allport's cognitive analysis of prejudice. *Personality and Social Psychology Bulletin*, 5, 461–476.

Piaget, J. (1930) *The child's conception of physical causality*. London: Routledge.

Pittman, T.S. and Pittman, N.L. (1980) Deprivations of control and the attribution process. *Journal of Personality and Social Psychology*, **39**, 337–389.

Pleban, R. and Richardson, D.C. (1979) Research and publication trends in social psychology: 1973–1977. *Personality and Social Psychology Bulletin*, 5, 138–141.

Poliakov, L. (1980) *La Causalité diabolique*. Paris: Calmann-Lévy.

Quattrone, G.A. (1982) Overattribution and unit formation: When behaviour engulfs the person. *Journal of Personality and Social Psychology*, **42**, 593–607.

Rachman, S. (1981) The primacy of affect: Some theoretical implications. *Behaviour Research and Therapy*, **19**, 279–290.

Rescorla, R.A. (1967) Pavlovian conditioning and its proper control procedures. *Psychological Review*, **74**, 71–80.

Rescorla, R.A. and Solomon, R.L. (1967) Two-process learning theory: Relationships between Pavlovian conditioning and instrumental learning. *Psychological Review*, **74**, 151–182.

Ring, K.E. (1967) Experimental social psychology: Some sober questions about some frivolous values. *Journal of Experimental Social Psychology*, **34**, 641–653.

Robinson, D. (1978) *Patients, practitioners and medical care: Aspects of medical society*, London: Martin Robinson.

Rodin, J. (1975) Menstruation, reattribution and competence. *Journal of Personality and Social Psychology*, **43**, 345–353.

Rodin, J. (1978) Somatopsychics and attribution. *Personality and Social Psychology Bulletin*, **4**, 531–540.

Rommetveit, R. (1974) *On message structure*. London: John Wiley.

Rommetveit, R. (1979) On the architecture of intersubjectivity. In R. Rommetveit and R.M. Blakar (eds), *Studies of language, thought, and verbal communication*. London: Academic Press.

Roqueplo, P. (1974) *Le Partage du savoir*. Paris: Le Seuil.

Rosenberg, C.E. (1976) *No other gods: On science and American social thought*. Baltimore: Johns Hopkins University Press.

Rosenberg, M.J. (1969) The conditions and consequences of evaluation apprehension. R. Rosenthal and R.L. Rosnow (eds), *Artifact in behavioural research*. New York: Academic Press.

Rosenstock, I. (1966) Why people use health services. *Milbank Memorial Fund Quarterly*, **44**, 94–127.

Rosenstock, I. (1974) The Health Belief Model and preventive health behaviour. *Health Education Monographs*, **2**, 354–386.

Ross, L. (1977) The intuitive psychologist and his shortcomings: Distortions in the attribution proces. In L. Berkowitz (ed.), *Advances in experimental social psychology* (vol. 10). New York: Academic Press.

Ross, L., Lepper, M.R. and Hubbard, M. (1975) Perseverance in self-perception and social perception: Biased attributional processes in the debriefing paradigm. *Journal of Personality and Social Psychology*, **32**, 880–892.

Ross, L., Rodin, J. and Zimbardo, P.G. (1969) Toward an attribution therapy: The reduction of fear through induced cognitive–emotion misattribution. *Journal of Personality and Social Psychology*, **12**, 279–288.

Rotter, J.B. (1966) Generalized expectancies for internal versus external control of reinforcement. *Psychological Monographs*, **80**; 1 (whole no. 609).

Ruble, D.N. and Feldman, N.S. (1976) Order of consensus, distinctiveness and consistency information and causal attributions. *Journal of Personality and Social Psychology Bulletin*, 34, 930–937.

Rumelhart, D.E. (1980) Schemata; the building blocks of cognition. In R. Spiro, B. Bruce and W. Brewer (eds), *Theoretical issues in reading comprehension*. Hillsdale, NJ: Erlbaum.

Ryan, W. (1971) *Blaming the victim*. New York: Pantheon.

Sabini, J. and Silver, M. (1980) Baseball and hot sauce: A critique of some attributional treatments of evaluation. *Journal for the Theory of Social Behaviour*, **10**, 83–95.

Sackett, D. and Haynes, R. (1976) *Compliance with therapeutic regimens*. Baltimore: Johns Hopkins University Press.

Sampson, E.E. (1977) Psychology and the American ideal. *Journal of Personality and Social Psychology*, **35**, 767–782.

Sampson, E.E. (1981) Cognitive psychology as ideology. *American Psychologist*, **36**, 730–743.

Sanford, A.J. and Garrod, S.C. (1981) *Understanding written language: Explorations of comprehension beyond the sentence*. Chichester: John Wiley.

Schachter, S. (1964) The interaction of cognitive and physiological determinants of emotional arousal. In L. Berkowitz (ed.), *Advances in experimental social psychology* (vol. 1). New York: Academic Press.

Schachter, S. and Singer, J.E. (1962) Cognitive, social, and physiological determinants of emotional state. *Psychological Review*, **69**, 379–399.

Schachter, S. and Singer, J.E. (1979) Comments on Maslach and Marshall–Zimbardo experiments. *Journal of Personality and Social Psychology*, **37**, 989–995.

Schank, R.C. (1982) *Dynamic memory: Learning in computers and people.* New York: Cambridge University Press.

Schank, R.C. and Abelson, R.P. (1977) *Scripts, plans, goals and understanding.* Hillsdale, NJ: Erlbaum.

Schank, R.C. and Riesbeck, C. (1981) *Inside computer understanding.* Hillsdale, NJ: Erlbaum.

Schuman, H. and Johnson, M. (1976) Attitudes and behaviour. In A. Inkeles (ed.), *Annual Review of Sociology* (vol. 2). Palo Alto, Calif.: Annual Review.

Schwartz, T. (1981) The acquisition of culture. *Ethos*, **9**, 4–17.

Scott, M.B. and Lyman, S. (1968) Accounts. *American Sociological Review*, **33**, 46–62.

Segall, M.H. (1979) *Cross-cultural psychology: Human behavior in global perspective.* Monterey, Cal.: Brooks/Cole.

Selby, H.A. (1975) Semantics and causality in the study of deviance. In M. Sanches and B.G. Blount, *Sociocultural dimensions of language use.* London: Academic Press.

Seligman, M.E.P. (1975) *Helplessness.* San Francisco: W.H. Freeman.

Seligman, M.E.P., Abramson, L.Y., Semmel, A. and von Baeyer, C. (1979) Depressive attributional style. *Journal of Abnormal Psychology*, **88**, 242–247.

Semin, G. (1980) A gloss on attribution theory. *British Journal of Social and Clinical Psychology*, **19**, 291–300.

Semin, G. and Manstead, A.S. (1983) *The accountability of conduct: A social psychological analysis.* London: Academic Press.

Shaver, K.G. (1970) Defensive attributions: Effects of severity and relevance on the responsibility assigned for accidents. *Journal of Experimental Social Psychology*, **16**, 100–110.

Shaver, K.G. (1975) *An introduction to attribution processes.* Cambridge, Mass.: Winthrop.

Shaw, M.E. and Iwawaki, S (1972) Attribution of responsibility by Japanese and Americans as a function of age. *Journal of Cross-Cultural Psychology*, **3**, 71–82.

Shirer, W.L. (1972) *The rise and fall of the Third Reich: A history of National Germany.* London: Pan Books.

Shultz, T.R. and Schleifer, M. (1983) Towards a refinement of attribution concepts. In J. Jaspars et al. (eds), *Attribution theory and research: Conceptual, developmental and social dimensions.* London: Academic Press.

Shweder, R.A. (1982) On savages and other children (review of *The foundations of primitive thought* by C.R. Hallpike). *American Anthropologist*, **84**, 354–366.

Shweder, R.A. and Bourne, E.J. (1982) Does the concept of the person vary cross-culturally? In A.J. Marsalla and G.M. White (eds), *Cultural conceptions of mental health and therapy.* Dordrecht, Holland: D. Reidel.

Sillars, A.L. (1981) Attributions and interpersonal conflict resolution. In J.H. Harvey, W. Ickes and R.F. Kidd (eds), *New directions in attribution research* (vol. 3). Hillsdale, NJ: Erlbaum.

Silver, R.L. and Wortman, C.B. (1980) Coping with undesirable life events. In J. Garber and M.E.P. Seligman (eds), *Human helplessness*. New York: Academic Press.

Simon, H.A. (1968) Causation. *International Encyclopaedia of the Social Sciences* (vol. 2), 350–356.

Singerman, K.J., Borkovec, T.D. and Baron, R.S. (1976) Failure of a 'misattribution therapy' manipulation with a clinically relevent target behaviour. *Behaviour Therapy*, 7, 306–313.

Singh, R., Gupta, M. and Dalal, A.K. (1979) Cultural difference in attribution of performance: an integration-theoretical analysis. *Journal of Personality and Social Psychology*, 37, 1342–1351.

Slovic, P., Fischhoff, B. and Lichtenstein, S. (1979) Perceived risk: Psychological research and public policy implications. Paper presented at the American Psychological Association, 87th Annual Convention, New York.

Smith, E.R. and Miller, F.D. (1979a) Attributional information processing: A response time model of causal subtraction. *Journal of Personality and Social Psychology*, 37, 1723–1731.

Smith, E.R. and Miller, F.D. (1979b) Salience and the cognitive mediation of attribution. *Journal of Personality and Social Psychology*, 37, 2240–2252.

Smith, F.R. (1977) On the concept and measurement of cause in studies of causal attribution. Paper presented at the annual convention of the American Psychological Association, San Francisco.

Smith, S.S., Richardson, D. and Hendrick, C. (1980) Bibliography of journal articles in personality and social psychology: 1979. *Personality and Social Psychology Bulletin*, 6, 606–636.

Smith, T.W. and Brehm, S.S. (1981) Person perception and the type A coronary-prone behaviour pattern. *Journal of Personality and Social Psychology*, 40, 1137–1149.

Smock, C.D. (1955) The influence of psychological stress on the 'intolerance of ambiguity'. *Journal of Abnormal and Social Psychology*, 50, 177–182.

Snyder, M. and Gangestad, S. (1981) Hypothesis-testing processes. In J.H. Harvey, W. Ickes and R.F. Kidd (eds) *New directions in attribution research* (vol. 3). Hillsdale, NJ: Erlbaum.

Snyder, M., Stephan, W.G. and Rosenfield, D. (1976) Egotism and attribution. *Journal of Personality and Social Psychology*, 33, 435–441.

Snyder, M. and Swann, W.B. (1978) Behavioral confirmation in social interaction: From social perception to social reality. *Journal of Experimental Social Psychology*, 14, 148–160.

Solomon, S. (1978) Measuring dispositional and situational attributions. *Personality and Social Psychology Bulletin*, 4, 589–594.

Sølvberg, H.A. and Blakar, R.M. (1975) Communication efficiency in couples with and without a schizophrenic offspring. *Family Process*, 14, 515–534.

Springer, S. and Deutsch, G. (1981) *Left brain, right brain*. San Francisco, Cal.: W.H. Freeman.

Spuhler, J.N. (1982) Review of S.J. Gould, *The mismeasure of man*. *Contemporary Psychology*, 27, 933–935.

Stebbing, L.S. (1950) *A modern introduction to logic*. London: Methuen.

Steiner, I.D. (1974) Whatever happened to the group in social psychology? *Journal of Experimental Social Psychology*, 10, 94–108.

Stephan, W.G., Rosenfield, D. and Stephan, C. (1976) Egotism in males and females. *Journal of Personality and Social Psychology*, 34, 1161–1167.

Stimson, G.V. and Webb, B. (1975) *Going to see the doctor: The consulation process in general practice*. London: Routledge and Kegan Paul.

Stitt, A. (1971) Emergency after death. *Emergency Medicine*, **3**, 270–279.

Stoeckle, J. and Barsky, A.J. (1980) Attributions: uses of social science knowledge in the 'doctoring' of primary care. In L. Eisenberg and A. Kleinman (eds), *The relevance of social science for medicine*. Mass.: D. Reidel.

Stokes, T.F. and Baer, D.M. (1977) An implicit technology of generalization. *Journal of Applied Behaviour Analysis*, **10**, 349–367.

Storms, M.D. (1973) Videotape and the attribution process: Reversing actors' and observers' points of view. *Journal of Personality and Social Psychology*, **27**, 165–175.

Storms, M.D., Denney, D.R., McCaul, K.D. and Lowery, C.R. (1979) Attribution and insomnia. In I.H. Frieze, D. Bar-Tal and J.S. Carroll (eds), *Attribution theory: Applications to social problems*. San Francisco: Jossey-Bass.

Storms, M.D. and McCaul K.D. (1976) Attribution processes and the emotional exacerbation of dysfunctional behavior. In J.H. Harvey, W.J. Ickes and R.F. Kidd (eds), *New directions in attribution research* (vol. 1). Hillsdale, NJ: Erlbaum.

Storms, M.D. and Nisbett, R.E. (1970) Insomnia and the attribution process. *Journal of Personality and Social Psychology*, **16**, 319–328.

Strickland, B.R. (1978) Internal–external expectancies and health-related behaviours. *Journal of Consulting and Clinical Psychology*, **46**, 1192–1211.

Strickland, B.R. and Janoff-Bulman, R. (1980) Expectancies and attributions: Implications for community mental health. In M.S. Gibbs, J.L. Lachenmeyer and J. Sigal (eds), *Community psychology: Theoretical and empirical approaches*. New York: Gardner Press.

Strong, S.R. (1978) Social psychological approach to psychotherapy research. In S.L. Garfield and A.E. Bergin (eds), *Handbook of psychotherapy research and behaviour change*. New York: John Wiley.

Stryker, S. and Gottlieb, A. (1981) Attribution theory and symbolic interactionism: A comparison. In J.H. Harvey et al. (eds), *New directions in attribution research* (vol. 3). Hillsdale, N.J: Erlbaum.

Sue, S. and Nolan, Z. (1980) Learned helplessness theory and community psychology. In M.S. Gibbs, J.L. Lachenmeyer and J. Sigal (eds), *Community psychology: Theoretical and empirical approaches*. New York: Gardner Press.

Surber, C.F. (1981) Necessary versus sufficient causal schemata: Attributions for achievement in difficult and easy tasks. *Journal of Experimental Social Psychology*, **17**, 569–586.

Swann, W.B., Stephenson, B. and Pittman, T.S. (1981) Curiosity and control: On the determinants of the search for social knowledge. *Journal of Personality and Social Psychology*, **40**, 635–642.

Symonds, M. (1974) Data reported in *Newsweek*, 17 June 1974, p. 66.

Tajfel, H., (1969) Cognitive aspects of prejudice. *Journal of Social Issues*, **25**, 79–97.

Tajfel, H. (ed.) (1978) *Differentiation between social groups*. London: Academic Press.

Tajfel, H. (1981) Social stereotypes. In J. Turner and H. Giles (eds), *Intergroup behaviour*. Oxford: Basil Blackwell.

Tajfel, H. and Turner, J.C. (1979) An integrative theory of intergroup conflict. In W.G. Austin and S. Worchel (eds), *The social psychology of intergroup relations*. Monterey, Cal.: Brooks/Cole.

Tarpy, R.M. (1982) *Principles of animal learning and motivation.* Glenview, Ill.: Scott Foresman.

Taylor, D.M. and Jaggi, V. (1974) Ethnocentrism and causal attributions in a South Indian context. *Journal of Cross-cultural Psychology,* 5, 162–171.

Taylor, S.E. (1981) The interface of cognitive and social psychology. In J.H. Harvey (ed.) *Cognition, social behaviour and the environment.* Hillsdale, NJ: Erlbaum.

Taylor, S.E. and Levin, S. (1976) The psychological impact of breast cancer: Theory and practice. In A. Enelow (ed.), *Psychological aspects of breast cancer.* San Francisco: West Coast Cancer Foundation.

Taylor, S.E. and Thompson, S.C. (1982) Stalking the elusive 'vividness effect'. *Psychological Review,* 89, 155–181.

Tedeschi, J.T. and Reiss, M. (1981) Verbal strategies in impression management. In C. Antaki (ed.), *The psychology of ordinary explanations of social behaviour.* London: Academic Press.

Tedeschi, J.T., Schlenker, B.R. and Bonoma, T.V. (1971) Cognitive dissonance: Private ratiocination or public spectacle? *American Psychologist,* 26, 685–695.

Tetlock, P.E. and Levi, A. (1982) Attribution bias: On the inconclusiveness of the cognition-motivation debate. *Journal of Experimental Social Psychology,* 18, 68–88.

Thibaut, J.W. and Riecken, H.W. (1955) Some determinants and consequences of the perception of social causality. *Journal of Personality,* 24, 113–133.

Thomas, K. (1971) *Religion and the decline of magic.* London: Weidenfeld & Nicholson.

Thompson, S.C. and Kelley, H.H. (1981) Judgments of responsibility for activities in close relationships. *Journal of Personality and Social Psychology,* 41, 469–477.

Thorngate, W. (1976) Must we always think before we act? *Personality and Social Psychology Bulletin,* 2, 31–35.

Thorngate, W. (1979) Memory, cognition and social performance. In L.H. Strickland (ed.), *Soviet and Western perspectives in social psychology.* Oxford: Pergamon Press.

Tolman, E.C. (1948) Cognitive maps in rats and men. *Psychological Review,* 55, 189–208.

Triandis, H.C. (1975) Social psychology and cultural analysis. *Journal of the Theory of Social Behaviour,* 5, 81–106.

Triandis, H.C. (1976) On the value of cross-cultural research in social psychology: Reactions to Faucheux's paper. *European Journal of Social Psychology,* 6, 331–341.

Triandis, H.C. (1978) Some universals of social behavior. *Personality and Social Psychology Bulletin,* 4, 1–16.

Triandis, H.C. (1981) Some dimensions of intercultural variation and their implications for interpersonal behavior. Unpublished manuscript. University of Illinois.

Turner, J.C. and Giles, H. (eds) (1981) *Intergroup behaviour.* Oxford: Basil Blackwell.

Tversky, A. and Kahneman, D. (1974) Judgement under uncertainty: Heuristics and biases. *Science,* 185, 1124–1131.

Tversky, A. and Kahneman, D. (1980) Causal schemas in judgements under uncertainty. In M. Fishbein (ed.), *Progress in social psychology* (vol. 1). Hillsdale, NJ: Erlbaum.

Valins, S. and Nisbett, R.E. (1971) *Attribution processes in the development and treatment of emotional disorders*. Morristown, NJ: General Learning Press.

Vayda, A.P. (1967) Foreword. In R.A. Rappaport, *Pigs for the ancestors: Ritual in the ecology of a New Guinea people*. New Haven, Conn.: Yale University Press.

Wallston, K. and Wallston, B. (1978) Development of the multidimensional Health Locus of Control scales. *Health Education Monographs*, **6**, 160–169.

Wallston, K. and Wallston, B., (1981) Health Locus of Control scales. In H.M. Lefcourt (ed.), *Research with the locus of control construct*. Vol 1: *Assessment methods*. London: Academic Press.

Walster, E. (1966) Assignment of responsibility for an accident. *Journal of Personality and Social Psychology*, **3**, 73–79.

Wan, K.-C. and Bond, M.H. (1982) Chinese attributions for success and failure under public and anonymous conditions of rating. *Acta Psychologica Taiwanica*, **24**, 23–31.

Wann, T.W. (ed.) (1964) *Behaviourism and phenomenology: Contrasting bases for modern psychology*. Chicago: University of Chicago Press.

Watzlawick P., Beavin, J. and Jackson, D. (1967) *Pragmatics of human communication: A study of interactional patterns, pathologies and paradoxes*. New York: W.W. Norton.

Watzlawick, P., Weakland, J. and Fisch, R. (1974) *Change: Principles of problem formation and problem resolution*. New York: W.W. Norton.

Weary Bradley, G. (1978) Self-serving biases in the attribution process: A reexamination of the fact or fiction question. *Journal of Personality and Social Psychology*, **36**, 56–71.

Weary, G. (1979) Self-serving attributional biases: Perceptual or response distortions? *Journal of Personality and Social Psychology*, **37**, 1418–1420.

Weary, G. (1981) Role of cognitive, affective and social factors in attribution biases. In J.H. Harvey (ed.), *Cognition, social behavior and the environment*. Hillsdale, NJ: Erlbaum.

Weary, G., Harvey, J.H., Schwieger, P., Olson, C.T., Perloff, R. and Pritchard, S. (1983) Self-presentation and the moderation of self-serving attributional biases. *Social Cognition*, forthcoming.

Wegman, C. (1979) Psychoanalyse en cognitieve psychologie. Unpublished doctoral dissertation, University of Nijmegen.

Weimer, W.B. (1976) *Psychology and the conceptual foundations of science*. Hillsdale, NJ: Erlbaum.

Weiner, B. (ed.) (1974) *Achievement motivation and attribution theory*. Morristown, NJ: General Learning Press.

Weiner, B. (1976) An attributional model of educational psychology. In L. Shulman (ed.), *Review of research in education* (vol. 4). Itasca, Ill.: Peacock

Weiner, B. (1979) A theory of motivation for some classroom experiences. *Journal of Educational Psychology*, **71**, 3–25.

Weiner, B. (1980) *Human motivation*. New York: Holt, Rinehart and Winston.

Weiner, B., Frieze, I., Kukla, A., Reed, I., Rest, S.A. and Rosenbaum, R.M. (1971) *Perceiving the causes of success and failure*. Morristown, NJ: General Learning Press; reprinted in E.E. Jones et al. (eds), *Attribution: Perceiving the causes of behaviour*. Morristown, NJ: General Learning Press, 1972.

Weiner, B., Russell, D. and Lerman, D. (1978) Affective consequences of causal ascriptions. In J.H. Harvey et al. (eds), *New directions in attribution rsearch* (vol. 2). Hillsdale, NJ: Erlbaum.

Weiner, B., Russell, D. and Lerman, D. (1979) The cognition–emotion process in achievement related contexts. *Journal of Personality and Social Psychology*, **37**, 1211–1220.

Wells, G. (1981) Lay analyses of causal forces on behaviour. In J.H. Harvey (ed.), *Cognition, social behavior and the environment*. Hillsdale, NJ: Erlbaum.

Wertheimer, M. (1923) Untersuchungen zur Lehre von der Gestalt, II. *Psychologische Forschung*, **4**, 301–350.

White, R.W. (1959) Motivation reconsidered: The concept of competence. *Psychological Review*, **66**, 297–333.

Wicklund, R.A. (1975) Objective self-awareness. In L. Berkowitz (ed.) *Advances in experimental social psychology* (vol. 8). New York: Academic Press.

Wilensky, R. (1978) Why John married Mary: Understanding stories involving recurring goals. *Cognitive Science*, **2**, 235–266.

Wilson, G.T. (1982) Psychotherapy process and procedure: The behavioral mandate. *Behavior Therapy*, **13**, 291–312.

Wilson, G.T. and Wilson, M. (1945) *The analysis of social change*. Cambridge: Cambridge University Press.

Windisch, U. (1978) *Xenophobie*. Geneva: L'Age d'Homme.

Witkin, H.A. and Berry, J.W. (1975) Psychological differentiation in cross-cultural perspective. *Journal of Cross-Cultural Psychology*, **6**, 4–87.

Witkin, H.A., Dyk, R.B., Faterson, H.F., Goodenough, D.R. and Karp, S.A. (1962) *Psychological differentiation*. New York: John Wiley.

Wong, P.T. and Weiner, B. (1981) When people ask 'why' questions, and the heuristics of attributional search. *Journal of Personality and Social Psychology*, **40**, 650–663.

Woody, E.Z. and Costanzo, P.R. (1981) The socialization of obesity-prone behaviour. In S. Brehm et al. (eds), *Developmental social psychology*. New York: Oxford University Press.

Wortman, C.B. (1975) Some determinants of perceived control. *Journal of Personality and Social Psychology*, **31**, 282–294.

Wortman, C.B., (1976) Causal attributions and personal control. In J.H. Harvey, W.J. Ickes and R.F. Kidd (eds), *New directions in attribution research* (vol. 1). Hillsdale, NJ: Erlbaum.

Wortman, C.B. and Dintzer, L. (1978) Is an attributional analysis of the learned helplessness phenomenon viable? A critique of the Abramson–Seligman–Teasdale reformulation. *Journal of Abnormal Psychology*, **87**, 75–90.

Wyer, R.S. and Srull, T.K. (1981) Category accessibility: Some theoretical and empirical issues concerning the processing of social stimulus information. In E.T. Higgins, P.C. Herman and M. Zanna (eds), *The Ontario symposium on personality and social psychology: Social cognition*. Hillsdale, NJ: Erlbaum.

Yarkin, K.L., Harvey, J.H. and Bloxom, B.M. (1981) Cognitive sets, attribution, and social interaction. *Journal of Personality and Social Psychology*, **41**, 243–252.

Zajonc, R.B. (1968) Cognitive theories in social psychology. In G. Lindzey and E. Aronson (eds), *Handbook of social psychology* (vol. 1). Reading, Mass.: Addison–Wesley (2nd edn).

Zajonc, R.B. (1980) Cognition and social cognition: A historical perspective. In L. Festinger (ed.), *Retrospections on social psychology*. New York: Oxford University Press.

Zillig, M. (1928) Einstellung und Aussage. *Zeitschrift für Psychologie*, **106**, 58–106.

Zillman, D. (1978) Attribution and misattribution of excitatory reactions. In J.H.

Harvey, W.J. Ickes and R.F. Kidd (eds), *New directions in attribution research* (vol. 2). Hillsdale, NJ. Erlbaum.

Zito, G.V. and Jacobs, J. (1979) Attribution and symbolic interaction – impasse at the generalized other. *Human Relations*, **32**, 571–578.

Zuckerman, M. (1979) Attribution of success and failure revisited, or: The motivational bias is alive and well in attribution theory. *Journal of Personality*, **47**, 245–287.

Index of Subjects

Index of Names